A READING OF THE
CANTERBURY TALES

A READING OF THE
CANTERBURY
TALES

TREVOR WHITTOCK

CAMBRIDGE
AT THE UNIVERSITY PRESS
1968

Published by the Syndics of the Cambridge University Press
Bentley House, 200 Euston Road, London, N.W. 1
American Branch: 32 East 57th Street, New York, N.Y. 10022

Library of Congress Catalogue Card Number: 68–12063
Standard Book Number: 521 06795 2 clothbound
521 09557 3 paperback

Printed in Great Britain
at the University Printing House, Cambridge
(Brooke Crutchley, University Printer)

1466018

Contents

Acknowledgements

I should like to thank those friends and colleagues who read earlier drafts of this book, and who helped with advice and corrections. In particular I am indebted to Professor Christina van Heyningen, Professor W. H. Gardner, Professor Geoffrey Durrant, Professor Donald Stuart, and Mrs Margaret Macpherson. Any errors or perverse opinions that remain are to be blamed squarely on me. I wish also to thank the editors of *Theoria* who published earlier versions of some chapters.

INTRODUCTION

ON READING CHAUCER

What is the function of the critic? So far as I am concerned, he can do me one or more of the following services:

1 Introduce me to authors or works of which I was hitherto unaware.
2 Convince me that I have undervalued an author or a work because I had not read them carefully enough.
3 Show me relations between works of different ages and cultures which I could never have seen for myself because I do not know enough and never shall.
4 Give a 'reading' of a work which increases my understanding of it.
5 Throw light upon the process of artistic 'Making'.
6 Throw light upon the relation of art to life, to science, economics, ethics, religion, etc.

W. H. AUDEN

THE reputation of any writer rises and falls as succeeding ages find, or fail to find, in his work a meaning pertinent to the spirit of their times. In his own life, and for a short period after his death, Chaucer earned a widespread admiration that not even Shakespeare's contemporaries accorded Shakespeare.[1] But as the language changed, and people became uncertain about the meanings of his words and the true rhythms of his lines, Chaucer's status declined or, with honourable exceptions, was paid lip-service only. The nadir of his general reputation was reached in the late seventeenth and early eighteenth centuries when not only his language but also his sensibility were regarded as obsolete. After that, admiration for his poetry grew steadily again. But however opinion among general readers has varied, on the whole, among poets, his fellow-craftsmen and fellow-makers throughout the ages, his pre-eminence has never been doubted. (The main exceptions are Addison and Byron, who were both very young when they committed themselves, and Dr Johnson who, apparently, was not well acquainted with his work.) From William Dunbar's, 'O reverend Chaucere, rose of rethoris all', to, say, D. H. Lawrence's, 'Nothing could be more lovely and fearless than Chaucer',[2] poets have proclaimed their admiration. Nor should we forget to mention Dryden who, at a time when Chaucer was most despised, courageously preferred him to Ovid and wrote the first argued criticism of his work. Doubtless, this acclamation by so many poets arises from a recognition of his natural genius ('here is God's plenty') and also, where ignorance of Chaucer's language did not prejudice the issue, of his superb craftsmanship. Certainly it bespeaks a sound consensus of opinion that has come as near as any to being unruffled by the whirligig of fashion.

[1] For a summary of critical attitudes towards Chaucer's poetry see the *Introduction to Five Hundred Years of Chaucer Criticism and Allusion, 1357–1900* by Caroline F. E. Spurgeon (C.U.P. 1925).

[2] William Dunbar, 'The Golden Targe', *Poems*, ed. J. Small, Scott. Text Soc. (1893), II, 10; D. H. Lawrence, *Phoenix* (Heinemann, 1936), p. 551.

When others have attempted to 'translate' Chaucer then it is, beside the clumsiness of their efforts, that his craftsmanship shines most brightly. Dryden, Pope and Wordsworth all tried their hands. Of these the most successful, I think, was Wordsworth. Dryden and Pope, for all their admiration and insight, were too much influenced by the current opinion of Chaucer's language. Thus Dryden wrote: 'Chaucer, I confess, is a rough Diamond, and must first be polished, e'er he shines.' In consequence both rewrote and amended Chaucer, and produced something rather different and quite inferior: the shine on their lines looks too much like enamel or varnish. But Wordsworth came closer to his original, and had an affinity for Chaucer's simplicity. For this reason a comparison of Wordsworth's rendering with Chaucer's own is all the more telling. Here are three stanzas from Book v of *Troilus and Criseyde*, the Wordsworth version first.

> Forth from the spot he rideth up and down,
> And everything to his rememberance
> Came as he rode by places of the town
> Where he had felt such perfect pleasure once.
> Lo, yonder saw I mine own Lady dance,
> And in that Temple she with her bright eyes,
> My Lady dear, first bound me captive-wise.
>
> And yonder with joy-smitten heart have I
> Heard my own Cresid's laugh; and once at play
> I yonder saw her eke full blissfully;
> And yonder once she unto me 'gan say—
> Now, my sweet Troilus, love me well, I pray!
> And there so graciously me did behold,
> That hers unto the death my heart I hold.
>
> And at the corner of that self-same house
> Heard I my most beloved Lady dear,
> So womanly, with voice melodious
> Singing so well, so goodly, and so clear,
> That in my soul methinks I yet do hear
> The blissful sound; and in that very place
> My Lady first took me unto her grace.

Now Chaucer.

> Fro thennesforth he rideth up and down,
> And every thyng com hym to remembraunce
> As he rood forby places of the town
> In which he whilom hadde al his plesaunce.
> 'Lo, yonder saugh ich last my lady daunce;
> And in that temple, with hire eyen cleere,
> Me kaughte first my righte lady dere.
>
> 'And yonder have I herd ful lustyly
> My dere herte laugh; and yonder pleye
> Saugh ich hire ones ek ful blisfully.
> And yonder ones to me gan she seye,
> "Now goode swete, love me wel, I preye;"
> And yond so goodly gan she me biholde,
> That to the deth myn herte is to hire holde.
>
> 'And at that corner, in the yonder hous,
> Herde I myn alderlevest lady deere
> So wommanly, with vois melodious,
> Syngen so wel, so goodly, and so clere,
> That in my soule yet me thynketh ich here
> The blisful sown; and in that yonder place
> My lady first me took unto hire grace.'

Wordsworth captures a lot of the original feeling. But finally his very fidelity to the original betrays him. The English language had changed too much over the centuries, and what in Chaucer is straightforward becomes in Wordsworth's version archaic and artificial: for example, 'I yonder saw here eke full blissfully'. Furthermore, even where the words and the word-order are unchanged, the medieval words carry a resonance almost lost by Wordsworth's time. When Chaucer wrote, 'and in that yonder place/My lady first me took unto hire grace', the tradition of courtly love, drawing upon the divine worship of the Virgin, was alive, and gives a rightness and *spontaneity* to Troilus' exclamation; but 'grace' as it appears in Wordsworth's version sounds arch. Even where Wordsworth changes the lines to capture some of the implications of

the original, the effect is slightly clumsy. Wordsworth probably put in 'joy-smitten heart' in the lines,

> And yonder with joy-smitten heart have I
> Heard my own Cresid's laugh,

to make explicit the heartiness of Troilus' pleasure. But in
Chaucer's lines,

> And yonder have I herd ful lustyly
> My dere herte laugh,

the natural rhythm, throwing the emphasis on 'lustyly' and
'laugh' does this, while at the same time wholly identifying
Troilus' heart with Cressida whom he loves, so that we can
comprehend how any joy she shows finds immediate response
within him. How simply Chaucer has managed it. It is fitting
that at such a moment in *Troilus and Criseyde* the poetry should
be transparent, so that we behold only Troilus' sweet pain
and forget the poetic medium. But the art which conceals art,
which can become so pellucid, is the hard-won product of
great craftsmanship. Wordsworth's translation does not fal-
sify the feelings Chaucer depicts (as most other translators
do), but in so far as he loses the dramatic fullness and immediacy
of the original he does distort. Let one last example suffice.

> And in that Temple she with her bright eyes,
> My lady dear, first bound me captive-wise.

This loses the sudden shock of the moment when Troilus fell
in love; the word-order in Chaucer's lines suggests the actual
sequence: his first glimpse of her, the transformation of love,
and finally the fond adoring.

> And in that temple, with hire eyen cleere,
> Me kaughte first my righte lady dere.

Poetry can never be adequately translated—we all know
that. The unique meaning, created by the interwoven elements
of language, overtones and rhythms, can never be more than
approximated to, and many adaptations become different poems
in their own right. But the corollary to this should not be
forgotten: the closer a reading of a poem is to the organised

particulars, the more valid it will be. Criticism which abstracts the ideas from their poetic expression, which discusses the meaning of words apart from the context in which the poet has used them, which subordinates a poem to a tradition and fails to see that a tradition is made up of individual poems, falsifies. This is not to deny that philosophical, historical or philological awareness may be helpful, but rather to emphasise that at best it is no more than a guide, and at worst may be treacherous distraction. The reader must subordinate himself to the poem, sensitively responding to *it*, and using with discretion whatever aids he selects.

Yet what is it that a reader must subordinate himself to? Is the poem simply an historical object, becoming more yellow and indecipherable with the passing of time? Certainly not, for the oldest poets are not lost to us. Is the poem then something unaffected by time and the flux of change? Certainly not, for appreciation and understanding are not fixed from generation to generation. We have already seen how there can be change of opinion on Chaucer's poetry, and yet a firm consensus which has fairly consistently held him in honour; we have already had some inkling of how his art can be time-bound and yet timeless. Perhaps I should preface my study of a reading of the *Canterbury Tales* with a brief outline of my attitude to these problems and paradoxes.

A poem, it seems to me, may be understood as a *mode of communication*, as *a game*, and as *an imitation*.

A poet attempts to communicate what he has thought, imagined or experienced to another mind through the shared medium of words. As we all know from common experience, no communication between one person and another can be absolutely assured: misunderstanding easily arises, and either speaker or auditor may make mistakes. But this is not to deny that communication is possible, nor that we can distinguish degrees of understanding. As at a lecture some in the audience will have gleaned a better comprehension of the speaker's meaning than others, so we may say that one reader has come closer to the poet's mind than another. Though we can ultimately only judge what went on in another's mind by what he has said, interpreting it by our training in the processes of a shared language and our understanding of our own mental make-up, we know that the meeting of minds is possible. Our very humanity is very largely created by what others have taught us, by our being able to overcome the limitations of self to share in the meaning of other selves. The degree of error is unimportant set beside the degree of understanding. Doubtless a modicum of error always remains, particularly where the communication is of any complexity. But the amount of error can also be diminished. 'What did you mean by that?' 'Well, I meant that...' 'What did he mean by that?' 'Well, his stress fell here, and I think by that word he meant such and such.' Or, 'In the context I don't think that interpretation fits'. We do it all the time, and acquire a variety of techniques for testing and improving our comprehension of communications we receive. Thus one of the functions of literary criticism is to offer improved readings of what an author has written. A final, absolutely right reading can perhaps never be attained, but one interpretation can be matched against another to see which is the better.

Where we are faced with a communication which is strange to us, we are more likely to misinterpret it than where it deals with what is familiar. Someone speaking to us from a different culture holds unrecognised assumptions, and a brief explanation of these may be all we need to clear up our confusion. This is where historical or philological explanations may be particularly helpful to the critic. For example, an African of some distinction once showed me round the house he was having built. When we came to the servants' quarters he showed me an extra room he was having added on for his mother to stay in when she visited. When I looked startled, he explained that in his tribe it was not the custom for a mother to sleep under the same roof as her son. Probably on further reflection I could have deduced this from his words and what else I knew about him. Thus, while historical or philological information may help the critic, they are usually most relevant when it is possible for that information to be deduced from the poetry itself. Obtaining the information from elsewhere is frequently only a short-cut to fuller comprehension: it is largely a matter of convenience.

With the next step in the argument this must be further qualified. When speaking of poetry as communication we are thinking of the relation between the mind of a poet and the mind of the reader: between, say, a fourteenth-century mind and a twentieth-century one. But let us now turn to the relationship between poet and poem. A poem is more than simply language used to communicate: to some extent it is an autonomous structure. The poet often feels that in writing it is not so much that he is setting down his thoughts or experience, as that he is being employed by the poem to give it birth. At a certain stage in the act of creation the poet does not ask himself, 'What do I want to say?' but, 'How can I complete this structure, this meaning, which has somehow revealed itself to me, without spoiling it?' Thus W. H. Auden writes, 'As a rule, the sign that a beginner has a genuine original talent (as a poet) is that he is more interested in playing with words than in saying something original; his attitude is that of the old lady, quoted by E. M. Forster—"How can I know what I think till I see what I say?"'[1] In this way poetry is like a game, and by pursuing the analogy further perhaps we can clarify some of its peculiar characteristics. Take a game like chess. There is a basic intention (to mate your opponent), and certain well-defined rules (the bishop can only move diagonally). To these, in poetry, might correspond the general intention (to write a lyric, or a satire), and the more clearly defined rules of language or form. Then come the subtler points of the game which an experienced player soon comes to know: the advantages of a concealed check, or the shifting values of different pieces in the opening, middle or end game. To these would correspond, of course at a much more complex level, the poet's feeling for the language, the possibilities of form and rhythm. Finally we come to a specific game of chess, or a specific poem. The tighter

[1] W. H. Auden, *The Dyer's Hand* (Faber, 1936), p. 22.

the 'logic' of a particular game, when every move becomes a crucial one, the more interesting the play. Such a game acquires a shape of its own, its own rhythm, moments of deadlock, moments of climax. To appreciate such a game one has to play it, either by being one of the players, or by following the sequence of moves oneself and comprehending their purpose. An interesting and important point arises here. In such a game there are no 'accidental' moves. One of the players may in reality have made a move arbitrarily, with no definite purpose, out of a whim or from impatience; but the move is immediately incorporated into the 'logic' of the game as a bad or good move. The spectator can only understand the move in relation to the progress of the game, and any other motive for it is irrelevant and beyond the spectator's grasp. (Only if someone played below his form might the spectator ask, 'Was the player feeling ill today?') In other words, the player's *intention* can only be conceived in terms of the game itself when the game is a good one. Returning to poetry we find the same characteristics. A good poem attains a coherence and 'inner logic' entirely its own. To comprehend that poem one has sensitively to apprehend the unique development it possesses. Furthermore, the poet's *intention* must be apprehended in terms of the poem's own structure, its own 'inner logic'. There may be exceptions to this, but in my experience it is only poor poems which raise questions of the poet's intention outside the poem he has made.

The appreciation of a poem depends, then, on 'performing' the specific piece, which has developed something of an autonomous being of its own. This is why there is a strict limit to the assistance historical or biographical information can provide the critic. The point has been very well put by H. D. F. Kitto, himself both a scholar and a critic:

Bowra declares that in order to understand the classical Greek drama we must seek to understand fifth-century Greek ideas as fully as possible. It is, I suppose, the chief contribution that present-day scholarship has made to the understanding of art, that it has tried to set it in its contemporary intellectual and social context. This is the contribution which scholarship ought to make; but scholarship should remember that it is *only* a contribution; the interpretation of art is not itself a work of scholarship but of criticism, and when the critic has absorbed what scholarship can tell him, he still has all his work to do. Indeed, I am not sure if the critic, even though he worked independently of scholarship, could not in the end tell the scholar more about fifth-century Greek ideas than the scholar could tell him about the play. His task would naturally be more difficult without scholarship than with it, but, at least ideally, it would be possible for him, after he had pondered on the style and form of the drama as being the outward expression of its inner meaning, to say: In matters concerning Man, and the Gods, the nature of the Universe and of human life, this and this and this are what Sophocles meant and expected his audience to understand.[1]

But there are boundaries to the analogy between poetry and games. A game is autonomous in one sense that a poem is not: it has no reference to anything outside itself, and is played for its own sake. To some extent the pleasure of poetry lies in its form and unity, but much of the delight experienced by a reader comes from his recognition that the poem is saying something true about life. It would be meaningless, however, to ask whether a particular game of chess was true or accurate. It is a highly relevant question to ask of a poem. It is this characteristic of poetry, that it refers to a reality outside itself, which makes it an act of imitation.

Clearly the reference poetry makes to reality is not a simple one, and we cannot test its truth merely by how well it corresponds. Again let us take a simple analogy to start with. Consider a good mimic. When he 'takes off' someone we know, what is it we are admiring? It is not the mimic's ability to become *identical* to the person he is portraying, for, though we may be astonished to see how much one person can change himself into another, even this pleasure would be lost if we did not remember the mimic was not the person he is mimicking. Nor do we necessarily relish a mimic for his ability to act like the person we know; rather it is that we enjoy the

---

[1] H. D. F. Kitto, *Form and Meaning in Drama*, University Paperbacks (Methuen, 1960), p. 91.

way he selects certain characteristics and forcefully puts these across. These characteristics may be ones with which we are familiar in the person depicted, or they may be characteristics we have only unconsciously noted and now observe with a thrill of recognition. Or they may be characteristics we have not observed at all, but which we will now look for next time we meet the person who has been mimicked. Often we may feel that these are characteristics which we might find in many people if we looked. Thus imitation is more than a matter of observation and authenticity: it requires a selection and organisation of the material, in such a way that the audience recognises a pattern, or, as important, begins to seek for such a pattern in real life. In either case, each member of the audience is beginning to reshape his own experience.

What is true of mimicry is, I think, generally true of poetry. Part of the truth of a poem comes from the reader's seeing freshly experience he has already had ('What oft was thought, but ne'er so well express'd'), and part from its power of making the reader seek and discover certain patterns in his future experience. Indeed, every poem is like an open equation which invites the reader to assign his own values to the variables. Since different readers will have different backgrounds of experience, and different opportunities for further experience, to some extent they will fill out the references of a poem differently. There is always more likely to be agreement about the verbal content of a poem than about its application to life: yet the poem's meaning consists not only in its verbal organisation but also in its faculty of alluding to life. This is why there can never be such a thing as a final and authoritative reading of a poem: each reader's interpretation depends so much on what knowledge and sensitivity to life he himself brings to the poem. Discussion of interpretation then should revolve round not only the verbal content—what the words mean, their valid connotations—but also, and more cautiously, round how readers comprehend the poem's allusions to life.[1]

---

[1] See chap. 19, for example, for a discussion of the relevance for the modern world of *The Canon's Yeoman's Tale*.

When Pope castigates bad critics such as

> The bookful blockhead, ignorantly read
> With loads of learned lumber in his head,

each reader is invited to name his own candidate for the post. Unless a reader is capable of recognising such a vice in the critics of his own time, he can scarcely be said to have understood Pope's lines. Yet probably no group of readers would agree completely on any list of actual names.

The issues of a poem's reference to the world outside and to the personal experience of readers are particularly acute when we consider the meaning of a poem for its author's contemporaries and for succeeding ages. There are many experiences we share with our contemporaries which those to come will probably neither know nor care about. Thus, to some extent, non-contemporary poetry is always read differently from contemporary poetry: the shared allusions are gone, and new and strange allusions replace them. This is not to say that the interpretation put by people on poetry of their own age is the best. Often it is not, its very contemporaneity blinding people to the merits or defects of the poetry. What the poem says and how it says it might seem so novel and shocking that many readers are inhibited from responding as sensitively as they are able. Perhaps it is easier for the reader today to appreciate Wordsworth's poetry than it was for many shortly after the publication of the *Lyrical Ballads*. Conversely, an age may grow out of sympathy with an earlier poet because, their attitudes and assumptions being what they are, the experience they bring to the poetry may not be suitably valid. This may be illustrated by the contempt most writers and critics felt for Chaucer's poetry in the early eighteenth century. The important thing, though, is to remember that a poem demands that its readers fill out its implications by bringing in their own experience: we must always move out from the verbal level to an experiential one. Hence it is not surprising that ages disagree often in their assessment and understanding of a writer's work. And the critics of each age must anew be witnesses to the applicability of any writer's work. (We might also add that not only does an age assign its value to a poem—a poem may also itself pass judgment on a whole age: thus the inability of the early eighteenth century to appreciate Chaucer is itself the mark of a serious limitation in that period's sensibility.)

If the argument being presented here is true, then the notion that the critic's function is to interpret a poem as its contemporaries would have understood it is clearly misguided. A twentieth-century reader cannot identify himself with a reader of the fourteenth or seventeenth century: his sense of the earlier context would always be abstract and acquired, not part of the air he breathes. Furthermore, and perhaps more important, he would have to renounce the poem's relevance to his own life and age, and forgo much that the poem could teach him about his own experience. Even Helen Gardner, who advocates an historical approach to the reading of poetry, is forced to confess, 'In trying to set *Hamlet* back into its own age, I seem to have found in it an image of my own. The Elizabethan Hamlet assumes the look of the Hamlet of the twentieth century.'[1] There is no need to be rueful about such a conclusion; rather we should be delighted that Shakespeare's play has an abiding but fresh significance for succeeding ages, that it can still challengingly shape and redirect our apprehension of our twentieth-century lives.

On the other hand, for a reader to ask himself what would a contemporary of a poet dead some three hundred years have made of a particular poem, is neither a foolish nor an irrelevant question. Just as every reader has limitations of perception and assumptions that prejudice his responses, so we tend to share the limitations of our own age. And just as a reader, by comparing his interpretation with someone else's, can modify and enrich his reading, so an attempt to appreciate what earlier ages have understood by the poem may contribute towards a less bigoted reading. Our own prejudices may be discovered

---

[1] See Helen Gardner, *The Business of Criticism* (O.U.P. 1959), chap. II and particularly p. 51.

to us by detecting the prejudices of others. But this is mainly a reminder that criticism is, or should be, a common pursuit.[1]

The reality that a poem imitates (in the sense that I have used this word) is not something fixed and definite, but changes and grows with time and sensibility. Even those experiences a poet himself might have had in mind may pass away, yet the pattern of observation the poet created may find new material and new relevance. That a poem generates such a significant pattern which, like a magnetic field transforming the behaviour of objects within it, leads people to reinterpret their own experience, this is the important thing. For all the rise and fall of Chaucer's reputation throughout the centuries, it is this quality in Chaucer's poetry that most poets have recognised and acclaimed. Let me conclude this section by quoting one of these poets who points to the abiding pattern in the midst of change, and its ever renewing applicability. William Blake wrote: 'Of Chaucer's characters, as described in his Canterbury Tales, some of the names or titles are altered by time, but the characters themselves for ever remain unaltered; and consequently they are the physiognomies or lineaments of universal human life, beyond which Nature never steps. Names alter, things never alter. I have known multitudes of those who would have been monks in the age of monkery, who in this deistical age are deists ... Chaucer's characters live age after age. Every age is a Canterbury Pilgrimage; we all pass on, each sustaining one of these characters; nor can a child be born who is not one or other of these characters of Chaucer.'[2]

[1] 'The critic, one would suppose, if he is to justify his existence, should endeavour to discipline his personal prejudices and cranks—tares to which we are all subject—and compose his difference with as many of his fellows as possible in the common pursuit of true judgment' (T. S. Eliot in 'The Function of Criticism', *Selected Essays*, Faber, 1951, p. 25).

[2] William Blake, *Descriptive Catalogue* (1809), no. 111.

II

Until the middle of the eighteenth century the poem of Chaucer's which received most mention, and was most highly regarded, was *Troilus and Criseyde*. Only later did the *Canterbury Tales* surpass it in general estimate. Probably the earlier preference for *Troilus and Criseyde* is partly accounted for by the popularity of poems dealing with the theme of love— Caroline Spurgeon points out that up to 1650, with the exceptions of *Hamlet* and *Henry IV*, there are more allusions to Shakespeare's *Venus and Adonis* than to any other work. And the swing in opinion towards the *Canterbury Tales* may be partly explained by the turn towards 'realism'. The development of the novel in the eighteenth and nineteenth centuries led to a special emphasis on the naturalistic portrayal of society and character, and other modes of literary representation, such as allegory, for example, were neglected and despised. Thus the accepted view of Chaucer came to be that he began his career as a poet caught in the artificial conventions of medieval poetry and that gradually he freed himself from the straitjacket of this medievalism, his originality manifesting itself more and more in the discovery and perfection of a 'realistic' style. In *Troilus and Criseyde* it seemed that Chaucer had emancipated himself to some extent: his treatment of Criseyde and, particularly, Pandarus, moved away from the courtly love convention that bound much of the material. But in the *Canterbury Tales*, and especially in the *General Prologue* and the links between the tales, Chaucer seemed to have left behind at last the distorting methods and assumptions of medieval literary artifice. Recently, however, Chaucerian scholarship has tended to challenge this view. A closer study of Chaucer's poetry, together with its sources and literary background, has led writers to recognise that Chaucer's style is much more complex than any theory about 'realism' would suggest.[1] (Doubtless

---

[1] The most interesting study of Chaucer's style I have read is Charles Muscatine's *Chaucer and the French Tradition* (University of California Press, 1960).

this shift in critical opinion is not unrelated to the decline in 'realism' and the growing recognition that the naturalistic mode is only one method of imitating life, and that it too has its limitations and distortions.) Far from growing away from the use of literary conventions, it would now seem that Chaucer delighted in mingling conventions, playing one off against another, and that in his later poetry he became more adept at doing this. Certainly this is my view, and it was something I had begun to feel even before I found corroboration in recent Chaucerian criticism. But if, indeed, this is Chaucer's method, what does it signify, and in particular, what implications does this have for a reading of the *Canterbury Tales*?

Before attempting to answer these questions let us briefly glance at a couple of the earlier poems.

In *The Parliament of Fowls* the main convention is the dream-allegory, but this French mode is overlaid with borrowings from Italian authors such as Dante and Boccaccio. The debate of the fowls themselves ranges from the high decorum of courtly love speech to the comic and vulgar chatter of some of the lower birds. Together with this mixing of conventions, and often created by it, goes a rapid shift from one tone to another, so that the reader scarcely knows what to expect next. The reader also finds sudden leaps in the argument, sudden jumps from one topic to another not necessarily expected: thus in the opening the initial idea of *Ars longa, Vita brevis* is surprisingly applied to love, presumably the art of courtly love, but almost immediately passes on to a Christianised version of Cicero's 'Dream of Scipio' which describes how the heroic soul is taken up into the heavens and shown the mysteries of the future life. The garden of the narrator's dream is part allegorical, part fresh landscape painting. The question of who deserves to be loved is not settled, since the formel asks for a year to make up her mind, and the poem ends inconclusively (turning a full circle) with the narrator awaking and selecting more books to read for his betterment! The reader is puzzled and intrigued, and it is perhaps not surprising to find that this poem has attracted more critical interpretations than any of Chaucer's other shorter poems. The poem does not express a point of view but draws the reader in to puzzle out for himself some of the many diverse attitudes mankind has towards love (and one cannot but suspect that to a considerable extent this was Chaucer's intention). Certainly the poetry seems quite deliberately to be creating polar tensions between such opposites as artifice and reality, idealism and practicality, sensuality and salvation, decorum and absurdity; and to be doing this in a manner which can only be called *witty*. There can be no doubt that Chaucer enjoyed, and invites the reader to enjoy, the juggling with styles and tones within the poem. The rhythms of the poem are too confident for us to believe that Chaucer did not know what he was doing in this poem.

In his study of Chaucer's early poetry Wolfgang Clemen writes:

Again and again we are struck by the ease with which Chaucer recalls past conventions or imitates former models, but then proceeds to reverse what had at first appeared to be his intention. Much as his contemporaries, with their knowledge of literary tradition, admired it, however, this art of combining and apparently imitating is only a means to an end. Chaucer makes use of these various literary themes and genres to find symbols which fit and indeed illustrate the experience or meaning he wishes to convey. He could thus rely upon what his readers were bound to expect and associate with these themes, and so he was able to employ an abbreviated, inferential style to present his ideas—an advantage enjoyed by all poetry rooted in tradition.[1]

In the same study Clemen says:

Chaucer almost invariably speaks clearly and plainly. But in regard to the significance of whole sections or poems, he developed a new art of silence, of reserve, of cautious suggestion, unique in his own age...The reader is always left to draw his own conclusions... Chaucer did not want to present his reader with a complete answer and dismiss him, accurately primed, at the end of the poem; what he was seeking to do was rather to induce in him a state of questioning disquiet, of 'wonderment', to awaken his faculty of imagination

[1] Wolfgang Clemen, *Chaucer's Early Poetry*, trs. C. A. M. Sym (Methuen, 1963), p. 124.

and in this way to set him thinking. When we read Chaucer's early poems we feel the author's awareness of how complex and involved the events and circumstances of life are, of how they defy any single interpretation.[1]

With *Troilus and Criseyde* Chaucer found the perfect story for his technique. To dramatise the delicately changing relationships between the main characters, their behaviour, feelings and motives at different levels of consciousness, and to create a compassionate sense of human frailty, Chaucer had evolved the appropriate method, and he now used it with a firmer confidence. Literary conventions are employed in the portrayal of character, but in such a way that the limitations of human awareness are revealed. Thus behind Troilus is the literary world of the courtly lover, and behind Pandarus the cynical world of the fabliau, but through their interaction within the poem the values and sensibility of both are constantly reassessed. Though the shifts of tone are not as abrupt as in the earlier poems—Chaucer tends to work in larger units which are relatively constant in tone, and rather juxtaposes one unit against another—they are still there to modify the response and undercut the complacency of the reader. Many of the scenes showing Troilus, the heartsick courtly lover, are described with an edge of exaggeration which greatly criticises his surrender to passion and mocks the rituals of courtly love itself. Human reality is never lost, always illuminated. We may be told how the God of Love, wroth at Troilus' contempt for his power, suddenly subjects him to love—but what is depicted is the uncertainty of man's pretensions, his subjugation to powers he cannot comprehend: the brash confidence of Troilus, at ease with his fellow-bachelors, gives way to the confusion of the lover, at a loss about what to do, tormented by feelings strange to him. Parallel to the shifts of tone and convention, and often working through them, goes the change of perspectives in portraying character. Sometimes we see a person's behaviour from outside, how he speaks and what he does; sometimes the narrator himself speculates about a charac-

[1] *Ibid.* pp. 10–11.

ter; sometimes he makes us privy to the character's innermost thoughts; sometimes that person's feeling is rendered directly; sometimes obliquely through symbols or formalised songs. By these means Chaucer evokes a completeness of understanding without losing the mystery and wonder that attend the labyrinth of any human personality. And by these means Chaucer retains a sense of humility without which the passing of judgment on human beings, in art as in life, is facile and arrogant. In establishing this latter attitude in the reader Chaucer makes skilful use of his narrator. Sometimes the narrator is omniscient, taking us into the innermost depths of a character's being; frequently he is foolish, a man as fallible and bedevilled by love and the complexities of the world as any of the characters he speaks about (or as any reader of the work). There has been much critical speculation about the last stanzas of the poem, whether the Christian vision at the end was an afterthought or indeed written by Chaucer at all. To my mind there can be no doubt. The last stanzas merely clinch the overall tone implicit in the whole poem through all these techniques I have been speaking of: a tone of one humbly striving to understand, charitably inclined to forgive, recognising the frailties and unrealities of human endeavour, and yet rejoicing in the 'yonge, fressh folkes', the 'fair' of this world, while reaching beyond to a serener wisdom.

To illustrate what I have been saying really requires lengthy quotation. But let one brief episode suffice to suggest something of the range of stylistic devices employed by Chaucer, and their cumulative effect. I have chosen the point in the story where Criseyde succumbs to Diomede's blandishments.

(Book v, 946–1099)

What sholde I telle his wordes that he seyde?
He spak inough, for o day at the meeste.
It preveth wel, he spak so that Criseyde
Graunted, on the morwe, at his requeste,
For to speken with hym at the leeste,
So that he nolde speke of swich matere.
And thus to hym she seyde, as ye may here,

As she that hadde hire herte on Troilus
So faste, that there may it non arace;
And strangely she spak, and seyde thus:
'O Diomede, I love that ilke place
There I was born; and Joves, for his grace,
Delivere it soone of al that doth it care!
God, for thy myght, so leve it wel to fare?

'That Grekis wolde hire wrath on Troie wreke,
If that they myght, I knowe it wel, iwis.
But it shal naught byfallen as ye speke,
And God toforn! and forther over this,
I woot my fader wys and redy is;
And that he me hath bought, as ye me tolde,
So deere, I am the more unto hym holde.

'That Grekis ben of heigh condicioun,
I woot ek wel; but certeyn, men shal fynde
As worthi folk withinne Troie town,
As konnyng, and as parfit, and as kynde,
As ben bitwixen Orkades and Inde.
And that ye koude wel yowre lady serve,
I trowe ek wel, hire thank for to deserve.

'But as to speke of love, ywis,' she seyde,
'I hadde a lord, to whom I wedded was,
The whos myn herte al was, til that he deyde;
And other love, as help me now Pallas,
Ther in myn herte nys, ne nevere was.
And that ye ben of noble and heigh kynrede,
I have wel herd it tellen, out of drede.

'And that doth me to han so gret a wonder,
That ye wol scornen any womman so.
Ek, God woot, love and I ben fer ysonder!
I am disposed bet, so mot I go,
Unto my deth, to pleyne and maken wo.
What I shal after don, I kan nat seye;
But trewelich, as yet me list nat pleye.

'Myn herte is now in tribulacioun,
And ye in armes bisy day by day.
Herafter, whan ye wonnen han the town,
Peraunter, thanne so it happen may,
That whan I se that nevere yit I say,
Than wol I werke that I nevere wroughte!
This word to yow ynough suffisen oughte.

'To-morwe ek wol I speken with yow fayn,
So that ye touchen naught of this matere.
And whan yow list, ye may come here ayayn;
And er ye gon, thus muche I sey yow here:
As help me Pallas with hire heres clere,
If that I sholde of any Grek han routhe,
It sholde be youreselven, by my trouthe!

'I say nat therfore that I wol yow love,
N'y say nat nay; but in conclusioun,
I mene wel, by God that sit above!'
And therwithal she caste hire eyen down,
And gan to sike, and seyde, 'O Troie town,
Yet bidde I God, in quiete and in reste
I may yow sen, or do myn herte breste.'

But in effect, and shortly for to seye,
This Diomede al fresshly newe ayeyn
Gan pressen on, and faste hire mercy preye;
And after this, the sothe for to seyn,
Hire glove he took, of which he was ful feyn.
And finaly, whan it was woxen eve,
And al was wel, he roos and tok his leve.

The brighte Venus folwede and ay taughte
The wey ther brode Phebus down alighte;
And Cynthea hire char-hors overraughte
To whirle out of the Leoun, if she myghte;
And Signifer his candels sheweth brighte,
Whan that Criseyde unto hire bedde wente
Inwith hire fadres faire brighte tente,

Retornyng in hire soule ay up and down
The wordes of this sodeyn Diomede,
His grete estat, and perel of the town,
And that she was allone and hadde nede
Of frendes help; and thus bygan to brede
The cause whi, the sothe for to telle,
That she took fully purpos for to dwelle.

The morwen com, and gostly for to speke,
This Diomede is come unto Criseyde;
And shortly, lest that ye my tale breke,
So wel he for hymselven spak and seyde,
That alle hire sikes soore adown he leyde.
And finaly, the sothe for to seyne,
He refte hire of the grete of al hire peyne.

And after this the storie telleth us
That she hym yaf the faire baye stede,
The which he ones wan of Troilus;
And ek a broche—and that was litel nede—
That Troilus was, she yaf this Diomede.
And ek, the bet from sorwe hym to releve,
She made hym were a pencel of hire sleve.

I fynde ek in the stories elleswhere,
Whan thorugh the body hurt was Diomede
Of Troilus, tho wepte she many a teere,
Whan that she saugh his wyde wowndes blede;
And that she took, to kepen hym, good hede;
And for to helen hym of his sorwes smerte,
Men seyn—I not—that she yaf hym hire herte.

But trewely, the storie telleth us,
Ther made nevere woman moore wo
Than she, whan that she falsed Troilus.
She seyde, 'Allas! for now is clene ago
My name of trouthe in love, for everemo!
For I have falsed oon the gentileste
That evere was, and oon the worthieste!

23

'Allas! of me, unto the worldes ende,
Shal neyther ben ywriten nor ysonge
No good word, for thise bokes wol me shende.
O, rolled shal I ben on many a tonge!
Thorughout the world my belle shal be ronge!
And wommen moost wol haten me of alle.
Allas, that swich a cas me sholde falle!

'Thei wol seyn, in as muche as in me is,
I have hem don dishonour, weylaway!
Al be I nat the first that dide amys,
What helpeth that to don my blame awey?
But syn I se ther is no bettre way,
And that to late is now for me to rewe,
To Diomede algate I wol be trewe.

'But, Troilus, syn I no bettre may,
And syn that thus departen ye and I,
Yet prey I God, so yeve yow right good day,
As for the gentileste, trewely,
That evere I say, to serven feythfully,
And best kan ay his lady honour kepe';—
And with that word she brast anon to wepe.

'And certes, yow ne haten shal I nevere;
And frendes love, that shal ye han of me,
And my good word, al sholde I lyven evere.
And, trewely, I wolde sory be
For to seen yow in adversitee;
And gilteles, I woot wel, I yow leve.
But al shal passe; and thus take I my leve.'

But trewely, how longe it was bytwene
That she forsok hym for this Diomede,
Ther is non auctour telleth it, I wene.
Take every man now to his bokes heede;
He shal no terme fynden, out of drede.
For though that he bigan to wowe hire soone,
Er he hire wan, yet was ther more to doone.

Ne me ne list this sely womman chyde
Forther than the storye wol devyse.
Hire name, allas! is punysshed so wide,
That for hire gilt it oughte ynough suffise.
And if I myghte excuse hire any wise,
For she so sory was for hire untrouthe,
I wis, I wolde excuse hire yet for routhe.

Just before this episode the author presents brief descriptions of the appearance of Diomede, Criseyde and Troilus. Apart from a few lines at the very beginning of the poem this description is the only one we have had of Criseyde in the poem. On the whole the stanzas describing her now, and held over till this moment in the tale, are objective—objective in that the crucial issue at this moment, the moral significance of Criseyde's 'fall', is apparently bypassed.

(Book V, 806–26)

Criseyde mene was of hire stature,
Therto of shap, of face, and ek of cheere.
Ther myghte ben no fairer creature.
And ofte tyme this was hire manere,
To gon ytressed with hire heres clere
Doun by hire coler at hire bak byhynde,
Which with a thred of gold she wolde bynde.

And, save hire browes joyneden yfere,
Ther nas no lak, in aught I kan espien.
But for to speken of hire eyen cleere,
Lo, trewely, they writen that hire syen,
That Paradis stood formed in hire yën.
And with hire riche beaute evere more
Strof love in hire ay, which of hem was more.

She sobre was, ek symple, and wys withal,
The best ynorished ek that myghte be,
And goodly of hire speche in general,
Charitable, estatlich, lusty, and fre;
Ne never mo ne lakked hire pite;
Tendre-hearted, slydynge of corage;
But trewely, I kan nat telle hire age.

'Slydynge of corage', however, may suggest a clue to what happens. But what is as important is the throw-away last line, 'But trewely, I kan nat telle hire age.' This sudden reminder of the author's limitation of knowledge prepares the reader for a certain humility of judgment—there are things we cannot know, facts we cannot establish. (I suppose the line also hints at Criseyde's very feminine desire to conceal her age.)

In the scene that follows we have, dramatised for us, the actual exchange of speech between Diomede and Criseyde. The fascination of the poetry here is in guessing at the motives behind the speaker's words. Diomede is marvellously virile and glib, and even his blushes (which must be beyond the control of his will) and his quavering voice seem part of a calculated seduction. The mixture of motives, and changing of attitudes, in Criseyde is even more exciting. At first she seems to be holding him off with polite exchanges, but gradually she becomes more involved. All that we know of Criseyde from what has gone before presses upon us now, giving her slightest word or accent enormous implications.

(Book v, 974–8)
'But as to speke of love, ywis,' she seyde,
'I hadde a lord, to whom I wedded was,
The whos myn herte al was, til that he deyde;
And other love, as help me now Pallas,
Ther in myn herte nys, ne nevere was.'

Is this a denial of Troilus, or merely concealment of her love? Is she thinking of Troilus when she speaks of her dead husband, and if so does their separation seem already as final as death? When she goes on to say that she will change her attitude when Troy has fallen, is this a clever rebuke, putting-off Diomede, or is it already a breach in her own defences—we know how timid she is, and how obsessed she has been by her father's prediction of the Trojan defeat? In the very ambiguity of her speech Chaucer is showing how one attitude slides into another so softly that we (like Criseyde) are hardly aware of the transition. The growing awkwardness and vagueness of her speech dramatise the morass she is entering.

(Book v, 988–1004)

'Myn herte is now in tribulacioun,
And ye in armes bisy day by day.
Herafter, whan ye wonnen han the town,
Peraunter, thanne so it happen may,
That whan I se that nevere yit I say,
Than wol I werke that I nevere wroughte!
This word to yow ynough suffisen oughte.

'To-morwe ek wol I speken with yow fayn,
So that ye touchen naught of this matere.
And whan yow list, ye may come here ayayn;
And er ye gon, thus muche I sey yow here:
As help me Pallas with hire heres clere,
If that I sholde of any Grek han routhe,
It sholde be yourselven, by my trouthe!

'I say nat therfore that I wol yow love,
N'y say nat nay; but in conclusioun,
I mene wel, by God that sit above!'

The last line is particularly pathetic, suggesting perhaps that already she has sensed her own betrayal.

After Diomede has won her glove, and taken his leave, the stanza on the coming of night, with its tone of heroic grandeur, is curiously powerful and disturbing.

(Book v, 1016–22)

The brighte Venus folwede and ay taughte
The way ther brode Phebus down alighte;
And Cynthea hire char-hors overraughte
To whirle out of the Leoun, if she myghte;
And Signifer his candels sheweth brighte,
Whan that Criseyde unto hire bedde wente
Inwith hire fadres faire bright tente.

The glory and beauty of the night seem set off against Criseyde's pathetic betrayal which is so soon to occur. Yet, because of the associations of godhead in the names of the stars, there is too perhaps the suggestion of superhuman forces—Time, Fate, Destiny, the Passions—sweeping on inevitably and carrying small humanity in their course. The lines also work ironically[1]—they recall (in Venus and Phoebus) all the bright happiness of love Criseyde and Troilus have known, and are now to be so fatefully severed from. The effect of the stanza is to change one's perspective of Criseyde, so that the struggle in her soul may be seen against a cosmic background. The phrase, 'hire fadres faire brighte tente', by the contrast with the heavens, emphasises that the wealth and protection of the dwelling—after her manoeuvres with Diomede Criseyde yearns for security and relief there—are slight, even illusory. This, together with the next stanza, draws us into a compassionate concern for Criseyde which is incompatible with any easy condemnation of her behaviour.

(Book v, 1023–9)

> Retornyng in hire soule ay up and down
> The wordes of this sodeyn Diomede,
> His grete estat, and perel of the town,
> And that she was allone and hadde nede
> Of frendes help; and thus bygan to brede
> The cause whi, the sothe for to telle,
> That she took fully purpos for to dwelle.

Here the omniscient narrator gives us access to Criseyde's innermost thoughts: her fear and need for comfort and reassurance. 'Sodeyn' Diomede threatens her with his masculine power, but this same quality (as even his 'grete estat') suggests a strong arm to shield her from her greater anxieties—the 'perel of the town' (Troy threatened with destruction, as well as the strange Grecian camp). Here is the seed which will so terribly, and sadly, ripen into betrayal.

By the next two stanzas the betrayal is complete—though the full implications of it are somewhat obscured. We are not quite sure how much of herself Criseyde gives to Diomede. Phrases such as, 'He refte hire of the grete of all hire peyne'

---

[1] See Robinson's note: 'Criseyde had promised to return before the moon should pass out of Leo. See iv, 1590 ff.' (*The Complete Works of Geoffrey Chaucer*, O.U.P. 1957).

tease with speculative possibilities—her fears have clearly been calmed, but has she callously forgotten Troilus? We want to know more. The gifts she gives Diomede—are they all she is giving? At the same time Criseyde is presented at a further remove—an object for speculation—by the device of referring to it all as a story—'And after this the storie telleth us'. But in the next stanza there is a suggestion of different versions, and the other accounts suggest contrary possibilities.

(Book v, 1044–50)

> I fynde ek in the stories elleswhere,
> Whan thorugh the body hurt was Diomede
> Of Troilus, tho wepte she many a teere,
> Whan that she saugh his wyde wowndes blede
> And that she took, to kepen hym, good hede;
> And for to helen hym of his sorwes smerte,
> Men seyn—I not—that she yaf hym hire herte.

If the last line suggests that the far from omniscient narrator is attempting to be fair and impartial, the effect is also to make the reader question any too hasty judgment on Criseyde. When the narrator goes on to say,

(Book v, 1050–3)

> But trewely, the storie telleth us,
> Ther made nevere woman moore wo
> Than she, whan that she falsed Troilus,

he suggests the soberer version is the more reliable, and we are sure some lamentation was natural. But with 'She seyde', we are once more brought back to Criseyde's own tormented mind, and her words with their intermingling of pain and self-justification convince us that *this* is real. Furthermore, Criseyde's lament at what the world will make of her action, and indeed we know it has, makes us appreciate how false and facile general judgments can be.

(Book v, 1053–64)

> 'Allas! of me, unto the worldes ende,
> Shal neyther ben ywriten nor ysonge
> No good word, for thise bokes wol me shende.
> O, rolled shal I ben on many a tonge!

Thorughout the world my belle shal be ronge!
And wommen moost wol haten me of alle.
Allas, that swich a cas me sholde falle!'

Yet the exaggeration here ('unto the worldes ende') also reveals Criseyde's own sense of guilt and failure. The irony is
that Criseyde, who from the first in her love for Troilus feared
so much the blemishing of her name, should now become
notorious for infidelity. Her actions have produced the very
result she most wished to avoid, and hence, even while we
recognise her self-pitying shirking of her own responsibility,
we also feel that she too is a victim—'Allas, that swich a cas me
sholde falle'. Even her vain protestations, and her wishful
vowing add to the pathos of her situation rather than awaken
any stringent condemnation.

(Book v, 1069–71)

'But syn I se ther is no bettre way,
And that to late is now for me to rewe,
To Diomede algate I wol be trewe.'

We feel sad because we recognise here how futile her words
are. What is so marvellous about the poetry is the way Chaucer
reveals all the frailty and error of human flesh, while at the
same time increasing our love and compassion for the mortal
creature. When we contemplate the nature of God, we feel
sure that it is with such understanding He would love his
creatures. For example, of Troilus she can say,

'And certes, yow ne haten shal I nevere.'

Yes, how easily we do come to hate those we wrong: if the
line shows Criseyde's false reasoning and self-justification, it
also manifests her struggle to avoid subtler sins.

At the end of her 'soliloquy' we are taken back to what the
stories say, or rather what they do not say.

(Book v, 1086–8)

But trewely, how longe it was bytwene
That she forsok hym for this Diomede,
Ther is non auctour telleth it, I wene.

Introduction

Nothing could more clearly display the irrelevance and opacity of 'facts' than this casual dismissal: the important things happen in the 'soule', not in the world of confirmed observations and reports. This episode ends aptly with a stanza emphasising the narrator's limitations, and a plea for 'routhe'.

(Book v, 1093–9)

> Ne me ne list this sely womman chyde
> Forther than the storye wol devyse.
> Hire name, allas! is punysshed so wide,
> That for hire gilt it oughte ynough suffise.
> And if I myghte excuse hire any wise,
> For she so sory was for hire untrouthe,
> Iwis, I wolde excuse hire yet for routhe.

When later we see Troilus' suffering, and face the cruelty of Criseyde's letter to him, our condemnation of Criseyde is mitigated and softened because we have been made to recognise so clearly and feel so powerfully the misery of her change.

By the time that Chaucer had completed *Troilus and Criseyde* he had developed a technique which, by mixing styles, tones and viewpoints, could be employed to question and open out a subject as well as to portray a subject in all its roundness. We might say—to change our metaphor—that in *The Parliament of Fowls* the technique is employed for centrifugal effects, in *Troilus and Criseyde* for centripetal ones. Perhaps in the work he came to write next, *The Legend of Good Women*, it was precisely because the fixed intention of his subject gave him too little scope to develop his technique that he never completed the poem. But at last, with the *Canterbury Tales*, Chaucer found another ideal subject for his talents. The notion of a series of story-tellers, all bound on a common pilgrimage, offered maximum opportunity for a diversity of styles and interplay of characters, tones and beliefs. Yet, by the very fact they all were *pilgrims*, the possibility of some reconciling principle—an overall viewpoint which could see unity in multiplicity—was inherent in the whole design from the start. In this work lies the fulfilment of Chaucer's development as a poet.

In other words, to recognise the importance in Chaucer's poetry of this manipulation of multifold styles and tones is to suggest a new approach to the *Canterbury Tales*. Not that I wish to imply that such an emphasis on Chaucer's technique should be imposed upon anyone's experience of reading the *Canterbury Tales*; but rather that, out of my own attentiveness to the work, I began to feel that such was Chaucer's method. In my reading of the *Canterbury Tales* I hope to set out an interpretation which will not only take into account the great variety present in the poem, but one which also shows that the poem is more unified than is generally recognised. Furthermore, I shall attempt to support the validity of this reading by frequent references to the text and to the details of the poem's construction.

III

The Unity of the 'Canterbury Tales'

Before going any further let me first mention briefly some of the difficulties facing any discussion of the unity of the *Canterbury Tales*. First, the work is incomplete. Not only is the list of tales which the pilgrims were to tell unfinished, there is also some evidence to suggest that Chaucer's plan changed and grew as he wrote. How he would further have modified his arrangement, what other revisions he might have made, we can only guess. For all we know, had Chaucer lived to complete his great poem, some tales might have been scrapped altogether, and others substituted. We cannot even be sure of the exact sequence of tales. Despite the efforts of scholars the situation has changed little since Ten Brink wrote at the end of the last century: 'None of the manuscripts gives the pieces in a succession which could have suited Chaucer's intentions; and no criticism has succeeded in making out anything like a sound and satisfactory arrangement. And even the latest ingenious and applauded attempt of this kind was foredoomed to failure (except by violent and arbitrary proceedings) from the impossibility of reconciling contradictions which the poet did not remove.'[1] Briefly the situation is this. All the manuscripts that have come down to us are dated later than Chaucer's death, and none can be regarded as authoritative. These manuscripts show wide variation in the order of the stories, in the connections between them, and the presence and position of the links. The sequence of tales within certain Groups (or Fragments) seems fairly reliable, but the actual order of the Groups themselves is a matter of dispute.[2] So long as these facts are borne in mind there is no need for me to enter the dispute, and commit myself heavily to one group of scholars or another. What I shall be concentrating on are themes which reappear with variations throughout the tales. As far as possible I have attempted to avoid employing assumptions and reaching conclusions dependent on the more disputed arrangements of the tales. For convenience only I have accepted the sequence set out in Robinson's edition of Chaucer, as that is probably the most widely used at present.

I have also tried to keep my conclusions about the themes organically uniting the tales fairly tentative, letting these themes emerge (I would like to think) from the separate analysis of each tale rather than imposing them on the material. A question in the Cambridge English Tripos a few years ago asked whether the notion of unity in the *Canterbury Tales* was a modern principle quite alien to the world of medieval poetry. But the question of unity even in a modern work may be no easy matter to decide. For example, how unified are Ezra Pound's *Cantos*? Despite the repetition of themes, sources and techniques do they display much more unity than, say, the body of W. B. Yeats's poems where only the identity of the author is the final link? I doubt it. Certainly I would suggest Chaucer had a more definite overall scheme than Pound, and some of the themes to be found in different tales are as

---

[1] Bernhard Ten Brink, *History of English Literature*, vol. II, trans. Wm. Clarke Robinson (George Bell, 1895), p. 150.

[2] For a straightforward account of the situation see R. M. Lumiansky, *Of Sondry Folk, The Dramatic Principle in the Canterbury Tales* (University of Texas Press, 1955), pp. 10–14.

deliberately related by echoes and cross references as Pound's themes are. Provided dogmatic assertions are avoided, there can be little harm and much reward in seeking for unifying devices in Chaucer's poem. Whether my analyses and suggestions are sufficiently sensitive and flexible my readers must decide.

One notion with which I commenced my study and which I found later had to be modified was that all the tales were equally valid evidence of thematic unity irrespective of their poetic quality. The tales do vary in quality and yet even the poorest (I thought) should attest as much as the best to Chaucer's intention. Yet when I came to set down on paper what I had actually experienced in reading each tale I soon discovered that quality did make a difference: the good tales insistently proclaimed their integration in the whole poem, while the poorer tales, like shuffling outsiders, proved embarrassing and difficult customers. This should not have been surprising: it is indeed typical of how the imagination with its 'esemplastic power' (as Coleridge called it) works. When the imagination is most alive it assimilates all material into an organic whole; but when it is sluggish the matter remains intractable. Therefore, while I have tried not to shirk the problems of the poorer tales, I would suggest that those tales which are most important witnesses of the poem's integrity are indeed the tales where the poetic quality is most marked. The tales which are decidedly inferior are, I think, *The Man of Law's Tale*, *Sir Thopas* and *Melibeus*, *The Manciple's Tale* and (a real difficulty this) *The Parson's Tale*, and here one's conclusions about the significance in the scheme must be most tentative.

The tales that make up the collection belong to a number of different genres. This raises another issue—the problem of convention. The word itself is ambiguous and may easily lead to confusion. One sense refers to some fairly explicit pattern to which a piece of fiction or poetry should conform. Thus a sonnet should have fourteen lines, and a ballade requires a refrain and a certain rhyme scheme. This easily shades off into less explicitly stated criteria, which yet may evoke a sense of expectation and appropriateness. Thus, for example, a ballad not only implies a certain range of prosodic devices but also implies a certain kind of material. We may not be able to define exactly what a ballad is but, on the whole, given a poem we can fairly easily settle whether it is a ballad or not. We also use the word *convention* when we find certain material frequently reappearing in works of poetry or fiction. Thus the frequent use of a *carpe diem* motif in poetry is regarded as a certain convention in lyric poetry. This leads on directly to what is really a matter of sensibility—the interest of a society in and its concern with certain areas of experience (perhaps at the expense or to the neglect of other areas). Here it is a focus of attention which reflects the society's obsession with some partial aspect of life. In time, of course, the sensibility may change, yet some writers will always be found bringing in the same old stuff, merely imitating what their predecessors have written and relying upon the past interest of readers in the subject. Here the works have become conventional in a derogatory sense: they are the last twitchings and reflexes of a dying sensibility. The best way of illustrating what I am describing is to take an example from our literature at present. With D. H. Lawrence the novel began to include descriptions of the sexual act. Today it is scarcely possible to pick up a novel which does not contain a portrayal of such intimate experience. Clearly this is more than a literary choice: it is a manifestation of our society's obsession with the significance of sex. Even the worst writers, where copying others for commercial success is the main motive for this selection of material, are exemplifying something of our contemporary sensibility.

From this we can see that *convention* is closely bound up with sensibility, and may indeed be almost identical with it. Perhaps we may go farther and recognise that the employment of any convention, no matter how clearly defined or deliberately chosen, is related to a focus of consciousness. Even the sonnet, that most artificial and arbitrary of literary forms, flourishes or is modified as a society finds it an appropriate mode of expression. To explain why the sonnet was dropped in the eighteenth century, or why it is of only marginal interest in twentieth-century English poetry (W. H. Auden is almost alone in using a sonnet sequence purposefully) would be to plot the loci of feeling and belief of these ages. When we consider a less definite form, one which is even more intimately bound up with sensibility, such as say *tragedy* or *satire*, we realise how the flourishing or neglect of these genres are of cardinal significance in understanding the contours of an age's civilisation.

Hence, when studying a work of poetry it is not sufficient merely to identify the conventions found it it: the study should press on to comprehend the sensibility that gives rise to them, and to appreciate the writer's ability to make contact with living experience. Chaucer wrote his poetry towards the end of the middle ages, when the medieval world was already beginning to give way to the Renaissance. Furthermore, his age was criss-crossed with many traditions often at conflict with one another. To mention one example: between the eleventh and sixteenth centuries the place of love in marriage became a problem scarcely known in earlier and later ages. For the Church taught that love should be a rational state drawing the soul to God;[1] but the tradition of courtly love inculcated heretical notions of surrendering oneself to passion under an elaborate code of frustrations and enticements. Under the idea of marriage that derived from Roman tradition, the wife was primarily a piece of property. For the courtly tradition, love and marriage were entirely incompatible. The Church enjoined a somewhat abstract charity bound by many warnings and negations. Yet in the period in England roughly delimited by the birth of Chaucer and the death of Shakespeare these incompatible traditions drew together and created that ideal of marital love defined so admirably by the phrase in the Anglican marriage service: 'With my body I thee worship.' Indeed

---

[1] This attitude to love is summed up in St Augustine's words: 'I call "charity" the motion of the soul toward the enjoyment of God for His own sake, and the enjoyment of one's self and of one's neighbour for the sake of God; but "cupidity" is a motion of the soul toward the enjoyment of one's self, one's neighbour, or any corporal thing for the sake of something other than God' (*De doctrina*, 3. 10. 16).

Chaucer's affirmation, in *The Franklin's Tale*, that love attains greatest fulfilment in the life-long commitment of marriage, is one of the earliest of such declarations in English literature, and marks a crucial turning-point in the history of civilisation. Chaucer's interest in these traditions is not that of an artist standing aside from the stream of his time and merely toying with literary notions. Criticism which suggests this, and too often Chaucerian criticism does, distorts the significance of his work as much as any modern criticism would which suggested that D. H. Lawrence's writing on sexual love was merely intended to establish and exploit new literary conventions for the novel. I am not, of course, trying to make Chaucer into a revolutionary or prophet as Lawrence was, but emphasising that his use of conventions is profoundly related to the key movements and changes in the sensibility of his time.

Let me go further. C. S. Lewis has said of *Troilus and Criseyde* that Chaucer, in comparison with Boccaccio's treatment of the theme, *medievalised* the story.[1] There is much truth in his comment. But why, we might wonder, did Chaucer do so? Perhaps the answer is something along these lines. Chaucer, living towards the end of the medieval period, was actually conscious of the assumptions and implications inherent in modes of sensibility which were beginning to retreat before the new ways that finally made the Renaissance. That moment of time he inherited enabled him to set out and criticise these very assumptions and implications. (In the first flush of a 'convention' we are scarcely aware of falling into a pattern—we simply seem to be struggling with experience raw and naked. Only later, when the mode has somewhat tamed experience, can we recognise how we have been led into certain emphases and evaluations which have made their own shapes and limits.) *Troilus and Criseyde*, then, is a criticism of courtly love showing its wonders but also its terrible deficiencies as a pattern for people to live by. And Chaucer, as an artist, was consciously offering such a critique.

[1] C. S. Lewis, 'What Chaucer really did to *Il Filostrato*', *Essays and Studies* (1932), vol. XVII.

Furthermore, and most important for this study, when Chaucer came to write the *Canterbury Tales* he chose to write in many genres not simply because he liked trying his hand at different literary conventions, but because he wished to explore and assess many of the ways his contemporaries understood and experienced the world.

Criticism which concentrated on this side of Chaucer's work could easily slide into cultural history, and it would certainly be interesting to see some studies along these lines. But, as I argued earlier, poetry not only mirrors the poet's own times but also holds up a mirror for later ages to see themselves in; and criticism which seeks to bring out the abiding relevance of the poetry has its special function too. Not only should we strive to understand how a poet shaped the culture that has shaped us, we should also seek to see what he can still teach us. Because I have wished to emphasise what meaning Chaucer's poetry can still hold today I have quite deliberately, when writing of the effect of his poetry, used the phrase the *reader*. Sometimes this might include a hypothetical contemporary of Chaucer's, but normally by it I mean the modern reader. Yet perhaps I should not take this liberty without saying something about the difference between Chaucer's audience and those who read him today.

Modern man's chief experience of literature, even of poetry, comes from silent reading. An oral tradition of poetry scarcely exists for us. (I believe that schools and universities should do more to introduce poetry to students through the ear and not the eye.) Yet Chaucer lived in an age when the oral tradition was only just beginning to give way to a readership tradition. Though Chaucer was not a true singer of the old type, who composed in performance, he still read his poems aloud to an audience for many of whom this must have been their chief acquaintance with his work. Though Chaucer's later poetry was probably intended more and more for readers rather than auditors, even reading was still largely an aural activity. Silent reading to oneself is on the whole an accomplishment that was only developed much later in history. Perhaps this fact may explain to some extent why poetry matured earlier than prose. Even though the *Canterbury Tales* were possibly aimed more at the reader than at a listening audience, Chaucer's lines in *The Miller's Prologue* emphasise the importance of hearing:

> And therefore, whoso list it not yheere,   (3176)
> Turne over the leef and chese another tale...

But more important, Chaucer brought the habits of writing for a gathered audience into the *Canterbury Tales*. It is generally believed that he did himself actually read aloud many of the tales in the court. Indeed Chaucer's relation to his audience has its parallel in the relation of each pilgrim to the group of pilgrims. Therefore it is useful to bear in mind some of the characteristics that distinguish poetry meant to be heard from poetry intended to be read by oneself.[1]

In the most interesting study I have read of this problem of Chaucer's relation to his audience, Bertrand H. Bronson writes,

For the art of oral narrative resembles music in this, that its points must in the main carry their own significance as they advance, and cannot await interpretation in the lights of later development. Their significance may be clarified and deepened by subsequent revelation; but if it is to have its due effect, the meaning must have been already suggested.[2]

The author cannot afford to confuse his listeners.

If he pauses for a moment, or digresses, or drops one strand of his story to take up another, he tells you what he has done and what he intends to do.[3]

This has important implications for any study seeking to find unifying themes. We should expect to find the more deliberately intended thematic linkings fairly explicitly stated. Chaucer's habit of ringing changes on certain key phrases ('Pity runneth

[1] For a study of the true oral tradition and what it means see Albert B. Lord, *The Singer of Tales* (Harvard University Press, 1960).
[2] Bertrand H. Bronson, 'Chaucer's Art in Relation to his Audience', in *Five Studies in Literature* by B. H. Bronson, J. R. Caldwell, J. M. Cline, Gordon McKenzie and J. F. Ross (University of California Press, Berkeley, 1940).
[3] *Ibid.* p. 8.

soone in gentil herte') may be partly accounted for thus. The direct preacher's address so common to different tales too may be accounted for in this way: it holds the audience to some of the main ideas of the particular tale, and helps them to see how one narrator's viewpoint differs from another's. But the necessity for such explicitness need not rule out subtler linkings and connections. Much of poetry works unconsciously (no doubt in the writer as well as in his audience), and just as in Shakespeare's plays clusters of images create patterns of meaning so too in Chaucer's poetry it will not be unreasonable to seek and find more unobtrusive echoings.

Another difference between the poet who composes for ear and the poet who writes for the eye is in the use of allusion. Milton or T. S. Eliot can require their readers to trace their references to other poems. The poet with a listening audience cannot. Hence he must employ allusions which are very well known, such as *The Song of Solomon* (which Chaucer employs for ironic contrast in *The Merchant's Tale*). Frequently the poet like Chaucer who is probably better acquainted with what has been written than his audience, will delight them and himself by introducing them to the works of other writers through translation and paraphrase. But if most of Chaucer's audience could not be expected to know Dante, Petrarch or Boccaccio as he did, they could be expected to know and recognise the various conventions shaping poetry and story-telling. For it is important to a listening public that they should know from the start what sort of performance they are about to hear, so that they can give it the right attention and miss nothing. Hence literary conventions played an even more important role than they have done in literature since, and Chaucer was favourably situated to juggle with conventions before the more sophisticated audience one would find at court.

The most important of all advantages that a poet directly addressing an audience possesses is the control of tone. For tone is primarily the expression of a relationship between a speaker and his auditors, though it may also include the author's relationship to his own characters. A nuance of voice, a gesture of a hand, the merest pause can transform the meaning of a phrase for an attentive audience. By his delivery the poet can draw the audience in to share a whispered confidence, or push them away with an harangue. To keep changing his tone, shifting his relationship with his audience, is a means to suspense and drama, a way of holding the attention over a period of time. Certainly there is strong evidence for believing that Chaucer over the years, through frequent performances of his own poetry, became a master of the technique. As I have suggested earlier, this technique was also ideal for Chaucer's purposes of sceptically exploring a subject and surveying a character or a situation 'in the round'. Intention and opportunity matched for Chaucer. Even when he came to write the *Canterbury Tales* we may surmise that he had occasion to try out many of the individual tales on eager audiences, and the whole is composed with a clear reliance on the speaking voice. On the audience's side, they had ample training in listening through the regular sermons they attended. Indeed, the habit of reading for most of them must have been of little consequence compared with the habit of listening, and the man with a gift of the tongue must have stirred them as no manuscript could have done. They had become accustomed to the subtleties of speech and could appreciate its finest arts. They could distinguish and enjoy the tricks and figures of rhetoric even as they were being performed.[1] Here is where the modern reader is at most disadvantage. He lives in an age where silent reading and the appreciation of visual arts are more developed than the art of listening. The radio is not as enthusiastically attended to as television or the cinema. Yet to read Chaucer well he

[1] 'But when all due subtractions have been made, the audience which can be discerned from its reflected image in Chaucer's work must compel our admiration. Clearly they were far more highly civilized than the audience which Shakespeare and his contemporaries had to address. Sensitive in most things, quick to catch the refinements of the subtlest humour and the finest irony, they must have been perceptive to a degree seldom attained in our own day' (*ibid.* pp. 52–3). See also John Speir's excellent essay on the civilisation of Chaucer's audience in the introductory pages of his *Chaucer the Maker* (Faber, 1951). I should like to express here my great indebtedness to that stimulating and perceptive book.

must counter his own training, and *hear*, ringing aloud in his own imagination, the great debate of the Canterbury pilgrims passing through the voice of the greatest raconteur England has known.

IV

The General Prologue to the 'Canterbury Tales'

In *The Rainbow* there is a remarkable passage in which D. H. Lawrence describes how Christianity shaped and gave meaning to the spiritual inner consciousness of the people. Here it is:

Gradually there gathered the feeling of expectation. Christmas was coming. In the shed, at nights, a secret candle was burning, a sound of veiled voices was heard. The boys were learning the old mystery play of St George and Beelzebub. Twice a week, by lamplight, there was choir practice in the church, for the learning of old carols Brangwen wanted to hear. The girls went to these practices. Everywhere was a sense of mystery and rousedness. Everybody was preparing for something.

The time came near, the girls were decorating the church, with cold fingers binding holly and fir and yew about the pillars, till a new spirit was in the church, the stone broke out into dark rich leaf, the arches put forth their buds, and cold flowers rose to blossom in the dim, mystic atmosphere. Ursula must weave mistletoe over the door, and over the screen, and hang a silver dove from a sprig of yew, till dusk came down, and the church was like a grove.

In the cow-shed the boys were blacking their faces for a dress-rehearsal; the turkey hung dead, with opened, speckled wings, in the dairy. The time was come to make pies, in readiness.

The expectation grew more tense. The star was risen into the sky, the songs, the carols were ready to hail it. The star was the sign in the sky. Earth too should give a sign. As evening drew on, hearts beat fast with anticipation, hands were full of ready gifts. There were the tremulously expectant words of the church service, the night was past and the morning was come, the gifts were given and received, joy and peace made a flapping of wings in each heart, there was a great burst of carols, the Peace of the World had dawned, strife had passed away, every hand was linked in hand, every heart was singing.

It was bitter, though, that Christmas day, as it drew on to evening, and night, became a sort of bank holiday, flat and stale. The morning was so wonderful, but in the afternoon and evening the ecstasy perished like a nipped thing, like a bud in a false spring. Alas, that Christmas was only a domestic feast, a feast of sweetmeats and toys! Why did not the grown-ups also change their everyday hearts, and give way to ecstasy? Where was the ecstasy?

How passionately the Brangwens craved for it, the ecstasy. The father was troubled, dark-faced and disconsolate, on Christmas night, because the passion was not there, because the day was become as every day, and hearts were not aflame. Upon the mother was a kind of absentness, as ever, as if she were exiled for all her life. Where was the fiery heart of joy, now the coming was fulfilled; where was the star, the Magi's transport, the thrill of new being that shook the earth?

Still it was there, even if it were faint and inadequate. The cycle of creation still wheeled in the Church year. After Christmas, the ecstasy slowly sank and changed. Sunday followed Sunday, trailing a fine movement, a finely developed transformation over the heart of the family. The heart that was big with joy, that had seen the star and had followed to the inner walls of the Nativity, that there had swooned in the great light, must now feel the light slowly withdrawing, a shadow falling, darkening. The chill crept in, silence came over the earth, and then all was darkness. The veil of the temple was rent, each heart gave up the ghost, and sank dead.

They moved quietly, a little wanness on the lips of the children, at Good Friday, feeling the shadow upon their hearts. Then, pale with a deathly scent, came the lilies of resurrection, that shone coldly till the Comforter was given.

But why the memory of the wounds and the death? Surely Christ rose with healed hands and feet, sound and strong and glad? Surely the passage of the cross and the tomb was forgotten? But no— always the memory of the wounds, always the smell of the grave-clothes? A small thing was Resurrection, compared with the Cross and the death, in this cycle.

So the children lived the year of Christianity, the epic of the soul of mankind. Year by year the inner, unknown drama went on in them, their hearts were born and came to fulness, suffered on the cross, gave up the ghost, and rose again to unnumbered days, un-tired, having at least this rhythm of eternity in a ragged, incon-sequential life.[1]

D. H. Lawrence shows how the Christian rituals are begin-ning to fade and disappear before the coming of a secular, industrialised society, and yet what strength and profundity even the remnants possess. The ragged and inconsequential life of the bank holiday world, with its trivial satisfactions of sweetmeats and toys which do not really satisfy, is beginning to overwhelm the rhythm of eternity. The gulf between a divine pattern and the meaningless flux of daily event has been known to men at all times, but in some ages the gulf has seemed less: everyday action has not been wholly cut off from ritual, and the ordinary life has been closer to spiritual signi-ficance. Though by Chaucer's time the scepticism and doubts of the approaching Renaissance were already beginning to flood in, for Chaucer the cycle of creation still wheeled in the Church year. The historical changes had not yet weakened belief, but rather given it more edge and acerbity. Chaucer, in depicting the bustling world he saw before him, could still give utterance to the epic of the soul of mankind. Indeed it is just this harmony between the spiritual and the mundane that permeates the *General Prologue to the Canterbury Tales*. Where Lawrence, because he is so conscious of what is being lost, is forced to be explicit and insistent, for Chaucer the mystery and the ecstasy belong to the air he breathed, and can be implicit and taken for granted. Nor is there in Chaucer what Lawrence so hated in Christianity: its obsession with the negative aspects of the Christian myth, the Cross, the wounds, the suffering. Chaucer sings the Resurrection, he celebrates the Creation, he sees in this life with its great joys and mixed woes the eternal promise. Nowhere perhaps better than in the opening of the *Prologue*, that passage so filled with spring, and wonder, and praise.

> Whan that Aprille with his shoures soote   (1)
> The droghte of March hath perced to the roote,
> And bathed every veyne in swich licour

[1] D. H. Lawrence, *The Rainbow* (Penguin Books, 1949), pp. 282–4.

Of which vertu engendred is the flour;
Whan Zephirus eek with his sweete breeth
Inspired hath in every holt and heeth
The tendre croppes, and the yonge sonne
Hath in the Ram his halve cours yronne,
And smale foweles maken melodye,
That slepen al the nyght with open ye
(So priketh hem nature in hir corages);
Thanne longen folk to goon on pilgrimages,
And palmeres for to seken straunge strondes,
To ferne halwes, kowthe in sondry londes;
And specially from every shires ende
Of Engelond to Caunterbury they wende,
The hooly blisful martir for to seke,
That hem hath holpen whan that they were seeke.
    Bifil that in that seson on a day,
In Southwerk at the Tabard as I lay
Redy to wenden on my pilgrymage
To Caunterbury with ful devout corage,
At nyght was come into that hostelrye
Wel nyne and twenty in a compaignye,
Of sondry folk, by aventure yfalle
In felaweshipe, and pilgrimes were they alle,
That toward Caunterbury wolden ryde.

Not only does the passage give the freshness and awakening of the season after the cold-locked rigours of winter, it also portrays the essence of this key moment in the Christian year. For by ancient Christian conviction spring was not only the occasion for all natural and human beginnings, but was the general date of the Redemption through the sacrifice of Good Friday, and hence was that time of year in which man's chance for salvation was specially offered him.[1] The promise of redemption is re-enacted with each rejuvenation of spring; the orders of man and nature interpenetrate and move together in spiritual and creative harmony.

Many qualities combine in the transformation of spring.

[1] See Ralph Baldwin, *The Unity of the Canterbury Tales* (Rosenhilde and Bagger, Copenhagen, 1955), particularly pp. 24–7.

Tenderness and delicacy, suggested by phrases such as 'shoures soote', 'sweete breeth', 'tendre croppes', are united with images suggesting power, vastness and energy—'The droghte of March hath *perced* to the roote', 'every veyne', 'every holt and heeth', 'yonge sonne...yronne'. The mysterious thoroughness with which the change is wrought is evoked by images such as 'perced to the roote'—how the fine rain penetrates deep into the ground while stabbing *drought* to the heart—and 'inspired' with its suggestion that the wind, like some divine agent, actually breathes into the vegetation, stirring and awaking to life. The description of the sun being in Aries gives the time of the month, and also expresses lusty vigour ('Ram', 'yronne'). The sun is 'yonge' because the new year was reckoned from March, but since it was believed that the world itself was created in March some suggestion of pristine wonder also enters the phrase. All is sweetness, and freshness, and rejoicing. The birds that 'maken melodye' also 'slepen al the nyght with open ye': which not only records an astonishing and wonderful fact of nature (though, alas, not true), but also suggests that they do not close their eyes even in sleep lest something of all this wonderful and rare beauty be lost to them. The line 'So priketh hem nature in hir corages' looks back to the mysterious potency of the rain and the 'licour' (*liqueur* rather than common *liquor* in its potency) which engenders the flowers, creating a parallel, and leads on immediately to the next line, 'Thanne longen folk to goon on pilgrimages', creating another parallel which implies that the same forces which transform and shape the flora and fauna move and guide men's lives. The parallel is strengthened a few lines later when Chaucer depicts himself, the naive and literal-minded pilgrim, as setting out for Canterbury with 'ful devout *corage*'. Against the vastness of spring's transformation as well as the sense of adventure, strangeness and new possibilities are implicit in the reference to palmers being led

to seken straunge strondes,
To ferne halwes, kowthe in sondry londes.

The creative joy that is evoked throughout by the rhythm mounts and concentrates on the figure of the saint:

> And specially from every shires ende
> Of Engelond to Caunterbury they wende,
> The hooly blisful martir for to seke...

The saint's holiness and bliss are at one with, and are a culmination of, the wonder and joy of the natural world. Even the identity of the rhymes 'seke' (visit) and 'seeke' (sick) emphasises the curative and transforming power of the saint, and suggests gratitude (akin to relief of spring after deathbound winter) moving men to pilgrimage. Whatever other motives pilgrims may have, such as the Wife of Bath who doubtless is seeking another husband, the most important perspective has been established for seeing what essentially moves men to set off, like migrating birds, on pilgrimage in this season of the Christian year.

In the passage creative energy and joy, hope and fulfilment unite in tranquil confidence. The portrait of spring is no private vision, but is presented as a common experience in which all may harmoniously participate. It is indeed the view of a religious civilisation in which the natural and the artificial, the personal and the general, the divine and the secular have been combined and reconciled. And this affirmation found in the opening of the *Prologue* permeates the *Canterbury Tales* so that even in ragged and inconsequential details the rhythm of eternity can be discerned. To rejoice in the Creation is to sense the all-present harmony and at the time time to delight in the particular, the unique, the separated created being. This is Chaucer's achievement.

It is absolutely in keeping with this sensibility that Chaucer should immediately move from the large affirmation and joy of the opening to the ordinary and mundane world of the Tabard Inn where twenty-nine pilgrims happen to fall into fellowship. There is no conflict between the artistic skill of the 'smale fowles' carolling the mood of rebirth, and the problems of lodging in an inn ('The chambres and the stables weren wyde') or trying to make out what your companions are like. All *sub species aeternitatis* bespeaks the glory of the Creator. Thus from the first Chaucer establishes an inclusive understanding which links great and small, high and low matters.

If what I am suggesting here is true, it should profoundly affect the way in which we read both the portraits in the *Prologue* and the tales that follow. On the whole the tendency of critics has been to concentrate on Chaucer's psychological acumen, his social observation or his satirical comment. All these approaches are valid, and the poetry repays such concentration with overwhelming largesse. But perhaps a reading of Chaucer can go further than this. Chaucer depicts the individual personality and the social representative in his portraits of each pilgrim, but does he not also reveal and suggest something of their spiritual condition? A pilgrimage is a penitential journey as well as an act of gratitude and worship. The state of a pilgrim's soul is more important than the array he is in, or the extent to which he is socially acceptable. What he believes in, the values he lives by, the reality as opposed to the pretence in his actions—these are the important things. Nor, of course, are these separable from his role in society, for spiritual obligations take a different shape with different vocations. The duties of a knight, a prioress or a doctor are not the same, and each must be understood not only as a private individual but also as a functionary fulfilling, or failing to fulfil, his purpose in the hierarchical pattern. Thus Chaucer's gift of combining individual portrait with social generalisation, so often acknowledged and praised in criticism dealing with his satire or dramatic presentation, is closely bound up with his depiction of the spiritual state.

When we turn to the actual portraits of the pilgrims we can see how clearly Chaucer has suggested the values they live by and what they look for. But before proceeding to this, a word of warning, and an explanation of his technique. Ultimately only God can know the state of a man's soul: for any human being to claim certainty of another's spiritual condition would be pretension indeed. Even the conventional omniscient narrator would seem arrogant if he laid this down. So Chaucer employs a more modest method, one which works by suggestion, and by an appeal to the reader to probe behind the appearances. It is the method of the very fallible, possibly only too obtuse narrator. In much medieval poetry the 'I' of the poem is a dramatic entity, bearing little relation to the actual personality of the poet himself, and usually expresses the moral judgments and emotions proper to all men.[1] Chaucer has used his variant of the naive or simple-minded narrator to good effect in earlier poems but, with the exception of *Troilus and Criseyde*, never has his method been more integrated into the plan and spirit of the work than it is here in the *Canterbury Tales*. Chaucer, as a foolish though devout pilgrim, purports to present his fellows as he got to know them during their stay at the Tabard and perhaps on the road as well. The limits of his knowledge, the extent to which he relies upon their conversation or their appearance, are delicately stressed. At the same time, by a sleight-of-hand trick, the time-span is expanded to include more than the night's stay at the inn or the several days' travelling: subtly more extensive information is provided us. Further, the pilgrims seem to reveal more of themselves to us, the readers, than they did to poor Chaucer, the pilgrim who had not wit enough to see through fair words or specious arguments. While there is a joke in this at the expense of the simple poet, more important, Chaucer the pilgrim comes to epitomise the myopia of human insight. Even as the careful selection of details, with their calculated density of implication, challenge us to judge profoundly, Chaucer weaves into the cloth of his poem the theme of human fallibility.

There is surely no need to say much about how the portraits often quite explicitly reveal the goals on which the pilgrims' hearts are set. The Knight who loves 'chivalrie, Trouthe and honour, fredom and curtesie'; the Monk who

---

[1] See Rosemary Woolf, 'Chaucer as a Satirist in the General Prologue to the *Canterbury Tales*', *Critical Quarterly*, XLI, 2 (1959), 150–1.

loves 'venerie'; the Clerk who would gladly learn and gladly teach; the Franklin who wishes 'to lyven in delit'; the Doctor of Physic who thought gold the most precious of all his medicines; the poor Parson rich in holy thought and work; in these portraits as in others the basic motive is plain to see. But, without going through the group one by one, something should be said briefly about the subtlety of the techniques whereby Chaucer uncovers their spiritual condition. Many of the apparently 'realistic' details are actually symbolic, and reveal vistas. For example, take the Knight

> That fro the tyme that he first bigan
> To riden out, he loved chivalrie...

This glance back at when he was a young man shows how dedicated he has been all his life—even in his youth he was quite unlike what his son, the Squire, now is. It further stresses how much he has experienced since then, as indeed does the mention of all the places he has been in and the battles he has fought. Have actuality and the harsh toll of years blunted his idealism, we might wonder? The poetry suggests no sense of disillusionment—indeed almost the opposite. A phrase such as 'And of his port as meeke as is a mayde', besides the obvious reference to his modest demeanour, suggests a certain paradox about him: a tenderness in the man of battle, an innocence still retained fresh in the war-torn soldier. His surcoat of fustian may be all spotted with rust from his coat of mail because he set off on pilgrimage as soon as he returned from his last expedition, suggesting again the dedicated man: it also more subtly perhaps suggests how his arduous life is beginning to leave its marks upon him, though his vigour and manliness are all the more admirable for the marks of strain and struggle. His choosing only his Yeoman to ride with him 'at that tyme' hints at a person who knows when to cut out of his life the redundant and the luxurious. Much of the subtlety of the Knight's portrait too comes from the contrast implied between him and his son, and also between him and his Yeoman. Where the Knight has the hardened virtues of experience and endurance, the other two seem untested. The Squire's virtues are those of life-happy youth. 'He sleep namoore than dooth a nyghtingale' with its echo of the small 'fowles' that 'slepen al the nyght with open ye' in the opening gives his innocent delight-crammed wonder at all the opportunities he possesses, and also mocks gently the intensity with which he throws himself into his love-life. Where does delight in *being*, in existing vigorously as God made one, shade into vanity and egoism? The Squire, because of his youth, is still on the safe side. His self-regard is (again to stress the paradox) unselfconscious. Perhaps one day hardship and endeavour like his father's may temper a character too little tried, and so far given perhaps slightly too much to indulgence and delight. But his conduct in cavalry raids, where he bore himself well 'as of so litel space', promises well for the future man he will be. Despite the touch of vanity suggested by 'embrouded', the lines comparing him to May and nature flourishing in the spring-time affirm the grace of heedless youth:

> Embrouded was he, as it were a meede   (89)
> Al ful of fresshe floures, whyte and reede.
> Syngynge he was, or floytynge, al the day
> He was as fresshe as is the month of May.

The Yeoman has the vigour of full manhood, but his nature seems akin to the silent intricacies of a wooded landscape. His life is concentrated on the skills of his craft. Yet the repeated emphasis on the neatness and good shape he keeps his weapons in, particularly by contrast with the worn gear of his master, while it suggests competence and reliability, also perhaps suggests his interest is too narrowly on his own skill. He wears a St Christopher—as if the only religious figure that concerns him is the patron saint of foresters. He knows things by lore and practice ('of wodecraft wel koude he al the usage'), but we may suspect he has little imagination or interest in matters outside the woods he knows so well. His trees, his craft, his weapons are his life. In this portrait the limitations of the pilgrim are depicted by details omitted as much as by details selected.

Each of these characters we have discussed has different interests, different values, indeed a different way of seeing life. Their reasons for going on pilgrimage likewise differ. For the knight it is part of his chivalric duty, and perhaps too a desire to clear his soul after his period at war. For his son it is doubtless a pleasant journey; a chance to enjoy the season, the country, new places, new faces. The Yeoman is loyally following his master. 'The hooly blisful martir' carries a different meaning for each of them. Yet they embark on a common pilgrimage, and mysteriously the same spirit draws them despite their diversity. In the poetry of the *General Prologue* the extremes of individual humanity and divine purpose interlock.

Chaucer was certainly fascinated by the variety and particularity of his fellow-men. The 'God's plenty' of the *Prologue* proves it. But Dryden's metaphor is so apt because the abundance of humanity constantly reminds us of the Creator; and while each pilgrim will differently conceive Him and the reasons for his own journey, this pilgrimage is still a common one. Perhaps too any presentation of a pilgrimage will tend to suggest the reminder that life itself is a pilgrimage; and certainly the fullness and range of Chaucer's company enforce the symbolic overtone. Thus we not only are drawn to imagine a particular band of men taking a certain route to Canterbury at a given moment in history; we are led to perceive what forms mankind may take, and what their lives may be like, spiritually as well as materially, as they proceed to a place where redemption is offered. Literally their goal is the shrine of St Thomas à Becket; anagogically it is Christ's gift of salvation.

If St Thomas à Becket is one key figure in the cavalcade, and that foolish pilgrim, Chaucer, who so embodies the fallibility of human awareness is another, then the third is the grand secular figure of the Host. He accompanies the pilgrims to ensure that they will return to his inn; his concern is with their hospitality and entertainment. He is all that is gross and material, though he can change his speech from vulgarity to courtesy; he is all that is concerned with living well in this world. For him life is 'Pleying by the wey', and he invites the others to do likewise by telling stories. So they agree, and speak out. Their stories entertain, but they also reveal what the pilgrims are, how they conceive life, what values they hold, what they have made of their opportunities here in this world. The stories are revelation of spiritual *being* as well as of character. Of course, this does not hold equally true of all the tales, but it would seem that as Chaucer's purpose grew and unfolded itself to him, this is the direction his great plan took. At any rate, this is the pattern I have found growing clearer and clearer as I have reread the tales, and it is the thesis I shall attempt to propose in the analyses of the tales that follow.

THE
CANTERBURY TALES

Never trust the artist. Trust the tale.

D. H. LAWRENCE

CHAPTER 1

The Knight's Tale

JOHN DRYDEN wrote of Chaucer's Tales, 'I prefer far above his other stories, the noble poem of *Palamon and Arcite*, which is of the Epique kind, and perhaps not much inferior to the Ilias and the Aeneis'. High praise indeed. Yet praise amply warranted. Indeed, in English, perhaps the nearest thing to this tale is one of the great tragedies or one of the last 'romances' of Shakespeare. Certainly *The Knight's Tale* requires of the reader the same kind of attention that he would give to a Shakespeare play: by this I mean the kind of attention that appreciates, in every detail of the poetic structure, the confident intent of the creative intelligence.

What sort of a tale is it that Chaucer is making his Knight tell? It is of the epic kind, said Dryden. The opening lines set the tone of heroic grandeur. In the first lines of the poem Chaucer makes use of the device, frequently used throughout the tale, of reminding the reader what else could be told had the narrator time or space to tell it.

> And certes, if it nere to long to heere, (875)
> I wolde have toold yow fully the manere
> How wonnen was the regne of Femenye
> By Theseus and by his chivalrye;
> And of the grete bataille for the nones
> Bitwixen Atthenes and Amazones;
> And how asseged was Ypolita,
> The faire, hardy queene of Scythia;
> And of the feste that was at hir weddynge,
> And of the tempest at hir hoom-comynge;
> But al that thyng I moot as now forbere.
> I have, God woot, a large feeld to ere,
> And wayke been the oxen in my plough.
> The remenant of the tale is long enough.

The effect of this device is to suggest the tale's large realm of discourse in which the events of the story are to be seen. Every tale, novel, or play has what I have called a *realm of discourse*. By this I mean that the work of art defines within itself the range of experiences it will treat of and the structure of values that are to guide the reader's judgments. Let me briefly illustrate what I mean: in *Macbeth* it is roughly true to say that the action takes place within the intellectual framework of the medieval (Christian) world order: salvation and damnation are presented as part of the central issue, and the reader is required explicitly to consider the issues of the play in such terms. *Romeo and Juliet*, on the other hand, has quite a different realm of action: the action takes place in the secular Renaissance world (despite the priest): the main conflict is between death and accidental disasters, and life fulfilled and flourishing. In the lines quoted above we can see that the realm of discourse of *The Knight's Tale* will be the world of chivalry and 'romance'. It will be the world of courteous and courageous actions, of love and war waged with ritualistic formality. Indeed even from the opening we can guess that the story will treat of love and war—the most basic of all human themes. Furthermore, love and war will be described in bold and extravagant colours, and the verse will ring with grandeur and ceremony.

> He conquered al the regne of Femenye, (866)
> That whilom was ycleped Scithia,
> And weddede the queene Ypolita,
> And boughte hire hoom with hym in his contree
> With muchel glorie and greet solempnytee,
> And eek hir younge suster Emelye.
> And thus with victorie and with melodye...

The brief account of Theseus' deed of retribution upon Thebes and the 'tiraunt', Creon, that forms a prelude to the tale of Palamon and Arcite, has an important function. Not only does it tell us something about the character of Theseus which is to be important later—that he is a true knight, chivalrous and good, and somewhat easily moved by pity—the prelude also introduces the important theme of 'Fortune'.

> 'Som drope of pitee, thurgh thy gentillesse,   (920)
> Upon us wrecched wommen lat thou falle.
> For, certes, lord, ther is noon of us alle,
> That she ne hath been a duchesse or a queene.
> Now be we caytyves, as it is wel seene,
> Thanked be Fortune and hire false wheel,
> That noon estaat assureth to be weel.'

Fortune is the disruptive force in this ideal world of chivalric order and simplicity. No matter how good a man may be, how noble his motives, how secure his position, how great his degree, he is still a thrall to the fickle goddess. In a moment the spin of her wheel may turn his feasting and joy to pain and anguish. Life, for all its ceremony and honour, is precariously held.

Of course, reading the opening pages of the tale one does not consciously set out the 'romantic' framework as I have done here, one just comes to accept it without awareness. But for some modern readers this chivalric world may seem unreal, artificial and naive, and may lead to their thinking this tale has no significant bearing on their own lives. Indeed, one of the fundamental questions to be asked in criticism is, 'What meaning has this work of art for me, living today?' I have sketched the conventions of this tale because I want the reader to consider this question, and because I want to show how a poet may make use of a framework to say things of universal significance. For literary conventions are a means of controlling the reader's responses, and of directing his attention towards the artistic focus of the work.

After the somewhat grand opening dealing with Theseus the tale proper begins. Though at first the story of Palamon and Arcite may seem small in comparison to the grand sweep of poetry that has preceded it, it soon begins to grow in power and complexity. From the moment we are introduced to Palamon and Arcite on the battlefield, 'liggynge by and by, Both in oon armes', their similarity and sworn brotherhood are stressed. They are both knights, of royal blood, in the bloom and vigour of young manhood. On the whole Chaucer avoids detailed characterisation (such as he gave in many of his portraits in the *General Prologue*). This is part of his design. If he gave each a too elaborate individuality we might, depending on our own natures and prejudices, be inclined to sympathise more with one character than the other, and Chaucer wants our sympathies to be equally balanced between the two young men.[1] Similarly with Emelye Chaucer mainly wants us to see her as the archetype of feminine grace and innocence.

> Emelye, that fairer was to sene (1035)
> Than is the lylie upon his stalke grene,
> And fressher than the May with floures newe—
> For with the rose colour stroof hire hewe.
> I noot which was the fyner of hem two—.

Not only to these lines have a freshness and natural vigour, the description relates Emelye to the traditional lady of courtly love. The idea of the lady's beauty striking a lover suddenly like the thrust of a weapon is one of the traditional images of courtly love poetry, and is related to the modern convention of 'love at first sight'. That the poetry works within a convention, however, should not blind us to its beauty and force.

> 'The fresshe beautee sleeth me sodeynly (1118)
> Of hire that rometh in the yonder place,
> And but I have hir mercy and hir grace,
> That I may seen hire atte leeste weye,
> I nam but deed; ther nis namoore to seye.'

In the 'fresshe beautee' we feel concentrated both the bountiful life of spring and the startling charm of femininity—and these associations gain power by the contrast with the prison in which Palamon and Arcite are confined. As sunlight can dazzle, so sights experienced with awe and passion can be almost painful to behold. The word 'rometh' subtly associates the lady with natural creatures that wander freely with graceful spontaneity,

---

[1] See Charles Muscatine: 'His crowning modification (of Bocaccio's *Teseida*) is the equalization of Palamon and Arcite' (*op. cit.* p. 180).

and 'in the yonder place' suggests how far removed from her Arcite feels himself to be. 'Hir mercy and hir grace' join feelings of spiritual love and worship to the already established sensation of physical ecstasy. All this Chaucer presents with astonishing lyrical tact. In this kind of poetry simplicity and elegance merge and become one.

This passage, I said, was completely *in* the convention of courtly love, and it exploits the convention perfectly. But the poetry is not always in a convention: sometimes the poetry is partly inside and partly outside a convention, and sometimes it breaks completely away. When Palamon and Arcite begin to argue about the right of each to love Emelye exclusively, the poetry overflows the bounds of the convention.

> 'Thou shalt', quod he, 'be rather fals than I;   (1153)
> And thou art fals, I telle thee outrely,
> For paramour I loved hire first er thow.
> What wiltow seyn? Thou wistest nat yet now
> Wheither she be a womman or goddesse!
> Thyn is affecioun of hoolynesse,
> And myn is love, as to a creature;
> For which I tolde thee myn aventure
> As to my cosyn and my brother sworn.
> I pose that thow lovedest hire biforn;
> Wostow nat wel the olde clerkes sawe,
> That "who shal yeve a lovere any lawe?"
> Love is a gretter lawe, by my pan,
> Than may be yeve to any erthely man;
> And therfore positif lawe and swich decree
> Is broken al day for love in ech degree.
> A man moot nedes love, maugree his heed.
> He may nat fleen it, thogh he sholde be deed,
> Al be she mayde, or wydwe, or elles wyf.'

The humour here gently derides the way lovers rationalise their feelings and elaborately justify their actions, and provides a note of 'realism' which is played off against the convention. But there is more to the passage than this. One of the most serious and important themes of the tale begins to emerge here. Man is the torn victim of conflicting passions and duties.

The drive of love rends sworn amities and separates blood kinships. Love itself is split by the rival claims of Agape and Eros, spiritual love and physical love.

> 'Thyn is affecioun of hoolynesse,
> And myn is love, as to a creature.'

Codes of conduct demand one thing of man, the laws of his passionate nature demand another. Between what he desires and what he gets, between what he imagines and what falls, between his comings and goings man is stretched and racked.

> 'Allas, why pleynen folk so in commune   (1251]
> On purveiaunce of God, or of Fortune,
> That yeveth hem ful ofte in many a gyse
> Wel bettre than they kan hemself devyse?
> Som man desireth for to han richesse,
> That cause is of his mordre or greet siknesse;
> And som man wolde out of his prisoun fayn,
> That in his hous is of his meynee slayn,
> Infinite harmes been in this mateere.
> We witen nat what things we preyen heere:
> We faren as he that dronk is as a mous.
> A dronke man woot wel he hath an hous,
> But he noot which the righte wey is thider,
> And to a dronke man the wey is slider.'

This complaint is made by Arcite when he is given his freedom and is exiled from Emilye. We are amused by Arcite's lamentings because they seem a bit excessive for his situation, yet we are also touched by the serious resonances of this passage. The image of the drunk man staggering in search of his home is a distinctively Chaucerian image in its compassionate humour and humanity. It makes us recognise how the same terrible pattern can be felt even in the most minute, and ridiculous, particulars of life.

> Who hath the worse, Arcite or Palamoun?   (1348)
> That oon may seen his lady day by day,
> But in prison he moot dwelle alway:
> That oother wher hym list may ride or go,
> But seen his lady shal he nevere mo.

The tale of Palamon and Arcite, as it proceeds, is emblematic of man's conflicts and frustrations. This is given its fullest expression in the final sections of the tale—in the descriptions of the powers of Mars, Venus, Diana, and Saturn, in the account of the battle, the death of Arcite and the grief and celebrations that follow. The divisions in man's nature between his various passions and aspirations are given body and substance in the fable by the way Palamon, Arcite and Emelye appeal to the gods to answer their desires, by the wrangling of the gods and Saturn's grim compromise. Arcite's aggressive desire to win his love by defeating his opponent, Palamon's surrender to the charities of love, Emelye's yearning to retain the independence of virginity are presented as comedy through the way each, unknown to the others, appeals to the appropriate god; but it is comedy that shows the terrible irreconcilabilities inherent in life, and sets these particular people and their differences in a perspective which takes in almost the whole range of human experience. The magnitude of the poetic vision can be seen particularly in the renowned description of the temple of Mars.

> Ther saugh I first the derke ymaginyng (1995)
> Of Felonye, and all the compassyng;
> The crueel Ire, reed as any gleede;
> The pykepurs, and eek the pale Drede;
> The smylere with the knyf under the cloke;
> The shepne brennynge with the blake smoke;
> The tresoun of the mordrynge in the bedde;
> The open werre, with woundes al bibledde;
> Contek, with blody knyf and sharp manace.
> Al ful of chirkynge was that sory place...

> Yet saugh I brent the shippes hoppesteres; (2017)
> The hunte strangled with the wilde beres;
> The sowe freten the child right in the cradel;
> The cook yscalded, for al his longe ladel...

By the sudden change to first person narration, and by vivid and concentrated imagery Chaucer makes us feel that we ourselves as we read are eyewitnesses to these very deeds: the very sound of 'chirkynge' seems to ring in our ears, and we are as appalled as if we have for the first time experienced the vicious horrors in life. There is an incredible centrality to the images:—'the smylere with the knyf under the cloke' catches the essence of hypocritical treachery. The image of the sow eating a child in the cradle gives the horror of all life's meaningless accidents, while the following image of the cook being scalded extends a similar horror to even trivial and comic incidents. With such images we seem to have come a long way from the chivalric splendour the tale at first promised, and a long way from an heroic and glorious tapestry of life. What is the significance of this, and how does Chaucer reconcile his range of tones within the tale?

There is no reconciliation, argues Elizabeth Salter in a very interesting study of the tale.[1] Her conclusions are, to put it mildly, radical. Chaucer, she suggests, was in two minds about the significance of his story. From his sources he acquired a tale that touched upon the suffering of human life under the cruel and disproportionate strokes of destiny. In reshaping his material he made the mistake of permitting sympathy for that suffering to make too strong a claim on him, and so introduced elements which rend his version apart. His failure is reflected in the tale's uncertainties of tone. 'By choosing to lay stress upon these elements in the story, Chaucer considerably widened his range of emotional and descriptive poetry: by choosing also to encourage reflection, even criticism, he made his task of final and total reconciliation much more complex. We may think that we see, in the strange switches of tone and attitude, in the "double voice" of poet-narrator, his half-conscious understanding of this fact: on the one hand, he is impelled to recreate the older story with intelligent scepticism, compassion, dramatic insight—on the other, he is reluctant to admit what he has done. The imaginative advance and withdrawal of the poem is noticeable throughout.'[2] The supreme

[1] Elizabeth Salter, *Chaucer: The Knight's Tale and The Clerk's Tale* (Edward Arnold, 1962). [2] *Ibid.* p. 34.

example of this withdrawal, indeed the crux of the poem's failure, is to be found in Theseus' final speech which 'relies upon our willingness to put out of our mind many of the more uncomfortable aspects of the poem'.[1] But even this is only an example of a graver defect in Chaucer's writing. 'Chaucer allows the poem to raise imaginative issues which are not resolved by the final philosophic summing-up any more than they are resolved by the bland denouement of the final twenty lines. This is something we have to face in other works of Chaucer. *The Knight's Tale* presents us with it in a particularly urgent form. *Troilus and Criseyde* is an excellent example of a poem which uses a good deal of philosophic and religious material with an eye to *local* richness rather than to overall thematic consistency.'[2] Nor does Chaucer alone fail to comprehend that certain set narrative or dramatic structures prevent the full utilisation of certain material. 'The reader's predicament is somewhat similar in *The Winter's Tale*: there also a narrative full of extreme and unmotivated cruelty is brought to a "happy" conclusion, but the reconciliation is hardly sufficient to quieten our uneasiness, even disgust, at the harsh treatment of innocence which makes that reconciliation necessary.'[3]

Now all criticism is an act of impertinence in that it implies that a work of art needs an intermediary, someone who can make the meaning clearer than the writer has, or can call the reader's attention to that which he was stupid enough to miss. It is a forgivable act of impertinence since we, the readers, often *are* obtuse and are grateful for direction which puts us right. It is also a forgivable act when some struggling writer has his purposes clarified or his blunderings located. But it is an impertinence which is less forgivable when a critic, faced with some supreme achievement of literature which establishes what canons there can be, patronises the work in a manner which suggests that if only Shakespeare or Chaucer or Milton had had the benefit of the critic's advice they would not have erred so foolishly. I do not mean that such poets are beyond

---

[1] *Ibid.* p. 34.   [2] *Ibid.* p. 33.   [3] *Ibid.* p. 32.

criticism, only that their achievements impose on their critics the duty of some humility. It is a great pity that Elizabeth Salter, particularly by the tone she adopts and by some unfortunate phrases she uses, lays herself open to the charge of being wanting in such humility. The pity is all the greater in that her argument merits consideration, and in debating it we approach a crux of the tale.

There are two main reasons for Elizabeth Salter's devaluation of the tale. First, she misinterprets the function of the gods in *The Knight's Tale*. She sees them as sinister divinities who callously from above sport with their human puppets,[1] as the President of the Immortals is said to in the closing pages of *Tess of the D'Urbervilles*. But the gods in the tale are not transcendent beings who exist in their own right: they are manifestations of human passions or human experiences. Venus is believed in because men know fleshly desires, and Saturn or Fortune can be conceived because men can credit things to necessity or chance. Omit the gods from the poem and Palamon and Arcite could still behave as they do even down to the man of violence losing his love because he trusts in his violence more than in his love. But by including the divine machinery the tale becomes more than an account of three particular people: it portrays the passions, sufferings, conflicts and disasters all men are susceptible to. The subject of the poem is not some supernatural malice, but the actual lot of mankind. Hence Theseus' final speech is not an attempt to withdraw from issues raised in the poem, rather it is simply an expression of one attitude and possibly to the Knight the wisest attitude to adopt before the inescapable facts of human existence.

Secondly, there is Mrs Salter's account of the variety of tones in the tale. This is always a crucial issue in Chaucer's poems. Some points can be immediately affirmed. There is truth in her suggestion that there are two voices in the tale. The first voice is the Knight's. He is telling a tale appropriate to his character and background: a tale of chivalry, in which battles are fought with courage, love pursued with vigour, and

[1] Salter, *op. cit.* pp. 32 and 34.

death is paid with heroic rites. But his tale is the first of many, and together with the pilgrims' tales are to build up into one of the most extensive portrayals of humanity ever attempted. *The Knight's Tale* will interconnect with tales that follow. Issues in it must have a resonance that can still be discerned later. This means that, beyond the intentions of the Knight relating his story, something of the grander design of Chaucer himself must be apprehended in the first of the tales. The poem must be a unity within itself, yet prepare for an even larger unity; issues must be resolved, yet lead on to further explorations; and the overall tone of the tale must establish something of the ultimate tone of the *Canterbury Tales*. Thus the second voice is the voice of Chaucer, commencing the great narration of the *Canterbury Tales*.

The Knight's Tale is told in such a way that, tragic and terrible as some parts may be, we are never depressed or downcast by it. This is achieved by the intriguing delight of the narration, and by the tale's fertility of invention and detail. Furthermore, we are consistently astonished by the ease with which Chaucer's lyrical simplicity can catch the very essence of human experience. What other poets, such rich poets as Keats, Wordsworth and even Shakespeare, we feel have to strive for Chaucer seems to pour out as spontaneous benison.

> The bisy larke, messager of day,   (1491)
> Salueth in hir song the morwe gray,
> And firy Phebus riseth up so bright
> That al the orient laugheth at the light,
> And with his stremes dryeth in the greves
> The silver dropes hangynge on the leves.

The fertility and joy to be found in the world seem reflected in the fertility and joy of the poetry here. Similarly the contrariety found in life seems reproduced in the multifarious tones and images within the poem. But whatever the subject written about or the local tone adopted, the overriding sense is that of life's fascinating complexity and its essential harmony and pleasure. Consider, for example, one of the more terrible passages in the poem:

> 'My deere doghter Venus,' quod Saturne,   (2453)
> 'My cours, that hath so wyde for to turne,
> Hath moore power than woot any man.
> Myn is the drenchyng in the see so wan;
> Myn is the prison in the derke cote;
> Myn is the stranglying and hangyng by the throte,
> The murmure and the cherles rebellying,
> The groynynge, and the pryvee empoysonyng;
> I do vengeance and pleyn correccioun,
> Whil I dwelle in the signe of the leoun.
> Myn is the ruyne of the hye halles,
> The fallynge of the toures and of the walles
> Upon the mynour or the carpenter.
> I slow Sampsoun, shakynge the piler;
> And myne be the maladyes colde,
> The derke tresons, and the castes olde;
> My lookyng is the fader of pestilence.
> Now weep namoore, I shal doon diligence
> That Palamon, that is thyn owene knyght,
> Shal have his lady, as thou hast him hight.
> Though Mars shal helpe his knyght, yet nathelees,
> Bitwixe yow ther moot be som tyme pees,
> Al be ye noght of o compleccioun,
> That causeth al day swich divisioun...'

Here the poetry certainly immerses us in 'the destructive element'. But the feelings generated are awe and compassion, not despair or self-pity. The hard clarity of the images forces us to contemplate without flinching the suffering that exists in life, and such clearsightedness and courage are themselves rewards of the imagination. The poetry never pretends that life is only like this, nor does it belittle mankind. The pride of those that build 'hye halles', the modest endeavours of carpenters, the self-sacrificial heroism of Samson point to the rich variety of human behaviour. Death comes to all, by a hundred thousand ways, but that is necessity. The poetry does not shirk reality nor (what would be the same thing) attack the god.

Saturn/Jupiter speaks to his daughter Venus with all the stern truthfulness of a just father who will not deceive his children; and by dramatising the harsh aspect of events in this way the poetry leads us to infer a benign care behind the rigour. The implications of the passage also fit into the total pattern of the poem. In the working out of the tale of Palamon and Arcite is suggested the secret justice of Saturn: each gets what he requests, Saturn 'wol thy lust fulfille', men's rewards and endings are implicit often in the goals they choose to seek. 'Order, which characterises the structure of the poem, is also the heart of its meaning,' writes Charles Muscatine. '...What gives this conception of life its perspective, its depth and seriousness, is its constant awareness of a formidably antagonistic element —chaos, disorder—which in life is an ever-threatening possibility, even in moments of supremest assuredness, and which in the poem falls across the pattern of order, being clearly exemplified in the erratic reversals of the poem's plot, and deeply embedded in the poem's texture.'[1] But the pattern of the poem assimilates even this disorder itself, capturing it by irony. Saturn is not only the god of justice, but he is also the source of universal necessity and recreation. Creation and joy cannot exist without destruction and the pain it brings. The poem in its structure mirrors this necessary truth. And by the harmony of its own structure, it invites us to see and rejoice in the analogous harmony of life itself.

But let us now take a closer look at how the poetry manages this in the final sections of the tale.

The tournament between Palamon and Arcite for the possession of Emelye is presented with all the pageantry and colourful formality of a medieval painting. But basically it is the sexual struggle to win a mate that is being presented in the ritualistic splendour of the tableau. The primitive and instinctive drives of the human race are felt behind all the elaborate and civilised trappings of the courtesy. Even though the knights have been forbidden to fight to the death by the gentle-hearted Duke, this battle is emblematic of all human strife. The arche-

[1] *Op. cit.* p. 181.

typal nature of the battle is created partly by the ritual (even today we can still feel in cowboy films the duel as the inevitable expression and outcome of conflict; also we might remember the function of the duel at the end of *Lear*); it is also created by Chaucer's deliberately pitching his description in terms that bring to mind the whole alliterative tradition of heroic battle poetry.

> Ther is namoore to seyn, but west and est (2601)
> In goon the speres ful sadly in arrest;
> In gooth the sharpe spore into the syde.
> Ther seen men who kan juste and who kan ryde;
> Ther shyveren shaftes upon sheeldes thikke;
> He feeleth thurgh the herte-spoon the prikke.
> Up spryngen speres twenty foot on highte;
> Out goon the swerdes as the silver brighte;
> The helmes they tohewen and toshrede;
> Out brest the blood with stierne stremes rede;
> With mighty maces the bones they tobreste.

There is zest and delight in the description, though we are also made to feel the fundamental savagery of war.

As might be expected Arcite, who put martial victory first and appealed to the god of war, wins the tournament. But in his moment of triumph, he is mortally injured. In his dying moments we are made to feel the common end all men must share. Arcite's painful last words whisper a universal lamentation.

> 'Naught may the woful spirit in myn herte (2765)
> Declare o point of alle my sorwes smerte
> To yow, my lady, that I love moost;
> But I biquethe the servyce of my goost
> To yow aboven every creature,
> Syn that my lyf may no lenger dure.
> Allas, the wo! allas, the peynes stronge,
> That I for yow have suffred, and so longe!
> Allas, the deeth! allas, myn Emelye!
> Allas, departynge of our compaignye!
> Allas, myn hertes queene! allas, my wyf!
> Myn hertes lady, endere of my lyf!

What is this world? what asketh men to have?
Now with his love, now in his colde grave
Allone, withouten any compaignye...'

Life is seen as dwelling amid 'compaignye'—knowing mirth, and solace, and security—death is utter negation and loneliness. Yet what makes Arcite's death all the more pitiful is the realisation, present in the poetry, that 'compaignye' is never fully achieved. No man can make any one else understand more than 'o point of alle his sorwes smerte'. In life there is an anguish as keen as the pains of death itself: the anguish of frustrated desires and unanswered aspirations. The pains of his death and the woes of his love for Emelye are merged in one pathetic lamentation in the dying Arcite. And even what love *is* won, is won only to be snatched away: 'Now with his love, now in his colde grave.' This is the human condition. Yet the poetry of the tale makes us feel that the search to love and be loved is the very breath of life.

Arcite dies like a true knight, with magnanimity and the unselfish desire to have the friends he loves know the happiness he must forsake. In death the courtly spirit is victorious. The poetry is all the more moving because of the grim and unsentimental way it presents to us the physical process of death.

> And with that word his speche faille gan,   (2798)
> For from his feet up to his brest was come
> The coold of deeth, that hadde hym overcome,
> And yet mooreover, for in his armes two
> The vital strengthe is lost and al ago.
> Oonly the intellect, withouten moore,
> That dwelled in his herte syk and soore,
> Gan faillen whan the herte felte deeth.
> Dusked his eyen two, and failled breeth,
> But on his lady yet caste he his ye:
> His laste word was 'Mercy, Emelye!'
> His spirit chaunged hous and wente ther,
> As I cam nevere, I kan nat tellen wher.
> Therfore I stynte, I nam no divinistre;

Of soules fynde I nat in this registre,
Ne me ne list thilke opinions to telle
Of hem, though that they writen wher they dwelle.

Even the last six lines, with their unexpected humour, add to
the pathetic grimness of the scene. The Knight, eschewing
speculation and superstition, reminds us how ignorant we are
and holds our view firmly to this world which is the only
world we know. (This should again remind us not to take the
existence of the gods too literally but to keep our eyes fixed
on this life.)

Grief and lamentation follow Arcite's death. We are shown,
with another touch of humour, how even into the most
serious and genuine experiences dubious (and absurd) elements
enter.

Allas, the pitee that was ther,   (2833)
Cracchynge of chekes, rentynge eek of heer.
'Why woldestow be deed', thise wommen crye,
'And haddest gold ynough, and Emelye?'

But these women, despite their comic obtuseness in seeing
life's fulfilment as made up of no more than the enjoyment of
gold or sex, word the fundamental question: why should men
die thus? Theseus' father, the old Egeus, in the disillusionment
of age, and speaking with senile sententiousness, offers only
despair of life for comfort.

'Right as ther dyed nevere man', quod he,   (2843)
'That he ne lyvede in erthe in som degree,
Right so ther lyvede never man', he seyde,
'In al this world, that som tyme he ne deyde.
This world nys but a thurghfare ful of wo,
And we been pilgrymes, passyng to and fro.
Deeth is an ende of every worldly soore.'

Through Egeus the tale gives expression to a mood we genuinely feel when the thought of death troubles us, but by giving
expression to it Egeus makes us see that such a mood is one-
sided and inadequate.

A fuller and more balanced attitude to death is given expression in the description of the funeral pyre. This passage
is a remarkable *tour de force* in which Chaucer writes one sentence over forty lines long: the key verb is mentioned once
near the beginning and then held back till right at the end it is
repeated once. The effect is to bind the whole passage into one
enormous vision of ritualistic grief and tribute.[1]

> But how the fyr was maked upon highte,   (2919)
> Ne eek the names that the trees highte,
> As ook, firre, birch, aspe, alder, holm, popler,
> Wylugh, elm, plane, assh, box, chasteyn, lynde, laurer,
> Mapul, thorn, bech, hasel, ew, whippeltree,—
> How they weren feld, shal nat be toold for me;
> Ne how the goddes ronnen up and doun,
> Disherited of hire habitacioun,
> In whiche they woneden in reste and pees,
> Nymphes, fawnes and amadrides;
> Ne how the beestes and the briddes alle
> Fledden for fere, whan the wode was falle;
> Ne how the ground agast was of the light,
> That was nat wont to seen the sonne bright;
> Ne how the fyr was couched first with stree,
> And thanne with drye stikkes cloven a thre,
> And thanne with grene wode and spicerye,
> And thanne with clooth of gold and with perrye,
> And gerlandes, hangynge with ful many a flour;
> The mirre, th'encens, with al so greet odour;
> Ne how Arcite lay among al this,
> Ne what richesse aboute his body is;
> Ne how that Emelye, as was the gyse,
> Putte in the fyr of funeral servyse;
> Ne how she swowned whan men made the fyr,
> Ne what she spak, ne what was hir desir;
> Ne what jeweles men in the fyre caste,
> Whan that the fyr was greet and brente faste;
> Ne how somme caste hir sheeld, and somme hir spere,

---

[1] *Op. cit.* p. 15. Elizabeth Salter's comment on this passage is: 'The jewels
that are cast into the funeral flames seem to symbolise both the material and
emotional extravagance of this society.'

And of hire vestimentz, whiche that they were,
And coppes fulle of wyn, and milk, and blood,
Into the fyr, that brente as it were wood;
Ne how the Grekes, with an huge route,
Thries riden al the fyr aboute
Upon the left hand, with a loud shoutynge,
And thries with hir speres claterynge;
And thries how the ladyes gonne crye;
Ne how that lad was homward Emelye;
Ne how Arcite is brent to asshen colde;
Ne how that lyche-wake was yholde
Al thilke nyght; ne how the Grekes pleye
The wake-pleyes, ne kepe I nat to seye;
Who wrastleth best naked with oille anoynt,
Ne who that baar hym best, in no disjoynt.

The grandeur of this description of the obsequies conveys the preciousness and dignity of human life: the variety of trees cut down, the woods laid bare, the jewels and other precious things cast into the fire, all these are a courtesy towards the dead, and a gesture that shows how much we value human life. Thus the funeral rites are an affirmation of life and values, and grief is mingled with rejoicing:

> Ne how that lad homward was Emelye;
> Ne how Arcite is brent to asshen colde;
> Ne how that lyche-wake was yholde
> Al thilke nyght; ne how the Grekes pleye
> The wake-pleyes, ne kepe I nat to saye.

As the woes of disaster and the anguish of grief heal, men come to see life whole again. What is necessary must be accepted, and the goodness of the universe rejoiced in. This, as I understand it, is the affirmation to which the whole of *The Knight's Tale* moves; and it is given explicit expression in the final speech of Duke Theseus:

> thilke Moevere stable is and eterne.　　(3004)
> Wel may men knowe, but it be a fool,
> That every part dirryveth from his hool.

In his speech Theseus presents the disasters and pains of man's life in terms of the natural patterns of growth and decay.

> Loo the ook, that hath so long a norisshynge (3017)
> From tyme that it first bigynneth to sprynge,
> And hath so long a lif, as we may see,
> Yet at the laste wasted is the tree.
> Considereth eek how that the harde stoon
> Under oure feet, on which we trede and goon,
> Yet wasteth is as it lyth by the weye.
> The brode ryver somtyme wexeth dreye;
> The grete tounes se we wane and wende.
> Thanne may ye se that al this thyng hath ende.
> Of man and woman seen we wel also...

Though individual things droop and end, the source from which they came and which receives them again is unfinished, inexhaustible and everlasting.

> What maketh this but Juppiter, the kyng, (3035)
> The which is prince and cause of alle thyng,
> Convertynge al unto his propre welle
> From which it is dirryved, sooth to telle?

The speech is a summation of the whole tale, and the Knight clearly endorses the wisdom of Theseus' attitude towards things as they must be. What cannot be avoided must not only be endured but also celebrated, for only in this way can the riches of life be appreciated. Clearly too the speech points to a religious belief that pervades most of what Chaucer wrote, and that from the spring opening of the *Prologue* to the final sombre leave-taking at the end is in the bloodstream of the *Canterbury Tales*: a belief in the fundamental benevolence of the Creator and His Creation. No man can prove such a belief true or false. But we can say that this belief, as Chaucer held it, infused his art and enabled him to depict the world with clarity and compassion.

After having faced up to the inevitability of disaster and suffering in life, the tale ends by placing all its emphasis on the fulfilment of happiness and the celebration of joy.

> 'What may I conclude of this longe serye, (3067–72)
> But after wo I rede us to be merye,
> And thanken Juppiter of al his grace?
> And er that we departen from this place
> I rede that we make of sorwes two
> O parfit joye, lastynge everemo.

The union of Palamon and Emelye concludes the tale; in their happiness all the themes of the tale are reconciled, and we are shown how joy can exist despite, and because of, anguish and suffering.

> And thus with alle blisse and melodye (3097–3100)
> Hath Palamon ywedded Emelye.
> And God, that al this wyde world hath wroght,
> Sende hym his love that hath it deere aboght.

CHAPTER 2

The Miller's Tale

The Miller's Tale has often been acclaimed as one of the finest achievements of Chaucer's art, but what has been scarcely recognised about the tale is its wide scope, and its close connection with *The Knight's Tale* that precedes it. Behind the drunken Miller's boast that he will 'quite the Knyghtes tale' we should detect the voice of Chaucer giving us fair warning. Not only are there a number of parallels between the two tales but, as we shall see, *The Miller's Tale* picks up several themes from *The Knight's Tale*, and, by embodying them in a different realm of discourse, fills out their implications. In the first tale we were told of the rivalry of two knights for the love of the same lady, now we shall see two clerks competing for the same wench. Central themes of *The Knight's Tale* have been love and war, and though the tale dramatised them with heroic grandeur the poetry, through the rising and sinking of its images, has constantly reminded us that high and low are thrall to the same forces. In *The Miller's Tale* we meet the same themes, apparently scaled down to lechery and strife. We are introduced to them straight away, for the Miller tells his tale to taunt the Reeve, and their animosity could well appear on the temple of Mars. Other themes too will be echoed, and turns of the poetry in the second tale are often enriched by our remembering lines in the first. The bold repetition of one of the most moving lines in the description of Arcite's dying, 'Allone, withouten any compaignye' (l. 2779), where it epitomised man's tragic frustration and isolation in life and at death, is only the most obvious of these echoes. In *The Miller's Tale* Chaucer uses the line to proclaim sexual desire and to hint at the rich fulfilment soon to be attained by Nicholas. Clearly he is not mocking the earlier scene, but letting the new context modify and expand our understanding of human yearnings. And, in addition to these parallels and echoes, *The Miller's Tale* will introduce new themes which will, in their turn, be reshaped and re-explored by later tales. The bawdy comedy of *The Miller's Tale* possesses all the resonance of the romance epic preceding it, and the perfection of the poetry guarantees this.

Most of the significant strands of *The Miller's Tale* appear immediately in the *Prologue*. The hierarchical sequence of tales intended by the host is disrupted by the drunken Miller who, speaking in 'Pilates voys' and swearing by 'Goddes soule', demands to tell a tale at once.

> Oure Hoost answerde, 'Tel on, a devel wey! (3134)
> Thou art a fool; thy wit is overcome.'

Even if to others he seems to speak in the devil's name, the Miller has a truth to express and dare we really say it is not God-given? Indeed, much of the tale itself will hinge on the question of whether a thing is divinely ordained or not. The Miller is drunk, but all God's creatures are fallible, and in *The Knight's Tale* the whole human condition was compared to the state of drunkenness:

> We witen nat what thing we preyen heere: (1260)
> We faren as he that dronke is as a mous.
> A dronke man woot wel he hath an hous,
> But he noot which the righte wey is thider,
> And to a dronke man the wey is slider.
> And certes, in this world so faren we...

If the Miller mispeaks we can blame it on the ale of Southwark, or the human condition! The language employed by Chaucer, while not out of character for the Miller, possessed a poetic resonance greater than the occasion would seem to call for.

> An housbonde shal nat been inquisityf (3163)
> Of Goddes pryvetee, nor of his wyf.
> So he may fynde Goddes foyson there,
> Of the remenant nedeth nat enquere.

Literally the lines mean that, provided a wife gives a man all
he wants, he should not become too inquisitive about her
secrets. But the poetry also asserts that we should welcome
the God-given joys of life, and not poison our life pursuing
questions we cannot answer. In this emphasis on accepting
things as they are and admitting to ourselves that much is
mysterious, we may find an echo of the lines in *The Knight's
Tale*:

> His spirit chaunged hous and wente ther,   (2809)
> As I cam nevere, I can nat tellen wher.
> Therfore I stynte, I nam no divinistre;
> Of soules fynde I nat in this registre,
> Ne me ne list thilke opinions to telle
> Of hem, though that they writen wher they dwelle.

There it was the harsh fact of death we had to contemplate,
here it is the blessing of coital joy. The difference marks the
change from epic sadness to bawdy celebration, but both tales
imply that the truly religious spirit will welcome what God
bestows upon him, be it bane or boon.

The Miller is as much a creature of God as the Parson, and
we would be closing our eyes to His creation if we attempted to
ignore his witness. Such deep-held conviction lies behind
Chaucer's justification for repeating the tale.

> For Goddes love, demeth nat that I seye   (3172)
> Of yvel entente, but for I moot reherce
> Hir tales alle, be they bettre or werse,
> Or elles falsen som of my mateere.

I believe that Chaucer wholeheartedly meant that 'for Goddes
love'. But the tone of bland naivety in these lines and those
that follow, pokes fun at the kind of reader who finds offensive
the subject matter of the tale. The reader who prudishly looks
only for 'gentillesse', morality or holiness should not blame
Chaucer if, from a squeamishness akin to Absolon's, he ignores
the tale and *chooses amiss*.[1] The earnest mind cannot face all

---

[1] E. M. W. Tillyard, *Poetry Direct and Oblique* (Chatto and Windus, 1948),
p. 86.

the wonderful incongruities of life, and always attempts to diminish the gaiety of God's creation.

The person in the tale who sins most by this making 'earnest of game' is the carpenter. Though he loves his wife more than his own life, by his distrust he ruins the happiness he could have. His jealousy is a sin against truth, and against the enjoyment of God's plenty.

> This carpenter hadde wedded newe a wyf,   (3221)
> Which that he lovede moore than his lyf;
> Of eighteteene yeer she was of age.
> Jalous he was, and heeld hire narwe in cage,
> For she was wylde and yong and he was old,
> And demed hymself been lik a cokewold.
> He knew nat Catoun, for his wit was rude,
> That bad man sholde wedde his simylitude.
> Men sholde wedden after hire estaat,
> For youth and elde is often at debaat.
> But sith that he was fallen in the snare,
> He moste endure, as oother folk, his care.

The poetry reveals how the carpenter's jealousy springs not from suspicions founded on Alisoun's character but from envy of her youth and obsession with his own age: the expression '*lik* a cokewold' suggests not that he thought she had betrayed him but that he is being cheated of something she can enjoy. Certainly there is comedy behind the gravely offered notion that had the carpenter read Cato he could have avoided error[1] (as though reading could make men wise, or prudence be sufficient); the reference also emphasises the hard-won and long-experienced truth that age and youth have their incompatibilities, and their yoking demands most difficult adjustments. (Perhaps the kind of honesty his situation requires from the carpenter is that expressed so painfully by Shakespeare in Sonnet 138:

> But wherefore says she not she is unjust?
> And wherefore say not I that I am old?

[1] Tillyard, *op. cit.* p. 88.

O, love's best habit is in seeming trust,
And age in love loves not to have years told.
Therefore I lie with her and she with me,
And in our faults by lies we flatter'd be.)

Instead the carpenter is possessive, injuring the free selfhood
of Alisoun by holding her 'narwe in cage', and naturally we
will rejoice at her winning her liberty at her husband's expense.
The lines, however, which most fully 'place' the carpenter's
sin are the last two in the passage just quoted from Chaucer's
poem. The snare into which he has fallen is marriage with a
younger wife whom he loves, but again we can detect in the
lines profounder implications: the snare is that of life itself,
and the cares are those human troubles no one can escape.
In the emphasis on endurance we are reminded how much
weight was given to this quality in *The Knight's Tale*:

> So stood the heven whan that we were born. (1090)
> We moste endure it; this is the short and playn.

The parallel again shows the difference of perspective between
the two tales. In *The Knight's Tale* the disasters that befell,
though partially brought about by human choices, were of the
kind that ultimately are beyond any individual's control, and
reflected the helplessness of human beings before death and
mischance. In *The Miller's Tale* the sufferings are slighter,
and originate wholly in human fallibility; disaster takes the
shape of a retribution we enjoy and laugh at as amply merited.
The comedy, then, is always rooted in seriousness, and the
carpenter's denial of what he is manifests a sin against God.

Other aspects of the same fault are his turning to superstitious belief instead of genuine religious wisdom, and his
complacent satisfaction in his own ignorance. The lines which
show this are, as always in this tale, full of comic ironies that
radiate in all directions.

> (He) seyde, 'Help us, seinte Frydeswyde! (3449)
> A man woot litel what hym shal bityde.
> This man is falle, with his astromye,
> In som woodnesse or in som agonye.

> I thoghte ay wel how that it sholde be!
> Men sholde nat knowe of Goddes pryvetee.
> Ye, blessed be alwey a lewed man
> That noght but oonly his bileve kan!'

The echo, in 'Men sholde nat knowe of Goddes pryvetee', of the *Prologue* reminds us again of the carpenter's jealousy, sharpening the irony that he should be unsuspicious at the moment when his wife's lover is about to snare him. His denunciation of astrology is about to be played off against the scene following when he will so foolishly accept the 'prophecy' of the flood on Monday night. The lines also look forward to his *falling* into the madness of delusion, as well as his literal falling down with the tub. The ignorant, as well as the over-clever, may accept false beliefs. 'Lewd' is nicely ambiguous: the obvious reference is to the stupidity of the carpenter, but if we take up the word's secondary meaning of 'wanton' the lines would also hold true of Nicholas who will enjoy bliss with Alisoun, and will also experience 'woodnesse' and 'agonye' when his schemes rebound on him. As the tale affirms a little later:

> Lo, which a greet thyng is affeccioun! (3611)
> Men may dyen of ymaginacioun,
> So depe may impressioun be take.

Though no one dies in this tale, the moral is none the less seriously meant.

Yet Chaucer's satire is only one voice in his whole comic harmonising, and if he observes human error with a clear eye he also possesses a generous heart: he is never self-righteous. For all his ironical delineation of the carpenter, he can still touch us with the man's pathos. When the carpenter is first told of the flood, his first reaction is to think of his wife: 'Allas, my wyf! And shal she drenche?' (3522–3). Perhaps he would not have been so easily gulled had he not cared so passionately for her. Man is the only creature who can plague himself with false conceptions, but he can so conceive because he is capable too of love and caring passionately for things beyond himself. This warmth and sympathy are always implicit in Chaucer's tale.

We are not given any set description of the carpenter: he is revealed to us by his own actions or by the briefest comment in passing. But Nicholas, Absolon and Alisoun are each allotted a formal passage of description where their qualities are listed. By this device of the rhetorical *effictio*[1] Chaucer sets them in the courtly tradition, and lets the idealisation of this convention play against the down-to-earth realism of the fabliau. Thus in his manipulation of styles Chaucer reinforces the one main theme, the tension between 'ymaginacioun' and reality.

Though Nicholas and Absolon are each given their own particular character, the one carefully differentiated from the other, Chaucer also stresses the similarities between them. Both are accomplished in playing an instrument and in singing, and both are highly conscious of their musical talents and their attractiveness to women. Both are vain and self-indulgent in dressing themselves; both are slightly effeminate in appearance, and both take care to smell sweetly. They both address Alisoun in the high-flown language of courtly love, though just as with Arcite and Palamon, the one is more aggressive and down-to-earth while the other is idealistic and more prone to the 'softer' feelings. Absolon is the courteous lover, given to romanticising and indulging in his own feelings.

> Fro day to day this joly Absolon   (3371)
> So woweth hire that hym is wo bigon.
> He waketh al the nyght and al the day;
> He kembeth his lokkes brode, and made hym gay;
> He woweth hire by meenes and brocage,
> And swoor he wolde been hir owene page;
> He syngeth, brokkynge as a nyghtyngale;
> He sente hire pyment, meeth, and spiced ale,
> And wafres, pipyng hoot out of the gleede;
> And, for she was of towne, he profred meede.
> For som folk wol ben wonnen for richesse,
> And somme for strokes, and som for gentillesse.

[1] Muscatine, *op. cit.* pp. 228–30.

The poetry casts a lyrical enchantment over the wooing: we feel all the lover's small ecstasies, each as desirous as the (sensuously evoked) gifts that he gives. In the description of his singing there is even downright beauty. But throughout the poetry the undercurrent of laughter can be felt. Absolon's woe is so clearly part of his own pleasure, the lover's *service* so incongruously brought down to offering pies and wafers, that the affectation in his wooing is delicately uncovered. In the little touch of the proffering of money Chaucer reminds us of the lechery behind all the courtesy, and the last couplet, perhaps a popular saw Absolon quotes to himself, suggests a cold opportunism embedded in his character. The hint, that he might try to win a woman by striking her, prepares us for the streak of childish viciousness in him that comes out at the end of the tale when he fetches the hot coulter. In this passage we see enacted what Chaucer from the beginning sketched of Absolon's character: the curious mixture of the predatory and the 'romantic'.

> I dar wel seyn, if she hadde been a mous,   (3346)
> And he a cat, he wolde hire hente anon.
> This parissh clerk, this joly Absolon,
> Hath in his herte swich a love-longynge
> That of no wyf ne took he noon offrynge;
> For curteisie, he seyde, he wolde noon.

From the analysis that has been given we can see how the related themes of truthfulness and 'ymaginacioun' may be again discerned in the presentation of Absolon. His desire leads him to glorify the sensations of being a lover, and he gives expression to this in language which derived from courtly love, or more blasphemously, from the Song of Solomon. We see too how the inflation of his feelings and speech is a form of self-deception: he takes himself too seriously. So his affectations find a fitting 'objective correlative' in his fastidiousness about farting, and his punishment fits the crime. But afterwards we are told he did 'weep as dooth a child that is ybete', and in this reminder of his sensitivity and hint at immaturity, we feel again a note of pathos.

The epithet most frequently used of Absolon was 'joly' which suggests a certain self-complacence and an eagerness to be liked. But the other clerk is usually 'hende' Nicholas. As Charles Muscatine suggests, 'The error of clerk Nicholas is faith in intellect and in the sufficiency of wit. . . His quite enormous self-sufficiency, conveyed in the opening description (3199 ff.) is already touched with irony in the epithet "hende". It is fascinating to watch this term, which means "gracious" and "ready-handed" and "clever" and "comely" and "near at hand" sharpen as the poem progresses. It becomes a signal of his defeat.'[1] Nicholas's 'fantasye' is his study of astrology, the investigation of 'Goddes pryvetee' for personal profit, and the tale enacts this by making it the device for gulling the carpenter. His sin against truthfulness is his contempt towards others whom he intellectually despises. It is not that he fails to understand his own motives—he is cynically very aware of what pleasures him; but his egoism is inimical to others. If Chaucer gives us no sign of pathos in Nicholas, it may be because such egoism is too smoothly surfaced to permit any sympathy to cling.

One of the most amusing demonstrations of Nicholas's cynical self-sufficiency is his wooing of Alisoun.

> And prively he caughte hire by the queynte, (3276)
> And seyde, 'Ywis, but if ich have my wille,
> For deerne love of thee, lemman, I spille.'
> And heeld hire harde by the haunchebones,
> And seyde, 'Lemman, love me al atones,
> Or I wol dyen, also God me save!'
> And she sproong as a colt dooth in the trave,
> And with hir heed she wryed faste awey,
> And seyde, 'I wol nat kisse thee, by my fey!
> Why, lat be', quod she, 'lat be, Nicholas,
> Or I wol crye "out, harrow" and "allas!"
> Do wey youre handes, for youre courteisye!'
> This Nicholas gan mercy for to crye,
> And spak so faire, and profred him so faste,

[1] Muscatine, *op. cit.* pp. 226–7.

> That she hir love him graunted atte laste,
> And swoor hir ooth, by seint Thomas of Kent,
> That she wol been at his comandement,
> Whan that she may hir leyser wel espie.

His style of wooing is nothing if not to the purpose, his first loving words being perfunctory to the point of contempt. But Alisoun is more than a match for him (as she is for the others too): her bluntness of speech squashes his arrogance, and makes him sue more humbly. It is not that she cares for sweet words —the phrase 'hir love hym graunted atte laste' comes too pat after the rhyme-word 'faste' to suggest any long delay on her part—she just wants to put him in his place. She may well swear that she will be at his command, but it will depend on her naming the opportunity. Nicholas is no more able to hold her like a colt 'in a trave' than her husband will be in confining her 'narwe in cage'. She is a genuinely self-sufficient and resilient creature.

The positives of *The Miller's Tale* are largely embodied in Alisoun, and she may be seen as the touchstone by which the other characters are tested. The description of Alisoun and the dramatic revelation of her being are among the finest things in the tale, and have often been praised. But to appreciate them we must also see how they are set off against the characteristics of the other actors in the story.

> Fair was this yonge wyf, and therwithal   (3233)
> As any wezele hir body gent and smal.

She is young where her husband is old, but the second line suggests her identity with a creature whose appearance invites making it a pet though by nature it viciously defends its own freedom. The description that follows of her clothes displays her sexual attractiveness, feminine pride, and healthy neatness. Various contraries are marvellously unified in her: wantonness and innocence, primness and fertility, softness and strength, tenderness and independence, haughtiness and playfulness, repose and spontaneity: till we feel that here indeed is 'Goddes foyson'. She seems to have come fresh and unspoilt from her Creator's hands:

> Ful brighter was the shynyng of her hewe   (3255)
> Than in the tour the noble yforged newe.

And like the newly minted coin she rings true and provides the standard. Though like Nicholas and Absolon she can sing, her music has a more natural unselfconsciousness about it:

> But of hir song, it was as loude and yerne   (3257)
> As any swalwe sittynge on a berne.

Where they are affected she has all the simplicity of the rustic home she probably came from:

> Therto she koude skippe and make game,   (3259)
> As any kyde or calf folwynge his dame.

(In the height of his wooing Absolon says, 'I moorne as dooth a lamb after the tete', and there in its context the image is ridiculous.) Where the two clerks resort to perfumes to sweeten themselves, Alisoun is naturally fresh and fragrant:

> Hir mouth was sweete as bragot of the meeth   (3261)
> Or hoord of apples leyd in hey or heeth.

Such is the nature of her 'infinite variety' that she seems to offer men what they would most desire in a woman—whether it be an eager mistress or a faithful helpmate.

> She was a prymerole, a piggesnye,   (3268)
> For any lord to leggen in his bedde,
> Or yet for any good yeman to wedde.

There can be little doubt of Chaucer's wholehearted endorsement of Alisoun and all she represents: the animal vigour of unspoilt creation. From her laced shoes on her 'legges hye' to her delighted 'Tehee' at Absolon's kiss she is a creature wholly out to be freely herself and enjoy her life to the fullest. In appreciating this we recognise the importance of her role in the story: she is the very gift God has blessed men with, and the gift must be accepted on its own terms. She is also the model of selfhood, which by its very being worships the God from whom that being is derived. In saying this I am asserting that Chaucer has here elevated the fabliau to the status of religious fable.

In *Chaucer and the French Tradition* Charles Muscatine says of this tale that 'All the fabliau features are here so completely realised that the genre is virtually made philosophical... Even the stock triangle of fabliau—the lecherous young wife, the jealous husband, and the clever clerk (here two clerks)—is a self-assertive vehicle for the purest fabliau doctrine, the sovereignty of animal nature.'[1] But Chaucer, while pushing the latent morality of this type of tale as far as it will go, has also given full weight to the religious implications. *The Miller's Tale*, as much as *The Knight's Tale* with which it is so carefully linked, is an attempt to answer the question:

> What is this world? what asketh men to have?   (2777)
> Now with his love, now in his colde grave
> Allone, withouten any compaignye?

The realm of the tale is the bounty of God, the injunction of the tale is that it is there to be enjoyed, the purpose of the tale is to celebrate it.

From the opening in the Prologue, where a wife's secrets were linked with God's, to the impudent rhyme that concludes the tale:

> And Nicholas is scalded in the towte.   (3853)
> This tale is doon, and God save al the rowte!

the erotic and the sacred are conjoined. Now, of course, such mixture of the two is typical of fabliaux, but in this tale it is given a distinctive weight, and a tone of joy and wonder that impress themselves upon us. It is not that the erotic in *The Miller's Tale* merely travesties or usurps the spiritual, as is quite common in secular literature of this kind: the erotic and spiritual are married and made one.

[1] Muscatine, *op. cit.* p. 224.

Before considering how this is so in *The Miller's Tale* it may be rewarding to reflect briefly upon the very existence of such a body of bawdy tales in the Middle Ages: why were they so popular and why did they continue to exist despite the firm disapproval of the Church? No doubt the Church's disapproval was a fundamental reason for their existence, for they represent a popular literature of protest against those teachings of the Church which were sexually repressive. Any society which attempts to impose a rigid mode of behaviour on its citizens, and indeed to some degree this is true of every society, finds that there are limits to its success, limits celebrated by the dirty joke and the blasphemous snigger. (Beyond the limits are the rebels, the outlaws, the misfits and neurotics.) The limerick scrawled on the lavatory wall marks the boundaries of English puritanism, as the political jokes current behind the Iron Curtain mock the pretensions of all-embracing Communist theory.[1] This humour, challenging the official values of the society, may be healthy or sour. Healthy laughter says in effect, 'No, we're still human beings, much as They would like to make us something more constricted according to Their notions'. Sour humour comes from an obsessive sense of self-degradation and aims, by shocking others, either to degrade them as well (We're all nasty!) or to force them to confess that their beliefs are hypocritical (In public it pays us to tell lies!). But both forms of humour are an attempt to retain balance, and to affirm the rightful existence of all that society officially represses, ignores, omits and even persecutes.

The popular tradition of bawdy tales in the Middle Ages then witnesses to the successes and failures of the Christian

[1] 'They spoke of criticism of the system. I said, but apart from its utterance in tea-house gossip how did it reveal itself?...One Indian said a lot of the criticism came out in jokes and funny stories. It was then that I heard, for the first time, of Radio Armianski, the wireless station to which is attributed all sorts of satirical comment on the system of the Soviet Union. The station exists, of course, only as a figment in popular imagination, but its function is so compelling and active that while I was in Russia the Government appointed a commission to investigate the phenomenon and to recommend means for dealing with it' (Laurens van der Post, *Journey into Russia*, Hogarth Press, 1964, pp. 66–7).

Church in subduing and ordering the sexual life of the people. In part such a struggle was one between different conceptions of religion, for in Western Europe Christianity had imposed itself upon older fertility religions and had attempted to suppress or redirect their rites and practices. 'The whole of the epithalamic genre may be considered as a heritage of the remote past', writes Huizinga. 'In primitive culture marriage and nuptials form but one single sacred rite, converging in the mystery of copulation. Afterwards the Church, by transferring the sacred element of marriage to the sacrament, reserved the mystery for itself...'[1] This quotation may also serve to remind us that in some ways *The Miller's Tale* itself is an epithalamion, at least in so far as it celebrates the joy of sexual union between eager partners.

But in part such a struggle was an attempt by the Church to suppress the human animal, and the inevitable resistance of the human animal to being locked up in a 'narwe cage'. It may seem strange that a religion which praises God for his Creation should find such joyful aspects of His Creation so abhorrent that it should wish to abolish them. Religions, however, are shaped by men, and men are not always rational or capable of accepting themselves as they are. The distrust of the sexual life of man was introduced into Christianity at an early stage (some commentators trace it right back to Paul) and persists down to the present day. This is not to say that the Church (or later, the churches) had been in one mind on this issue, and in the Middle Ages, as today, arguments raged fiercely. But it is not untrue to say that the dominant tradition in the Church during the Middle Ages was that coitus was shameful and could never take place without sin.[2] Medieval theologians could not always explain why this was so, and their various attempts to produce arguments suggest that they were often merely attempting to rationalise an innate hostility. Hugo of Pisa, for example, thought, 'There is a certain passion (*fervor*), a certain pleasure

[1] J. Huizinga, *The Waning of the Middle Ages* (Penguin, 1955), pp. 110–11.
[2] Sherwin Bailey, *The Man–Woman Relation in Christian Thought* (Longmans, 1959), p. 133.

(*voluptas*), which is always sinful...'; while Aquinas located the seat of coital evil in the inordinate desire, inevitably exceeding the bounds of reason, which accompanies the act of copulation in fallen humanity.[1] But the niceties of theological dispute are of less importance to us than the impression of such teaching on the common people, who doubtless were simply recipients of the dogma that sexual love and its pleasures were sinful and to be avoided. It is upon such teaching Nicholas calls when he persuades the carpenter to stay in the tub separated from his wife:

> Thy wyf and thou moote hange fer atwynne;   (3589)
> For that bitwixe yow shal be no synne,
> Namoore in lookynge than ther shal in deede,
> This ordinance is seyd.

Tales of ribaldry, then, may be regarded as a literature of protest: as an attempt by the people to resist, mock, satirise or refute the restrictive sexual morality of the Church. Those who made up such tales or those who passed them on would not, of course, always be fully conscious of the import of such tales, for men express and grasp meanings beyond the threshold of the intellect. But it is highly unlikely that a maker as skilful and deliberate as Chaucer would be unaware of these meanings, and that in shaping his fabliau he should not be capable of controlling its implications. On the contrary we must assume that Chaucer was fully aware of what he was doing, and we must see in *The Miller's Tale* an artist's sophisticated reasoning on these matters. But his argument, deliberately intended and stated with the utmost intelligence, cannot be separated from the tale which embodies it. This is how poets always present their reasoning, through the discipline of their poetry, and this form of argument is perhaps the most subtle and reliable that can be achieved.

The suggestion that Chaucer, through the mouth of the bawdy Miller, was quite consciously criticising some of the Church's teachings on sexual love immediately calls to mind

[1] *Ibid.* pp. 133–6.

another poet renowned for doing this. I mean William Blake. But if Chaucer (I want to suggest) shares some of Blake's attitudes, in many ways his thinking is very different, and the similarities and dissimilarities can be apprehended in the texture of the poetry. *The Garden of Love* may be chosen as an example of Blake's explicit condemnation of the sexual repressiveness of Christianity.

> I went to the Garden of Love,
> And saw what I had never seen:
> A Chapel was built in the midst,
> Where I used to play on the green.
>
> And the gates of this Chapel were shut,
> And 'Thou shalt not' writ over the door;
> So I turn'd to the Garden of Love
> That so many sweet flowers bore;
>
> And I saw it was filled with graves,
> And tomb-stones where flowers should be;
> And Priests in black gowns were walking their rounds,
> And binding with briars my joys and desires.

Blake, like Chaucer, believed that man was blessed with God's foison: 'Every thing that lives is holy'. He saw, and it is embodied in this poem, that to suppress sexual joy is to commit a blasphemy against God and to pervert religion: the closed chapel desecrates the Garden of Innocence, and worship is blighted when negative commandments are written over the door. Sex and religion are intimately connected, perhaps because both express the human being's profoundest attempt to reach beyond himself to communion with Another, and both celebrate his deepest delight of his own very existence. In this poem of Blake's we feel a very personal commitment to what he is saying. By this I mean two things. First, that Blake believed that he himself had been personally injured by the restrictions placed on love. Secondly, in accusing the Church of doing wrong to himself and countless others, there is a dogmatic tone to his wisdom: with indignation he asserts thou shalt not preach that Thou Shalt Not. For all Blake's emphasis on the co-existence of contraries, there is often an attitude of intolerance to be detected in the forceful extremes of his imagery. Christian love is aligned with death, as free love embodies life: 'tomb-stones where flowers should be'. Blake is *par excellence* the rebel who, seeing only too clearly the faults of the system, and feeling strongly his own isolation, overbalances in the attempt to correct error. This scarcely detracts from his shorter poems, for their form is just right for what he has to say: their epigrammatic lyricism matches his passionate outspokenness. In the formless style of the prophetic works he succumbs to rant and tedium all too frequently. But even in the best of Blake, when placed against the highest poetry such as Chaucer's, there is the limitation of over-assertiveness. Blake too often neglected the wisdom of his own lines,

> He who binds to himself a joy
> Does the winged life destroy;
> But he who kisses the joy as it flies
> Lives in eternity's sun rise.

The rebel who expounds freedom often finds that with his doctrines he has woven his own bonds.

We miss in Blake a certain degree of Negative Capability. Keats's description of this quality in a poet can never be too often called to mind. 'I mean Negative Capability, that is when a man is capable of being in uncertainties, Mysteries, doubts, without any irritable reaching after fact and reason.' And again in a later letter: 'As to the poetical Character itself ...it is not itself—it has no self—it is every thing and nothing —It has no character—it enjoys light and shade; it lives in gusto, be it foul or fair, high or low, rich or poor, mean or elevated—It has as much delight in conceiving an Iago as an Imogen. What shocks the virtuous philosopher, delights the camelion Poet. It does no harm from its relish of the dark side of things any more than from its taste for the bright one; because they both end in speculation...It is a wretched thing to confess; but it is a very fact that not one word I ever utter can be taken for granted as an opinion growing out of my identical nature—how can it, when I have no nature?'[1] It is the possession of the Negative Capability that most clearly sets Chaucer apart from Blake in his criticism of the Church's teachings on sexual love. For Chaucer's criticism is such that it does not delimit, rather it invites speculation and opens possibility.

Of the many juxtapositions of the profane and the sacred in *The Miller's Tale* there are two that are particularly significant. After Nicholas and Alisoun have agreed to deceive her husband at the first opportunity we are told Nicholas

> ...thakked hire aboute the lendes weel,   (3304)
> He kiste hire sweete and taketh his sawtrie,
> And pleyeth faste, and maketh melodie.
>   Thanne fil it thus, that to the paryssh chirche,
> Cristes owene werkes for to wirche,
> This goode wyf went on an haliday.

The second one is even more startling. While the carpenter lies snoring in his kneading-trough Alisoun and Nicholas go off to make love:

> Withouten wordes mo they goon to bedde,   (3650)
> Ther as the carpenter is wont to lye.
> Ther was the revel and the melodye;
> And thus lith Alison and Nicholas,
> In bisynesse of myrthe and of solas,
> Til that the belle of laudes gan to rynge,
> And freres in the chauncel gonne synge.

How are we to take these lines? One of the most enjoyable qualities about them is the way they tease us with their innumerable possibilities. People who disapprove of ribaldry—those indeed who could have taken the warning of the *Prologue* that the tale would contain churlish 'harlotrie'—may find it shockingly blasphemous. They deserve to be shocked. For churls, like the Miller, the blasphemy is gloriously funny, a wonderful cocking the nose at the spiritually minded who never appreciate what goes on behind the scenes. Other readers

[1] John Keats, *Letters* (Oxford University Press, 1952), pp. 71, 226–7.

might stress the moralistic or ironic elements. There is a touch of hypocrisy in Alisoun's going off to Church to do Christ's own work when she is planning adultery; a callousness in her choosing to commit it in her husband's bed. Perhaps the lines reflect the dual and imperfect nature of Man as a creature who both seeks to please his own body and save his own soul. Does the profane action cast doubt on the validity of the spiritual, or the spiritual diminish the rewards of the profane? Shall we see them as incompatibilities, and praise the irrepressible realism of comic art which flourishes upon the wild incongruities of life? Or we might assert that the poetry fuses two forms of joy, the lovers' ecstasy and the hymn of praise to God, and suggests they are one and the same thing. This last meaning is certainly there. But then so are the other meanings. We pay our money and we take our choice. Or wiser still, we do not choose but open ourselves to possibilities. If the fabliau structure of *The Miller's Tale* affirms that the lust of the goat is the bounty of God, the moral is not exclusive, the glory and challenge of Creation not diminished.

CHAPTER 3

The Reeve's Tale

ALL the pilgrims enjoyed the Miller's tale, except Osewold the Reeve. What is the cause of the enmity between the two? It certainly cuts deeper than the traditional hostility that was supposed to exist between millers and reeves; it seems to be of a very personal nature. What had happened between these two Chaucer has not clearly delineated, perhaps intending to fill out the details later. Certainly the Miller's wife seems to have something to do with it. Perhaps the Miller had once joked about the Reeve's lusting after her. But this is pure speculation and not worth pursuing. It would not take much to set two people so different in character at odds with one another. The Miller abounds in physical energy. That he could break a door off its hinges by charging it with his head, that he led the pilgrims out of town with his bagpipe, such details give the brawny confidence and vigorous insensitivity of the man. He embraces life with a lusty hug. The Reeve, who significantly comes at the very tail of the company, is about as far apart from this as could be. He is old and emaciated in appearance. Though he has cunningly and secretly amassed quite a fortune and acquired a lovely place to dwell in,

> His wonyng was ful faire upon an heeth; (606)
> With grene trees yshadwed was his place,

he seems to derive little pleasure from life. His dress gives him an ascetic and clerical appearance. He is tormented by his own sinful desires, and this drives him to preach of moral rectitude. There are several hints of frustrated or impotent lust: 'And by his syde he baar a rusty blade.' He finds life bitter, and must hate and envy the Miller's gross exuberance. And their tales represent the bias of their natures.

The Miller's Tale has celebrated the vigorous enjoyments of the flesh. Pain or sickness or age are mocked at or ignored, affectations scorned, and life is portrayed with zest and praised for its naturalness. *The Reeve's Tale* now gives the other side of the picture. Bitterness, frustration and ugliness. Men's motives are sordid, their pleasures nasty, and life is a cheat. What do men ask to have? To be now with his love, says the Miller. What they are given, says the Reeve, is the 'colde grave'.

In the *Prologue to the Reeve's Tale* Chaucer gives us the pathos of the Reeve's age:

> But ik am oold, me list not pley for age;   (3867)
> Gras tyme is doon, my fodder is now forage;
> This white top writeth myne olde yeris...

The sad dignity of these lines enforces sympathy. But the poetry continues,

> Myn herte is also mowled as myne heris,
> But if I fare as dooth an open-ers.
> That ilke fruyt is ever lenger the wers,
> Til it be roten in mullok or in stree.
> We olde men, I drede, so fare we:
> Til we be roten, kan we nat be rype;
> We hoppen alwey whil the world wol pype.
> For in ouer wyl ther stiketh evere a nayl,
> To have an hoor heed and a grene tayl,
> As hath a leek...

The sympathy is not dropped, but mingled with it now is a feeling of distaste. Beginning with the image of his heart being as *mouldy* as his hairs, the portrayal of decay and rottenness is rendered with an unpleasant concreteness. The worst is that age rots not only the flesh but the spirit as well. The Reeve speaks with a terrible bitterness, soon bursting forth with the denunciation of a preacher. The sermon-like tone of his speech is perfectly in character, but the effect is to give the substance detachment and authority.

> Foure gleedes han we, which I shal devyse,— (3883)
> Avauntyng, liyng, anger, coveitise:
> Thise foure sparkles longen unto eelde.

97

> Oure olde lemes mowe wel been unweelde,
> But wyl uc shal nat faillen, that is sooth.
> And yet ik have alwey a coltes tooth,
> As many a yeer as it is passed henne
> Syn that my tappe of lif bigan to renne.
> For sikerly, whan I was bore, anon
> Deeth drough the tappe of lyf and leet it gon;
> And ever sithe hath so the tappe yronne
> Til that almoost al empty is the tonne.
> The streem of lyf now droppeth on the chymbe...

The last part of the passage enforces the sad and awful inevitability of death. No wonder the good Host objects. Yet for all the universality of the picture of age and death, Chaucer never lets us forget the Reeve's bitter conviction that life plays us a dirty trick, and he mingles some loathing with our compassion.

The Reeve's Tale then is almost an inversion of *The Miller's Tale*. It is not merely that a miller becomes the gull of the tale instead of a carpenter; the most important inversion is that of the way life is experienced. The changed values can be felt in every thread of the texture.

The characters are belittled and drawn with an ugliness not to be found in the previous tale. While the tale is almost as rich as the Miller's in its details of place and objects and behaviour, the cumulative effect of some details and the selection of particular images is on the whole derogatory to all the characters of the tale.

> Round was his face, and camus was his nose;   (3934)
> As piled as an ape was his skulle.
> He was a market-betere atte fulle.
> Ther dorste no wight hand upon hym legge,
> That he ne swoor he sholde anon abegge.
> A theef he was for sothe of corn and mele,
> And that a sly, and usaunt for to stele.

This exemplum of 'avauntyng, liying, anger, coveitise' is also proud of his own cleverness, and of the good marriage he made with the illegitimate daughter of the local parson. These will

be the occasion for his humiliation. His wife who is the feminine counterpart to him in her sauciness and vanity is as scorn-
fully dealt with:

> for she was somdel smoterlich,   (3963)
> She was as digne as water in a dich,
> And ful of hoker and of bisemare.

Their vices might justify some animosity in their presentation,
but the daughter, who can hardly be blamed for her parents,
receives little better shrift.

> This wenche thikke and wel ygrowen was,   (3973)
> With kamus nose, and eyen greye as glas,
> With buttokes brode, and brestes rounde and hye;
> But right fair was hire heer, I wol nat lye.

Her blue eyes merely emphasise her ugliness compared with the
traditional portrait of ladies in courtly romances. The one con-
cession is perhaps the more damning because it suggests the
speaker is trying to be just and mention what good he can.
(Though this one touch of beauty is to be picked up later in a
most significant way.)

Even her grandfather, the parson, does not escape the lash
of the Reeve's scorn: a few lines suffice to depict the parson's
clerical sing-song mode of speech, his vanity, hypocrisy and
perversion of the Church's teachings to his own ends.

> His purpos was for to bistowe hire hye   (3981)
> Into som worthy blood of auncetrye;
> For hooly chirches good moot been despended
> On hooly chirches blood, that is descended.
> Therfore he wolde his hooly blood honoure,
> Though that he hooly chirche sholde devoure.

The two clerks who will teach the miller a lesson are scarcely
admirable. The dialect of their speech betrays their social in-
feriority, and provides scope for mirth and mimicry.[1] Their
offer to take the corn to be ground arises from the desire 'for
hire myrthe and revelrye' and to show the miller that they are

---

[1] See Muscatine, *op. cit.* pp. 201–2.

smarter than he. But the miller quite easily makes fools of them. By the time the scene is set for the comic finale we can feel little respect for anyone. Now the poetry begins to mount in dramatic revulsion. In the portrayal of the miller and his wife going to bed the description attains an almost Swiftian disgust.

> Wel hath this millere vernysshed his heed; (4149)
> Ful pale he was for dronken, and nat reed.
> He yexeth, and he speketh thurgh the nose
> As he were on the quakke, or on the pose.
> To bed he goth, and with him goth his wyf...
> This millere hath so wisely bibbed ale   (4162)
> That as an hors he snorteth in his sleep,
> Ne of his tayl bihynde he took no keep.
> His wyf bar hym a burdon, a ful strong;
> Men myghte hir rowtyng heere two furlong;
> The wenche rowteth eek, *par compaignye*.

The archness of 'of his tayl bihynde he took no keep', the courtliness of '*par compaingye*' serve to emphasise the grossness, and despite the comedy of it this passage is appalling in a way *The Miller's Tale* never is.

Aleyn's motive for making love to the miller's daughter is simply to take revenge. His justification, that law allows it to him, drags law down to an eye for an eye, a tooth for a tooth— seduction for being shown up as a fool. But it is in the descriptions of the sexual act that *The Reeve's Tale* differs most from *The Miller's Tale*. 'Ther was the revel and the melodye,' we are told of Alisoun's and Nicholas's love-making, and the tale is full of song and music and joy. But the descriptions in *The Reeve's Tale* are closer to Iago's cold inhumanity when he sums up Othello and Desdemona's bridal night in the phrase: '(they) are making the beast with two backs'. When John tricks the miller's wife into coming to his bed after she had gone 'out to pisse' we get this description:

> Withinne a while this John the clerk up leep   (4228)
> And on this goode wyf he leith on soore.
> So myrie a fit ne hadde she nat ful yoore;
> He priketh harde and depe as he were mad.

The account of Aleyn is even nastier. First, through such a word as 'swonken', and through the comically inappropriate dialect, we are given a parody of an *aubade*:

> Aleyn wax wery in the dawenynge,   (4234)
> For he had swonken al the longe nyght,
> And seyde, 'Fare weel, Malyne, sweete wight!
> The day is come, I may no lenger byde;
> But evermo, wher so I go or ryde,
> I is thyn awen clerk, swa have I seel!'

When we are told the two clerks had a 'joly lyf' that night the phrase is clearly sarcastic, for neither of them appears to have derived much joy from their labour. Aleyn, hunting for his own bed,

> 'By God', thoughte he, 'al wrang I have mysgon   (4252)
> Myn heed is toty of my swynk to-nyght,
> That makes me that I ga nat aright.'

So to the climax of the tale where Aleyn's hypocrisy and heartlessness are brought together with the miller's quick temper and family pride.

> He wende have cropen by his felawe John   (4259)
> And by the millere in he creep anon,
> And caughte hym by the nekke, and softe he spak.
> He seyde, 'Thou John, thou swynes-heed, awak,
> For Cristes saule, and heer a noble game.
> For by the lord that called is seint Jame,
> As I have thries in this shorte nyght
> Swyved the milleres doghter bolt upright
> Whil thow hast, as a coward, been agast.'
>   'Ye, false harlot', quod the millere, 'hast?
> A, false traitour! false clerk!' quod he,
> 'Thow shalt be deed, by Goddes dignitee!
> Who dorste be so boold to disparage
> My doghter, that is come of swich lynage?'

And the fight follows. The fight is farcical, but with this difference: normally in farce though injuries occur their painfulness or seriousness are played down. Here the physical brutality is stressed.

> Doun ran the blody streem upon his brest;   (4276)
> And in the floor, with nose and mouth tobroke
> They walwe as doon two pigges in a poke.

Man is a nasty animal. This seems to be the moral of the tale told by the Reeve. He is, to use D. H. Lawrence's phrase, 'doing dirt on life'. But what is Chaucer's attitude? This brings us to a question which has been postponed long enough: the relationship of Chaucer to the teller of each tale and to the tale itself.

Chaucer allows to each of the Canterbury pilgrims the kind of tale appropriate to his character. The Knight tells a tale of chivalry and romance; the Miller a cheerfully ribald one aimed at the Reeve; the Reeve a bitter tale answering the Miller's. At the first level the tales portray the characters of the people who relate them. More than that, the tales depict the world as these people see and understand it, and in reading the tales we are invited to experience things through their eyes. But there is more to it than this. Chaucer, through the poetry, *realises* the implications of each story to the maximum, and these implications often criticise or clarify the limits of the pilgrim's own vision. Thus *The Knight's Tale* celebrates heroism and chivalry, but also shows the darkness and suffering that exist in the very centre of all the radiant pageantry.[1] *The Miller's Tale* praises the bounty of the Creator through the vigour and delight of natural being, but beyond its amoral gusto there is a clear-sighted morality and the story teases us with religious probings. Each story establishes its own realm of discourse, only to suggest realms beyond and above. This is managed partly by juxtaposing one tale against another, or others; mainly it is done within the tales by Chaucer's variety and control of tones. A sudden image or phrase or joke will release unexpected resonances. A strange voice will interject

[1] See Salter, *op. cit.* p. 13.

new possibilities beyond the speech of the tale itself, and a monologue is suddenly converted into a duologue, or into a conversation in which many voices may join. But when do we hear Chaucer's own voice? Only when all the other voices have sunk into the silence of our minds, if at all. For it exists in the control, the manipulating, juggling and balancing of the whole, human conversation.

So it is in *The Reeve's Tale*. Simply to share the Reeve's very bitter vision would be to turn away from the tale depressed and irritated. We do not. We have been shown too clearly the Reeve's own character to believe that what he says is not jaundiced. Life has its sordid and bestial side. Yes, this is partially valid. A good corrective to the noble idealism of *The Knight's Tale*, and the physical enjoyment of *The Miller's Tale*. But still it is a view of life that ignores too much. Other possibilities exist and are implicit in the tale itself: in the physical excitement and comedy of Aleyn and John chasing their horse; in the wonderful cunning of the miller's trick, and the even more astute stroke of John's shifting the baby's cot to his own bedside; in the pleasurable laughter at human folly, as when Aleyn catches the miller by the neck and softly tells him what he has done to his daughter. All these affirm, what the Reeve's moral would deny, that life is wealthy with pleasure. But perhaps most important of all is the compassionate portrayal of human beings. The miller, his wife, Aleyn and John are so much more than the pettiness of their motives or the ugliness of some of their behaviour. The moment they speak they are fascinating in the way living creatures are. For what delights us is that amalgam of the anticipated and the surprising every time we look at them. Not only that everything done asserts the unique selfhood: 'Selves—goes itself; *myself* it speaks and spells;/*Crying What I do is me: for that I came.*' But that selfhood is always newly unfolding, newly discovering. To make us feel this of his creatures of the imagination is one of the artist's supreme gifts. We feel it in this tale: the affirmation of the beauty of life. The finest instance of it in the tale is the sudden revelation given of the miller's daughter. After Aleyn has whispered his hypocritical *aubade*,

> 'Now, deere lemman', quod she, 'go, fareweel! (4240)
> But er thow go, o thyng I wol thee telle:
> Whan that thou wendest homward by the melle,
> Right at the entree of the dore bihynde
> Thou shalt a cake of half a busshel fynde
> That was ymaked of thyn owene mele,
> Which that I heelp my sire for to stele.
> And, goode lemman, God thee save and kepe!'
> And with that word almoost she gan to wepe.

Almoost! The poetry will not deviate from the strictest truth. So how telling it is! Affection is beautiful, even when it turns up so unexpectedly here and expresses itself through the gift of the stolen cake. Even this rather ugly-looking girl of such unbecoming parents has fair hair and a tender heart, and is really beautiful. Ironically, Aleyn will probably never think much about her again except as a thought of how he triumphed over her father. He collects the cake, but doesn't understand the gift. A further irony is that the Reeve himself does not seem to grasp the implications of this incident: he sees life as a cheat and a disappointment, cursing the chaff and missing the grain. In his sourness he has cheated himself, and the final lines of the tale, in their double-edged ambiguity, point the moral behind the moral.

> And therfore this proverbe is seyd ful sooth,   (4319)
> 'Hym thar nat wene wel that yvele dooth';
> A gylour shal hymself bigyled be.
> And God, that sitteth heighe in magestee,
> Save al this compaignye, grete and smale!
> Thus have I quyt the Millere in my tale.

The lines firmly judge the Reeve, but not without calling forth compassion upon him. There is a poem by W. B. Yeats called *Paudeen*:

> Indignant at the fumbling wits, the obscure spite
> Of our old Paudeen in his shop, I stumbled blind

Among the stones and thorn-trees, under morning light;
Until a curlew cried and in the luminous wind
A curlew answered; and suddenly thereupon I thought
That on the lonely height where all are in God's eye,
There cannot be, confusion of our sound forgot,
A single soul that lacks a sweet crystalline cry.

Because of Chaucer's art and humanity each of the characters
in *The Reeve's Tale* rings with a clear crystalline cry.

CHAPTER 4

The Man of Law's Tale

CHAUCER intended that *The Reeve's Tale* should be followed by a tale from the Cook. But only the prologue and a fragment of the tale exist, just enough to show that the tale would have been another fabliau, and that it would have dealt with a theme or themes raised by the two preceding tales. The Cook's first words explicitly refer to elements in the other two tales.

> 'Wel seyde Salomon in his langage,   (4331)
> "Ne bryng nat every man into thyn hous";
> For herberwynge by nyghte is perilous.
> Wel oghte a man avysed for to be
> Whom that he broghte into his pryvetee.'

With *The Cook's Tale* there is a break in the continuity of the *Canterbury Tales*. In the best manuscripts *The Man of Law's Tale* constitutes a section by itself, but scholarship considers the most likely position for it among the tales that have come down to us to be after *The Cook's Tale*. Considerations of a purely literary nature support this. Though we cannot know what, in his final plan, Chaucer might have put here, or how he might have revised *The Man of Law's Tale*, there are sufficient echoes of the first three tales for us to infer that it should appear fairly close to them. There are also strong grounds, which I shall discuss a little later, for believing that the tale should precede *The Wife of Bath's Prologue and Tale*. That some revision was required is indicated by the Man of Law's saying that the tale would be in prose, unless we read this as an ironic remark emphasising the tale's greater seriousness after the preceding fabliaux (or Gower's rhymed couplet version of the story). The *Prologue* on poverty does not seem accountable by what has gone before, and we might speculate that in some way *The Cook's Tale* would have touched upon poverty, thus putting the subject in the Man of Law's mind. But both in tone and subject it is a contrast to the tales we have dealt with so far.

One link between it and the first group is provided by the words the Host speaks to the company. The Host, after calculating the hour of the day in a rather ponderous fashion, proceeds to moralise about time.

> Lordynges, the tyme wasteth nyght and day, (20)
> And steleth from us, what pryvely slepynge,
> And what thurgh necligence in oure wakynge,
> As dooth the streem that turneth nevere agayn,
> Descendynge fro the montaigne into playn...
> It wol nat come agayn, withouten drede, (29)
> Namoore than wole Malkynes maydenhede,
> Whan she hath lost it in hir wantownesse.
> Lat us nat mowlen thus in ydelnesse.

What his moralising is leading up to is the request for another tale, but again the poetry has a resonance beyond the immediate occasion. The lines remind us of the Reeve's description of the inevitability of death, particularly when the image of *mouldering* is repeated. The poetry seems to be calling for something beyond this unsatisfactory and imperfect world where all is transitory and where even the surrender of virginity, as with the miller's daughter, is an aspect of irrevocable dissolution. The something beyond is provided by the moral allegory of the tale the Man of Law chooses to tell. Though the tale deals with the changes and uncertainties of circumstance, and even ends on a note of death and separation, it points to a higher realm, abiding virtues, and even miraculous preservation. The quality of fortitude endorsed by the tale contrasts with the grudging and discontented attitude displayed by the Reeve, and provides a comment on the fatalism of *The Knight's Tale*. The peculiarly medieval nature of *The Man of Law's Tale* together with the break from the couplet form have led commentators to suggest that the work is an earlier one which Chaucer had decided to include in the *Canterbury Tales*, but the appropriateness of the tale to issues already raised and the frequency of back-reference suggest that this is unlikely. The tale was probably written (or rewritten) with some larger unity in mind.

In *The Knight's Tale* the passions, conflicts and misfortunes afflicting man were largely dramatised through the agency of gods, and man's lot was presented as though patterned in the heavens. Palamon's lament near the end of part one is a particularly explicit expression of this. But when we reconsider his speech after reading *The Man of Law's Tale* we can see how the story of Constance is a variation on the same issues.

> Thanne seyde he, 'O crueel goddes that governe (1303)
> The world with byndyng of youre word eterne,
> And writen in the table of atthamaunt
> Youre parlement and youre eterne graunt,
> What is mankynde moore unto you holde
> Than is the sheep that rouketh in the folde?
> For slayn is man right as another beest,
> And dwelleth eek in prison and arreest,
> And hath siknesse and greet adversitee,
> And ofte tymes giltelees, pardee.
>   What governance is in this prescience
> That giltelees tormenteth innocence?

Indeed the story of Constance may be said to be a further attempt to answer this last question. In *The Knight's Tale* the issues were raised in a largely non-Christian context. *The Man of Law's Tale* gives them a specifically Christian context. Thus the picture of man going to the slaughter like a lamb becomes in the new tale a reminder of Christ's sacrifice for mankind:

> She blesseth hire, and with ful pitous voys (449)
> Unto the croys of Crist thus seyde she:
> 'O cleere, o welful auter, hooly croys,
> Reed of the Lambes blood ful of pitee,
> That wessh the world fro the olde iniquitee,
> Me fro the feend and fro his clawes kepe,
> That day that I shal drenchen in the depe.'

And a few stanzas later we not only find another echo of
Saturn's saying, 'Myn is the drenchyng in the see so wan',
but Palamon's question is given a Christian reply.

> God liste to shewe his wonderful myracle   (477)
> In hire, for we sholde seen his myghty werkis;
> Crist, which that is to every harm triacle,
> By certeine meenes ofte, as knowen clerkis,
> Dooth thyng for certein ende that ful derk is
> To mannes wit, that for oure ignorance
> Ne konne noght knowe his prudent purveiance.

> Now sith she was nat at the feeste yslawe,
> Who kepte hire fro the drenchyng in the see?
> Who kepte Jonas in the fisshes mawe
> Til he was spouted up at Nynyvee?
> Wel may men knowe it was no wight but he
> That kepte peple Ebrayk from hir drenchyng,
> With drye feet thurghout the see passynge...

> Where myghte this womman mete and drynke have (498)
> Thre yeer and moore? how lasteth hire vitaille?
> Who fedde the Egipcien Marie in the cave,
> Or in desert? No wight but Crist, sanz faille.
> Fyve thousand folk it was as greet mervaille
> With loves fyve and fisshes two to feede.
> God sente his foyson at hir grete neede.

And the lines certainly also echo 'Goddes pryvetee' and
'Goddes foyson' played on in *The Miller's Tale*.

These quotations suggest that *The Man of Law's Tale* inter-
connects with the earlier tales. But nothing is to be gained by
a mere numerical adding up of echoes and repeated phrases.
What is more to the purpose is to consider how these common
themes are expressed in the tale, and to what extent the tale
succeeds in justifying or making comprehensible the existence
of innocent suffering in the world.

The kind of tale the Man of Law tells requires a different
style from those that have preceded it.

> Me list nat of the chaf, ne of the stree,   (701)
> Maken so long a tale as of the corn.

Thus the rich pageantry of details found in *The Knight's Tale*, or the realism and particularity of the fabliaux are inappropriate here. Tales of this sort follow a different emotional pattern. The incidents display innocence and virtue undergoing various trials, till in the end a divine grace rewards the sufferer with merited bliss; the aim of the narrative is to move the reader to wonder and pity, and finally to relief and joy at the miraculous outcome. In these tales we are to glimpse the rewards of heaven or the mercy of divinity that shall be proffered to the pure in spirit dwelling in a world of woe and injustice. The dramatic problem in relating such a tale is to retain a sense of the human and pathetic while exemplifying absolute and divine virtues. Since human motives and divine purposes do not always run parallel their reconciliation can be extremely difficult. Where the demands of the exemplum result in characters behaving with psychological improbability, the manner of narrating must tone down or suppress awkward questions. Once the reader begins to wonder why Constance keeps her real identity secret, even after she has returned to Rome, doubt intrudes. The story of Constance, like others of the same genre, has its source in the simplifications of popular religious feelings. Fundamentally, such stories are naive and superstitious. It is easier to get such a story across if the reader is invited to accept it at a naive and simple level. The attempt to relate such a story at a level of sophistication creates enormous difficulties.

Though John Gower's version of the tale in *Confessio Amantis* is flat and dull, the story is told with an innocent directness which does fairly successfully fuse pathetic realism with credulous acceptance of improbabilities. The tone of the poetry seems to say, quite simply, well it happened like this: take it as you find it. The events are so swiftly narrated, so many incidents following one another within the same sentence, that the reader is swept along. Here, for example, is Gower's account of Constance's first trial:

> Whan al was slain bot sche al one,
> This olde fend, this Sarazine,
> Let take anon this Constantine

With al the good sche thider broghte,
And hath ordeined, as sche thoghte,
A nakid Schip withoute stiere,
In which the good and hire in fiere,
Vitailed full for yeres fyve,
Wher that the wynd it wolde dryve,
Sche putte upon the Wawes wilde.
  Bot he which alle thing mai schilde,
Thre yer, til that sche cam to londe,
Hire Schip to stiere hath take in honde,
And in Northumberlond aryveth;
And happeth thanne that sche dryveth
Under a Castel with the flod,
Which upon Humber banke stod
And was the kynges oghne also,
The which Allee was cleped tho,
A Saxon and a worthi knyght,
Bot he believeth noght ariht.[1]

At the other extreme from this we have the high sophistication
of Shakespeare's last 'romances'. The difficulty of reconciling
the psychologically probable with the requirements of the
fable are overcome by the sheer skill of the poetry which embodies the drama, the psychology and the moral. The supreme
example of this is the miracle of Hermione's statue being
brought to life. By the establishment of a ritualistic movement,
by the portrayal of Leontes' growing anguish and guilt, by
the evocation of the wonder and miracle of life itself, by the
generation of a mounting excitement, Shakespeare forces the
audience themselves to *wish* the statue to life. 'If this be magic,
let it be an art / Lawful as eating.' But the uncertainties of
Pericles, and the clumsiness of moments in *Cymbeline* show
that it was magic won only after much exercise and endeavour.
  Chaucer is more akin in his method to Shakespeare than to
Gower. His version is very sophisticated, and the complexity,
as usual, can be felt in the variety and extremes of style and
tone. The religiously didactic element is carried further than

[1] *The Complete Works of John Gower*, ed. G. C. Macaulay (O.U.P., 1901), I,
149–50.

it is in Gower's version. (Indeed, if Gower's tale were read in isolation from its context in *Confessio Amantis* it would be difficult to guess that the tale was exemplifying the deadly sin of Envy.) At the other extreme Chaucer permits the reader to linger on and contemplate the pathos of the human aspects. Gower, for example, has nothing to say about Constance's feelings when she has to depart to marry the Sultan, but Chaucer spends several stanzas on it.

> Allas! what wonder is it thogh she wepte,   (267)
> That shal be sent to strange nacioun
> Fro freendes that so tendrely hire kepte,
> As to be bounden under subjeccioun
> Of oon, she knoweth nat his condicioun?
> Housbondes been alle goode, and han ben yoore;
> That knowen wyves; I dar sey yow na moore.

> 'Fader', she seyde, 'thy wrecched child Custance,
> Thy yonge doghter fostred up so softe,
> And ye, my mooder, my soverayn plesance
> Over alle thyng, out-taken Crist on-lofte,
> Custance youre child hire recomandeth ofte
> Unto youre grace, for I shal to Surrye,
> Ne shal I nevere seen yow moore with ye.

> 'Allas! unto the Barbre nacioun
> I moste anoon, syn that is youre wille;
> But Crist that starf for our redempcioun
> So yeve me grace his heestes to fulfille!
> I, wrecche womman, no fors though I spille!
> Wommen are born to thraldom and penance,
> And to been under mannes governance.'

In the portrayal here of Constance a fine balance is established between the particular and the general. We are aware of her as a strongly devout girl, who has grown up surrounded with security and love, and who returns her parents' love and is dutiful and obedient. At the same time the pathos of her situation is that of any young girl who must leave home to marry a stranger and live among foreign people. This device of dramatising her feelings by relating her lot to a generalised human situation makes it possible for her character to be idealised without loss of humanity. When Constance is brought 'as the lomb' before the king to be accused of murdering Hermengyld we see the same method again being used.

> She sette hire doun on knees, and thus she sayde: (638)
> 'Immortal God, that savedest Susanne
> Fro false blame, and thou, merciful mayde,
> Marie I meene, doghter to Seint Anne,
> Bifore whos child angeles synge Osanne,
> If I be giltless of this felonye,
> My socour be, for ellis shal I dye!'

> Have ye nat seyn somtyme a pale face,
> Among a press, of hym that hath be lad
> Toward his deeth, wher as hym gat no grace,
> And swich a colour in his face hath had,
> Men myghte knowe his face that was bistad,
> Amonges alle the faces in that route?
> So stant Custance, and looketh hire aboute.

In this way *The Man of Law's Tale* generates a sympathy for innocent suffering and a wonder at the mercy and intervention of God that Gower's tale never approaches.

But Chaucer, unlike Gower, goes out of his way to stress the incredibility of what happens in the tale. For example, in the lines from *Confessio Amantis* quoted earlier, Gower 'explains' Constance's survival for three years on the ship by saying that it had been provisioned for five years. Chaucer asks how could she possibly have survived without meat and drink, and answers the question by referring to miracles in the Scriptures. With Gower it is relatively easy to suspend disbelief; with *The Man of Law's Tale* it is more difficult unless one accepts implicitly the authority of the Bible and the preachings of Christianity. What makes the incidents of *The Man of Law's Tale* credible, lies, as it were, 'outside' the tale itself. Again and again the tale, instead of drawing us in to share a belief, forces us back on our own beliefs. Yet the tale also dramatises the feelings of pathos and religious wonder in a way Gower's less incredible version never does. What are we to make of this paradox or contradiction?

A tempting answer is to explain it away historically. Chaucer himself was a Christian living in an age imbued with Christian belief: he intended and expected his readers to accept the tale in devout faith. Today, living in a more sceptical age, modern readers find doubts where the medieval world found only faith. A tempting answer perhaps, but fallacious. For one thing, Christian belief in the late middle ages was by no means as monolithic as this, and arguments as sceptical as any today had wide currency. For example, there is the dispute between Siger of Brabant and Thomas Aquinas which has been described as the most important intellectual episode of the thirteenth century. Siger taught the supremacy of reason over faith. Religion was necessary for the masses, but not for educated people. Dogmas were beneficial for faith, but were often contrary to reason and then reason was to be followed. There was also Boetius of Dacia who taught that the greatest beatitude was to be found in the practice of the good and the cognition of the true. Man's intellect, he wrote, could guide him to these, for if there is anything divine in man then it is the intellect, and it is by the exercise of the intellect that truth and justice are discerned and practised.[1] Though the teachings of both of these men were condemned by the Church, ideas are not so easily suppressed. 'In particular,' writes Wolfgang Clemen, 'England in the fourteenth century was permeated by a spirit of philosophical and theological criticism of such intensity that literary historians have even called it a century of "critical self-disintegration".'[2] But we need not look outside Chaucer for evidence of religious scepticism and doubt: we have already seen in *The Miller's Tale* how this world could be glorified at the expense of the spiritual world, and the degree of importance

[1] See Friedrich Heer, *The Medieval World* (Weidenfeld and Nicolson, 1961), particularly chap. 10: 'Intellectual Warfare in Paris'.
[2] See Clemen, *op. cit.* pp. 14–17.

that could be assigned to truth about the human lot. It is more reasonable then to assume that Chaucer was quite deliberate in so shaping *The Man of Law's Tale* that it may evoke belief *or* scepticism.

Chaucer's method is not to provide answers, but to open possibilities. *The Knight's Tale* introduced the issue of inexplicable suffering, and sought to affirm the essential goodness of things in terms that are, on the whole, non-Christian. *The Man of Law's Tale* has picked up the issue and attempted to settle it in a Christian exemplum. The devout can find in the tale of Constance much to satisfy them. For the hedgehog mind the tale may tell him all he needs to know. 'The fox knows many things, but the hedgehog knows one big thing.' And Chaucer is a fox. He knows that the answer the Man of Law gives is only one point of view, and that any point of view is limited, particularly on an issue as vast and crucial as this. Therefore, while creating a spiritual fable, he builds into it elements which can lead us to doubts and further questioning. The more perceptive readers are invited to recognise the bias of the teller in the tale told, and to seek further.

The tale of Constance is not inappropriately fitted to the character of the Man of Law. It is just the sort of tale such a respectable personage might choose to tell. But it is worth recalling the undertone of irony in the description of the Man of Law in the *Prologue*:

> A Sergeant of the Lawe, war and wys,   (309)
> That often hadde been at the Parvys,
> Ther was also, ful riche of excellence.
> *Discreet he was and of greet reverence—*
> *He seemed swich, his wordes weren so wise.*

There is one thing in the tale which more clearly than any other shows that Chaucer intended a critical approach to the Man of Law and the Christian standpoint he expresses. This is the attitude towards women. In its dualistic portrayal of the nature of womanhood the tale is symptomatic of the curious attitude towards the sex so prevalent in medieval Christianity

(and not always overcome today). On the one hand a woman
may epitomise the greatest purity and innocence, as in the
figure of the Virgin Mary. (That Mary *had* to be a virgin is
itself an illuminating fact about medieval Christianity.) Thus
Constance in the tale. On the other hand women represent
wickedness and sin. A woman caused the Fall, and the daughters
of Eve transmit the sin down through the generations.

> O sowdanesse, roote of iniquitee! (358)
> Virago, thou Semyrame the secounde!
> O serpent under femynynytee,
> Lik to the serpent depe in helle ybounde!
> O feyned womman, al that may confounde
> Vertu and innocence, thurgh thy malice,
> Is bred in thee, as nest of every vice!

> O Sathan, envious syn thilke day
> That thou were chaced from oure heritage,
> Wel knowestow to wommen the olde way!
> Thou madest Eva brynge us in servage:
> Thou wolt fordoon this Cristen mariage,
> Thyn instrument so, weylawey the while!
> Makestow of wommen, whan thou wolt bigile.

The plot does not require this rhetorical exposition of the
Sultaness's evil. (Nor is it to be found in the versions of
Nicholas Trivet or Gower.) Its sole justification is that it expresses the Christian vision. (The same anti-feminine and
pro-masculine bias can be seen in the lines quoted earlier of
Constance's departure where we were told 'Housbondes been
alle goode, and han ben yoore'.) The effect is to make the fair-
minded reader pause and query the validity of the Christian
picture. And in case the point should be missed, the Wife of
Bath's outburst on the Church's attitude towards her sex will
soon drive it home. For these lines are clearly a preparation
for her confession and tale to follow, and no doubt we are to
take it that it was hearing the Man of Law speak like this that
led to her speaking out. (Clearly too *The Man of Law's Tale*

must precede *The Wife of Bath's Prologue and Tale* for it would ruin the drama of the debate if these words could be spoken after her outburst.) Thus *The Man of Law's Tale* dramatises the teaching of the Christian Church, but in such a way that it may prepare us for the attack on Christian doctrines that the Wife of Bath will deliver. *The Clerk's Tale*, in its turn, will repeat the lesson of *The Man of Law's Tale*, but with wider and more intricate implications.

CHAPTER 5

The Wife of Bath's Prologue and Tale

IT was Professor Kittredge who first suggested that *The Wife of Bath's Prologue and Tale*, *The Clerk's Tale*, *The Merchant's Tale* and *The Franklin's Tale* belonged together and formed a debate between the Canterbury pilgrims on the subject of marriage. 'The Wife of Bath's *Prologue*', he wrote, 'begins a Group in the *Canterbury Tales*, or, as one may say, a new act in the drama. It is not connected with anything that precedes.'[1] This is not my view. I have already suggested that it was the Man of Law's orthodox comments on the nature and role of women that set off the Wife of Bath. Indeed to some extent her confession may be seen as a parody of the life of Constance, for the Wife of Bath too has many misadventures before she (ultimately) finds bliss with her fifth husband. The satirical realism of the Wife of Bath's *Prologue* is set off against the divine idealism of *The Man of Law's Tale*. Further, this group of tales deals with much more than marriage: issues from earlier tales find new expression, and novel issues are introduced. This group is not self-contained but fits into the larger, human debate of the *Canterbury Tales*.

The central subject of *The Wife of Bath's Prologue and Tale* is the war between the sexes. The struggle for 'maistrye', for 'sovereignty', is more than a mere struggle as to who should wear the trousers in the home (though it is this as well). It is the eternal struggle between male and female, in which the one attempts to deny the challenge and being of the other by

---

[1] George Lyman Kittredge, 'Chaucer's Discussion of Marriage', reprinted in *Chaucer: Modern Essays in Criticism*, ed. Edward Wagenknecht (Galaxy Books, 1959). See p. 189. The same point has recently been repeated by Charles Muscatine: 'Though the *Prologue* may have been intended to follow the *Nun's Priest's Tale*, and thus to stand in some relationship to the matrimonial matter therein, as we have it there is no link with what goes before' (*op. cit.* p. 207).

domination or aggression. This struggle is represented in the *Prologue* in a number of different ways.

First, it is represented through the Wife of Bath herself. It is completely inadequate to see her as a mere character-drawing or, even worse, as a portrayal of a real woman. She is larger than life-size. I am not saying that Chaucer has not given us a convincingly drawn individual—he has.[1] But the Wife of Bath is much more than this. She is more than merely an aggressive, uninhibited, vulgar woman dominating the particular men fortunate or unfortunate enough to have been married *by* her. She is also a matriarchal figure who has declared war on *man*kind. She embodies the eternal female in revolt against a male-ordered and male-centred civilisation. Such was the medieval civilisation the Wife of Bath (and Chaucer) lived in; and the *Prologue* portrays that society as well as her nature.

Before demonstrating what I have said by an examination of the *Prologue* itself, it would be well to reflect further on medieval sexual ideals and attitudes.

It was about the tenth century that the Church began to develop the enormously strict system which ruled in the Middle Ages. A series of 'penitential books' began to appear which explored the subject of sex in all its details: every misdeed was described and elaborated at length, and penalties were prescribed for each...All who could were urged to attempt the ideal of complete celibacy, while for those with priestly functions it was obligatory. In this direction the medieval Church could scarcely go further than had the early fathers. Jovinian had been excommunicated for daring to deny, what St Augustine had asserted, that virginity was a better state than marriage simply because it provided the world with potential virgins...

[An absolute ban was placed] on all forms of sexual activity other than intercourse between married persons, carried out with the object of procreating.[2]

[1] See John Livingstone Lowes, *Geoffrey Chaucer* (O.U.P., 1939), pp. 187–90.
[2] G. Rattray Taylor, *Sex in History* (Thames and Hudson, 1953). See chap. III, 'Medieval Sexual Morality'.

The sexual act, even in marriage, was held to be accompanied by lust and sin unless performed solely for the object of procreating.

St Gregory the Great [wrote that] the marriage act is in itself lawful and pure, 'but in practice husbands and wives are far from respecting fully the serene beauty of this act. They do not respect its extremely lofty purpose, seeing that all too often they mix lust in with it and the desire to gratify their craving for pleasure; they make immoderate use of it, not confining themselves to what the Divine Will calls for. That is why the marriage act is always tainted with a fault...It is a slight fault, no doubt...; but after all it is a fault, and David could with reason assert that we are all conceived in sin.'[1]

Because of this belief all sorts of prohibitions were placed upon the sexual act even within marriage.

[What is not generally realised today] is the extensive nature of the attempt which was made to limit and control the sexual act when performed *within* the marital relationship. Thus the sexual act must be performed in only one position, and numerous penalties were prescribed for using variants. Not content with this, the Church proceeded to cut down the number of days per annum upon which even married couples might legitimately perform the sexual act. First, it was made illegal on Sundays, Wednesdays and Fridays, which effectively removed the equivalent of five months in the year. Then it was made illegal for forty days before Easter and forty days before Christmas, and for three days before attending communion (and there were regulations requiring frequent attendance at communion). It was also forbidden from the time of conception to forty days after parturition. It was, of course, forbidden during any penance...It was ordered that no one might marry for a second time, even if the first partner had died...[2]

The position of women in those days was an unenviable one.

The sexual obsessions of the Church bore with especial hardness on women. By the Saxons she had been treated as property; now she was treated as the source of all sexual evil as well. Chrysostom, less vindictive than some, spoke of women as a 'necessary evil, a

[1] Quoted by Dr Jacques Leclercq in *Marriage and the Family*, (Frederick Pustet, 1941), p. 147.
[2] Rattray Taylor, *op. cit.* chap. III.

natural temptation, a desirable calamity, a domestic peril, a deadly fascination, and a painted ill'. But by the Middle Ages even these qualifications were no longer acceptable. 'A Good Woman (as an old Philosopher observeth) is but like one Ele put in a bagge amongst 500 Snakes, and if a man should have the luck to grope out that one Ele from all the snakes, yet he hath at best a wet Ele by the Taile.' It was argued that sexual guilt really pertained to women, since they tempted men, who would otherwise have remained pure...By the Middle Ages married women ceased even to have a legal existence. Though unmarried women had certain legal rights, and could dispose of their own property on reaching their majority, married women were mere shadows of their husbands. The very being or legal existence of the woman is suspended during the marriage...for this reason a man cannot grant anything to his wife or enter into any covenant with her: for the grant would be to presuppose her separate existence, and to covenant with her would be only to covenant with himself', says Blackstone.

Furthermore any suit against a woman automatically made the husband a defendant: hence husbands must have the power to prevent their wives from doing anything which might so involve them. It was upon this proposition that the husband's right to inflict 'moderate chastisement' on his wife was based. Though the common law enjoined husbands to treat their wives mercifully, the civil law said that he could 'beat her violently with whips and sticks'. It was permissible to thrash a woman with a cudgel but not to knock her down with an iron bar.[1]

'Allas! allas! that evere love was sinne', says the Wife of Bath.

Clearly, an important part of *The Wife of Bath's Prologue* is the satire (Chaucer's satire) directed at the sex-obsessed and guilt-ridden attitudes of medieval Christianity. At all times the male attitude towards woman involves a certain amount of distrust: the male suspects her of undermining and betraying his manhood. But the sexual repressions of medieval Christianity pushed this fear to insane and absurd lengths.

> Thou liknest eek wommenes love to helle,   (371)
> To bareyne lond, ther water may nat dwelle.
> Thou liknest it also to wilde fyr;

[1] *Ibid.* chap. III.

> The moore it brenneth, the moore it hath desir
> To consume every thyng that brent wole be.
> Thou seyest, right as wormes shende a tree,
> Right so a wyf destroyeth hire housbonde;
> This knowe they that been to wyves bonde.

Every one of the ridiculous images here could be capped by quotations from the seriously intended anti-feminist writings of the times (e.g. St Jerome's phrase upon which Chaucer based this speech: *Infernus, et amor mulieris, et terra arens, et ignis exaestuans*). But this passage, put in the mouth of the Wife of Bath, makes preposterous the whole business of the male projecting his sexual guilt on to the female. Indeed, what better vehicle for the satire could there be than the comic, guilt-free, indignant Wife of Bath! Again and again, with devastating common-sense she upturns official morality.

> Telle me also, to what conclusion   (115)
> Were membres maad of generacion,
> And for what profit was a wight ywrought?
> Trusteth right wel, they were nat made for noght.

And

> For hadde God comanded maydenhede   (68)
> Thanne hadde he dampned weddyng with the dede.
> And certes, if ther were no seed ysowe,
> Virginitee, thanne wherof sholde it growe?

The last passage, with its image of the seed, shows the Wife of Bath to be on the side of life, and opposed to the forces of falsehood and death. She stands for naturalness, vigour, spontaneity, joy and fertility. The only time she speaks sadly is when for a moment the reflection of inevitable age and death touches her, but she shakes off such morbid thoughts with her next breath. (This passage echoes the Reeve's and the Host's speeches on the passing of time, but the attitude here is wholly the Wife of Bath's and contrasts particularly with the bitterness and defeatism of the Reeve.)

> But, Lord Crist! whan that it remembreth me   (469)
> Upon my yowthe, and on my jolitee,
> It tikleth me aboute myn herte roote.

Unto this day it dooth myn herte boote
That I have had my world as in my tyme.
But, age, allas! that al wole envenyme,
Hath me biraft my beautee and my pith.
Lat go, farewel! the devel go therwith!
The flour is goon, ther is namoore to telle;
The bren, as I best kan, now moste I selle;
But yet to be right myrie wol I fonde.
Now wol I tellen of my fourthe housbonde.

'The innocent and the beautiful/Have no enemy but time', wrote W. B. Yeats, but Chaucer's achievement is to make one feel the essential innocence and beauty in the Wife of Bath—in a way that is more profound than Yeats's romantic idealisation. Chaucer achieves this largely through the centrality and homeliness of his images, such as 'myn herte roote' with its suggestions of deep and solid connectedness with the source of life. 'The flour is goon' is another such image. Here the associations of pure and good fare are mingled with associations of delight and beauty in the ambiguous word 'flour'. It is achieved also through the presentation of the Wife of Bath's courageous and joyful acceptance of sorrowful things: 'The bren, as I best kan, now moste I selle.'

'I have had my world as in my time.' The Wife of Bath is essentially a secular figure. Without shame she confesses that God's commands are for those that would live perfectly, and that she has never aspired to do.

He spak to hem that wolde lyve parfitly: (111)
And lordynges, by youre leve, that am not I.
I wol bistowe the flour of al myn age
In the actes and in fruyt of mariage.

Hers is a rejection of transcendental religion. She is, to refer to a Yeats poem again, the self as opposed to the soul. She sometimes aspires to speak piously but the effect is usually a parody of false clerical arguments, or else a revelation of the blasphemy that often lies in common piousness ('By God! in erthe I was his purgatorie./For which I hope his soule be in glorie'). Yet she is not really an anti-religious or amoral figure. Just as in her piety she sometimes utters blasphemy, so in her blasphemy we sometimes find the profoundest piety and morality.

> Crist was a mayde, and shapen as a man,　　(139)
> And many a seint, sith that the world bigan;
> Yet lyved they evere in parfit chastitee.
> I nyl envye no virginitee.
> Lat hem be breed of pure whete-seed,
> And lat us wyves hoten barly-breed;
> And yet with barly-breed, Mark telle kan,
> Oure Lord Jhesu refresshed many a man.

Her sexual prodigality is in a curious way profoundly religious. In its bawdy exuberance it is an expression of life, and of gratitude to God who made her.

> In wyfhod I wol use myn instrument　　(149)
> As frely as my Makere hath it sent.

I have stressed the 'innocence and beauty' in the Wife of Bath, but clearly this 'innocence and beauty' contains within it a great deal that is also satirised and criticised. The Wife of Bath is the vehicle for satirising male attitudes, but she is also the vehicle for satirising female attitudes. She herself is a grotesque examplar of most of the female vices: nagging, scolding, deceiving, chiding, grumbling, spending, gossiping, lying and betraying. She is vain, egotistic, hypocritical (as when she attends the funeral of her fourth husband), possessive and licentious. Chaucer brilliantly catches the smothering destructiveness of females in these lines:

> Thow seyst that droppyng houses, and eek smoke,　(278)
> And chidyng wyves maken men to flee
> Out of hir owene hous; a! *benedicitee!*
> What eyleth swich an old man for to chide?

But while she possesses most of the vices that woman-hating clerics could think up she still remains, despite these and thus giving lie to the clerics who saw women as agents of the devil, a very human and sympathetic figure. We are more amused by her than angry with her.

Her prime fault, however, and here we return to the central theme of the war between the sexes, is that she wishes to assert female domination over the male. 'Sovereignty' means breaking the male will, and possessing him completely.

> An housbonde I wol have, I wol nat lette,   (154)
> Which shal be bothe my dettour and my thral,
> And have his tribulacioun withal
> Upon his flessh, whyl that I am his wyf.
> I have the power durynge al my lyf
> Upon his propre body, and noght he...

This aspect of the Wife of Bath is comically terrifying. Here is the ugliness that co-exists with her 'beauty', making her such a complex figure. She is a terrible, matriarchal goddess, demanding complete subservience to herself. Law, order, discipline are cast over.

The climax of the *Prologue* is reached in the conflict between the Wife of Bath and her fifth husband, the clerk. All the elements of the poem are here united in the scene between the two, the servant of Venus and the servant of Mercury.

> The children of Mercurie and of Venus   (697)
> Been in hir wirkyng ful contrarius;
> Mercurie loveth wysdom and science,
> And Venus loveth ryot and dispence.

In the grand comedy at the end not only does Chaucer give the clash between the 'self' and the 'soul', between the natural vigour of the secular and the contemptuous asceticism of the ecclesiastical, but he also portrays for us in a scene of high absurdity the ruthlessness, aggression and fierceness lurking in the male–female relationship.

It is easy to see why the Wife of Bath chooses to tell the tale she does tell. To her the moral seems an obvious one: that the man gets his reward by handing over the mastery to the woman. But there is irony in the fact that the Wife of Bath should choose to tell this tale, for the real moral of the tale is quite different from what she thinks it is. Indeed, the important thing about the tale is that it condemns the desire for mastery. Mastery involves the subordination of the beloved's will, and the swallowing up of his or her personality. It is the refusal to recognise the 'otherness' of the other person (to use D. H. Lawrence's phrase), or the desire not to recognise it by destroying it. The real moral of the tale told by the Wife of Bath is that this 'otherness' must be recognised.

The Knight in the tale rapes a woman. This means that he sees women only as adjuncts to his own personality, as objects he can ravish by force. In punishment for this crime his life is made dependent on the will of women, and they (i.e. the queen) tell him that his life is forfeit unless he can find out what women most desire. The answer he finds, with the aid of the ugly, old woman, is that

> Wommen desiren have sovereynetee (1038)
> As wel over hir housbond as hir love,
> And for to been in maistrie hym above.

That is to say, they claim the right, as much as men, to assert their own identity and dominate the opposite sex. This is the first lesson the knight has to learn.

But then the knight is forced to marry the old woman, and a more searching problem is posed him. In the more common version of the folk-tale on which *The Wife of Bath's Tale* is based, the knight has to choose between having his old and ugly wife beautiful by day, or having her beautiful by night.[1]

---

[1] E.g. *Weddynge of Sir Gawen and Dame Ragnell*:

> 'Syr', she sayd, 'thus shalle ye me have,
> Chese of the one, so God me save,
> My beawty wolle nott hold;
> Wheder ye wolle haue me fayre on nyghtes,
> And as foulle on days to alle men sightes,
> Or els to haue me fayre on days,
> And on nyghtes on the fowlyst wyfe,
> The one ye must nedes haue.'

See W. F. Bryan and Germaine Dempster (eds.), *Sources and Analogues of Chaucer's Canterbury Tales* (Routledge and Kegan Paul, 1958).

That is, he has to choose which is the more important, physical love or ideal love. Chaucer changed this: the knight has to choose between having his wife ugly and faithful, or beautiful and unfaithful. This choice is in line with anti-feminist complaints: one can only be sure of a wife if she is ugly. Implied in the choice is this dilemma: *possession* of a woman can give a man no joy, since he can only hold dominion over her by making her show him the loveless side of her nature. On the other hand allowing her independence may allow her to be too free with her love, and cause the man to taste all the doubtful joys of jealousy and betrayal.

The knight in the *Tale* gives the correct answer, which is not to choose either of these alternatives. Both these alternatives involve a selfish, egocentric choice: the being of one partner is sacrificed for the pleasure of the other. The knight chooses rightly by giving the choice to her: he makes no claim at all upon her, subordinating his desires to her responsibility, letting her decide what is to their mutual benefit.

> 'Cheseth yourself which may be best plesance,   (1232)
> And moost honour to yow and me also.'

By doing this the Knight finds that the lady will be both beautiful and faithful. By his full recognition of her 'otherness' he is rewarded by her free acceptance of him. Thus, in the mutual recognition of the other, in each giving only to find that the giving is the taking, in this lies the ideal love–marriage relationship. This is the true moral of the *Tale*. What enables the knight to make his right decision? It is what he learns from the old woman about the nature of 'gentilesse'. 'Gentilesse' is a word almost impossible to translate into modern English. What W. B. Yeats calls 'courtesy' is only part of it:

> In courtesy I'd have her chiefly learned:
> Hearts are not had as a gift but hearts are earned...

'Gentilesse' is more than a 'glad kindness', and it is more than custom or ceremony.

> Crist will we clayme of him oure gentilesse.   (1117)

We do not inherit it but get it of God out of His grace and charity. Indeed, God is the source of 'gentilesse' (the Parson in his *Tale* actually speaks of God's 'gentilesse'). Perhaps the closest to it would be something of what Shakespeare means by 'grace' in *The Winter's Tale*. At any rate, 'gentilesse' is a charitable nobility of spirit, which involves the full recognition of other people in thought and action. The importance of 'gentilesse' in the love–marriage relationship is to be found even more powerfully explored in *The Franklin's Tale*, but the spirit of 'gentilesse' pervades all Chaucer's art.

CHAPTER 6

The Friar and the Summoner

THE Wife of Bath began her tale by saying,

> In th'olde dayes of the Kyng Arthour,   (857)
> Of which that Britons speken greet honour,
> Al was this land fulfild of fayerye.
> The elf-queene, with hir joly compaignye,
> Daunced ful ofte in many a grene mede.

There is more to this than the conventional 'Once upon a time...' For the Wife of Bath is recalling a past, still dimly carried in the memories of the people, when the reigning religion in England was a fertility cult, and its rites were presided over by a woman often identified as the Queen of Faerie or as the Elfin Queen. The greater number of its ceremonies appear to have been practised for the purpose of securing fertility, and many of the rites—the feasts and dances—show that it was a joyous religion.[1] References to this cult can be found elsewhere in English literature, perhaps the most explicit example being Shakespeare's *A Midsummer Night's Dream*. That the fairies in the play are connected with sexual desire and fertility is manifest, the best illustrations being Titania's speech to Oberon in which she says their quarrel has injured the bounty of Nature (II, i—it is one of the most powerful speeches in the play, another mark of its importance), and the final blessing the fairies give to the bridal couples.

The Wife of Bath would clearly have been more in her element in an age ruled by the Elfin Queen—indeed might herself have been such a Queen. But, as she laments, the coming of Christianity spelled the decline of the earlier religion.

> I speke of manye hundred yeres ago.   (863)
> But now kan no man se none elves mo.

[1] See M. A. Murray, *The Witch-Cult in Western Europe* (O.U.P., 1962), particularly pp. 13–15.

For now the grete charitee and prayeres
Of lymytours and othere hooly freres,
That serchen every lond and every streem,
As thikke as motes in the sonne-beem,
Blessynge halles, chambres, kichenes, boures,
Citees, burghes, castels, hye toures,
Thropes, bernes, shipnes, dayeryes—
This maketh that ther ben no fayeryes.

In the poetry here there is more than an undercurrent of scorn
for Christianity. The representatives of the Church poke and
pry everywhere, as aggravating as dust that spreads in the air.
The sarcasm in 'grete charitee and prayeres' suggests that
they had less generous motives in ridding the land of elves,
that they wished to be freer in obtaining their own ends.
The irony in these lines is perhaps too poised to be the Wife
of Bath's alone, but the hostility to the Church is certainly
hers and we might say one function of Chaucer's irony is to
reveal what she feels in her heart of hearts about Christianity.
Doubtless, too, she was not unaccompanied in feeling like
this: many must have shared her nostalgia for the good times
past and her resentment at the inescapable interference of the
Church. For the introduction of Christianity meant that a religion of joy and fertility was replaced by one of guilt and
asceticism. Furthermore, by the time Chaucer came to write
this tale many of the Church's institutions, and the men running
them, had become thoroughly corrupt. In the best of circumstances the ideals of the Church must have chafed hard on
human nature, but when it became the main source of authority and wealth it inevitably gathered into itself many whose
personal interests were at odds with the body they pretended
to serve. It has been estimated that by the thirteenth century
one out of every twelve males in England were ecclesiastics of
some kind,[1] and it is not to be expected that such a high pro-
portion of the population could keep vows of celibacy or
maintain the strict rules of their calling. By Chaucer's day
certain sections of the Church were little more than collections

[1] Bailey, *op. cit.* p. 152.

of rogues and vagabonds. Many had become notorious for their avarice or lechery:

> For ther as wont to walken was an elf,   (873)
> Ther walketh now the lymytour hymself
> In undermeles and in morwenynges...
> Wommen may go now saufly up and doun.   (878)
> In every bussh or under every tree;
> Ther is noon oother incubus but he,
> And he ne wol doon hem but dishonour.

Thus *The Friar's Tale* and *The Summoner's Tale* that follow continue the satire on the Church that began in *The Wife of Bath's Prologue and Tale*. The satire may be said to work on two levels. By the juxtaposition with the Wife of Bath's attack on the teachings of Christianity and the way the Church supplanted a joyful worship of life here and now, the two tales illustrate how the people of England suffer under the exploitation of the clergy. Secondly, the satire reveals how the ideals of Christianity are themselves distorted and abused by the self-seeking behaviour of its corrupt members. The Wife of Bath's own twisting of the gospel is quite honest and religious, compared with what the Friar and the Summoner do to it. I do not wish to be taken as saying, however, that the satire here is wholly anti-Christian. The Wife of Bath, I have suggested, represents qualities in life that the Church has scorned and belittled; but what she stands for too has its own defects and limitations which Chaucer has not concealed. Again it is a question of viewing the same things from conflicting viewpoints, reaching towards responsible understanding by entertaining the many possibilities. Indeed the second level of satire is in keeping with what many devout Christians felt about their own body, and Chaucer is in no way ahead of popular feeling or ecclesiastical authority of the time in his unmasking of the Friar and Summoner. 'Certain religious, who even belong to one or the other of the mendicant orders, and some secular clerks, even endowed with privileged benefices', Boniface IX had said in a pontifical letter, '...proclaim to the faithful and simple people the real or pretended authorisations which they have received; and irreverently abusing those which are real, in pursuit of infamous and hateful gain, they carry further their impudence by mendaciously attributing to themselves false and pretended authorisations of this kind.'[1] The criteria which most fully condemn the Friar and the Summoner are often uttered by themselves when quoting scripture. Thus, if one element of the satire challenges Christianity as men preach and practise it, there co-exists another element which affirms the divine truth in the religion itself.

The quarrel between the Miller and the Reeve was a clash between opposite personalities; the quarrel between the Friar and the Summoner arises, we feel, from the rivalry of competitors. Each accuses the other of similar vices, with mutual justice. The characters of summoner and friar *within* the tales are drawn with darker lines than the portraits Chaucer gives us in the *Prologue to the Canterbury Tales* of the two antagonists, but the kinship of the malicious caricatures to their originals is unmistakable. The Friar and the Summoner are, though we know them to be rogues, not without likable qualities: the dark and detestable side of their being appears in the caricatures.

In the *General Prologue* Chaucer delineates the Friar's glib tongue, conceit, and attractive vitality.

> He was the beste beggere in his hous; (252)
> For thogh a wydwe hadde noght a sho,
> So plesaunt was his '*In pricipio*,'
> Yet wolde he have a ferthyng, er he wente.
> His purchas was wel bettre than his rente...
> Somewhat he lisped, for his wantownesse,
> To make his Englisshe sweete upon his tonge;
> And in his harpyng, whan that he hadde songe,
> His eyen twynkled in his heed aryght
> As doon the sterres in the frosty nyght.

[1] Quoted by J. J. Jusserand, *English Wayfaring Life in the Middle Ages* (University Paperbacks, 1961), pp. 178–9.

The tale he tells is in keeping, for the witty homiletic he delivers suggests with what style he puts across sermons; indeed fundamentally the same story was told by Master Rypon of Durham as a sermon, and termed by him a 'narratio jocosa'.[1] Of all the tales so far it is the most sparing in detail. In most the background of the characters is filled in by many small touches: here we learn very little about the carter and the wife, and what we learn about the summoner and the fiend emerges largely from their conversation. The effect of this, combined with the all-pervading irony of the tale, is to throw emphasis on the evil wills they possess and their mental manoeuvring. The fiend and the summoner become sworn brothers, they are fundamentally alike, but their dedication to wickedness entails a brotherhood of betrayal.

> 'Brother', quod he, 'where is now youre dwellyng,   (1410)
> Another day if that I sholde yow seche?'
> This yeman hym answerde in softe speche,
>   'Brother', quod he, 'fer in the north contree,
> Where-as I hope som tyme I shal thee see.
> Er we departe, I shal thee so wel wisse
> That of myn hous ne shaltow nevere mysse.'

The fiend, still speaking in the disguise of the yeoman, tells of the hard master he serves.

> 'My wages been ful streite and ful smale.   (1426)
> My lord is hard to me and daungerous,
> And myn office is ful laborious,
> And therfore by extorcions I lyve.
> For sothe, I take al that men wol me yive.
> Algate, by sleyghte or by violence,
> Fro yeer to yeer I wynne al my dispence.
> I kan no bettre telle, feithfully.'
>   'Now certes', quod this Somonour, 'so fare I.'

These lines, reminding us of the harsh archdeacon the summoner serves, point to the hierarchy of evil and lead on to the notion that God permits the existence of evil beings to warn men and to punish them. The agents of this punishment, of

---

[1] See G. R. Owst, *Literature and Pulpit in Medieval England* (O.U.P., 1961), pp. 161–3.

course, punish one another. A nice example of the piquant irony of the tale is found in, 'I take al that men wol me yive', which not only prepares us for the old wife giving the summoner to the fiend, but emphasises that the summoner has already given himself to the devil by following the vocation he has, and will endorse this by the bargain he is about to strike with the fiend. Occasionally a stroke of irony incorporates the Friar himself, as when the fiend a few lines later uses the phrase, 'My purchas is th'effect of al my rente', which echoes a similar phrase in Chaucer's description of the Friar in the *General Prologue* (l. 256).

At the core of the tale is the question of *intent*, and it is round this concept that the fundamental ironies revolve. The carter's wishing his horses and carts to the devil is without effect because 'it is nat his entente': he speaks one thing, but in his heart intends something else. Thus the tale enforces the Christian notion of man's conscience: what is said or done takes its meaning from what is really desired in our heart of hearts. The agents of hell may attempt to trick man and entrap him, but can never succeed unless their victim has himself already chosen the path of hell. There is a further elaboration on this in the shape of a paradox. Those whose intent is evil may yet find that they have only fulfilled the purpose of good. Again and again the devil is out-tricked and his fiends out-manoeuvred by the cunning of God.

> 'But, for thou axest why labouren we—   (1482)
> For somtyme we been Goddes instrumentz,
> And meenes to doon his comandementz.
> Whan that hym list, upon his creatures,
> In divers art and in diverse figures.
> Withouten hym we have no myght, certayn,
> If that hym list to stonden ther-agayn . . .
> And somtyme be we suffred for to seke
> Upon a man, and doon his soule unreste,
> And nat his body, and al is for the beste.
> Whan he withstandeth oure temptacioun,
> It is a cause of his savacioun,
> Al be it that it was nat oure entente . . .'

Thus God converts evil to good, and the fiend who outwits the summoner is himself outwitted. The tale focusses on the evil wills of the two, only to reveal the all-powerful will of God. The plot of the tale makes it a theological paradigm.

Nowhere is this better seen than in the climax, where the heartfelt curse of the old wife the summoner intended to cheat is the occasion for his doom. Occasion rather than cause, for the summoner could still have saved himself by repentance. But his own 'entente' betrays him.

> 'The devel', quod she, 'so fecche hym er he deye,   (1628)
> And panne and al, but he wol hym repente!'
>   'Nay, olde stot, that is nat myn entente,
> Quod this somonour, 'for to repente me
> For any thyng that I have had of thee.
> I wolde I hadde thy smok and every clooth!'
>   'Now, brother', quod the devel, 'be nat wrooth;
> Thy body and this panne been myne by right.
> Thou shalt with me to helle yet to-nyght,
> Where thou shalt knowen of oure privetee
> Moore than a maister of dyvynytee.'

In these lines is concentrated the Christian teaching on salvation and on damnation. The tale would be an appropriate parable for a master of divinity to tell. But it is in the nature of Chaucer's art to exploit the fullest significance of his story. And the full force of the tale is only appreciated when we recognise how the moral of the tale reflects back on the Friar who tells it. For him it is the sort of story he would employ to gull the people of money and gifts, here cleverly turned into a malicious gibe at the Summoner. When, a few lines later, the Friar enjoins the pilgrims to pray that summoners repent he does not mean it: his intention is merely to humiliate the Summoner. Indeed, his implication is that the Summoner, like his counterpart in the tale, is too far gone for repentance. But he fails to recognise that the story carries a sting in its tail for him. His own intent is malicious, and he himself is the 'maister of dyvynytee' who may come to make more intimate acquaintance with the devil's 'privetee'.

There is a parallel between the Friar and the summoner he drew; further there is a parallel between the Friar and the fiend of the tale. For just as the fiend's evil intentions were converted to good ends, so the Friar, himself a corrupt man who abuses his ecclesiastical position, even in a tale whose purpose is slander, still spreads the teaching of Christianity. Thus we reach Chaucer's ultimate irony. The tale, which satirises Christianity and the corruptions its ministers have fallen into, finally affirms Christian doctrines and asserts the divine Will manifest even behind men's venal intentions.

The Friar's Tale has a religious moral, *The Summoner's Tale* a social one. A paragraph in J. J. Jusserand's *English Wayfaring Life in the Middle Ages* may be said to sum it up. He writes: 'Begging friars go from door to door, pardoners grow rich, pilgrims live by alms and by the recital of their adventures, always on the way, always at work. What is this work? By constantly addressing the crowd, they in the end make themselves known for what they are, and cause their listeners to pass sentence on them; by disabusing them they render reform inevitable. Thereby, too, will the rust and superstition of the middle ages drop away...'[1] *The Summoner's Tale* dramatises just such an occasion. The focus of the tale is on, first, the way the friar reveals his own roguery, and, secondly, the contempt people hold for the friar and his order. The Summoner's personal malice against the Friar becomes submerged in the popular hostility, and functions as an instrument of the satire. Though the friar in the tale himself exemplifies all the deadly sins, and is the ironical subject of his own sermonising, the main delight of the tale lies in the delineation of the friar's behaviour.

Near the beginning of the tale there is one brief echo of the lines I quoted earlier from *The Wife of Bath's Tale*.

> Whan folk in chirche had yeve him what hem leste, (1735)
> He wente his wey, no longer wolde he reste.

---

[1] Jusserand, *op. cit.* p. 242.

> With scrippe and tipped staf, ytukked hye,
> In every hous he gan to poure and prye,
> And beggeth mele and chese, or elles corn.

That Thomas's illness does not deter the friar from begging, indeed becomes even an excuse for it, emphasises further his ubiquitous imposition. His glib speech, his smooth manner, his practised cleverness, his licensed authority, make him a difficult man to snub—only some strong and unequivocal action could hope to succeed. Almost any passage of his speech would serve to illustrate these characteristics, for it is all in the same groove. The imitation of his manner could become boring were it not for our rising amazement at each additional stroke of impudence.

> 'But herkne now, Thomas, what I shal seyn.   (1918)
> I ne have no text of it, as I suppose,
> But I shal fynde it in a maner glose,
> That specially oure sweete Lord Jhesus
> Spak this by freres, whan he seyde thus:
>   "Blessed be they that povere in spirit been."
> And so forth al the gospel may ye seen,
> Wher it be likker oure professioun,
> Or hirs that swymmen in possessioun.
> Fy on hire pompe and on hire glotonye!
> And for hir lewednesse I hem diffye.
>   Me thynketh they been lyk Jovinyan,
> Fat as a whale, and walkynge as a swan,
> Al vinolent as botel in the spence.
> Hir preyere is of ful greet reverence,
> Whan they for soules seye the psalm of Davit;
> Lo, "buf!" they seye, "*cor meum eructavit!*"'

It seems incredible that a man should condemn others for those faults he so typifies himself. Doubtless from long experience the friar has discovered the bigger the lie the better it pays. His eloquence is exemplified by the sharp images: how succinctly the line, 'Fat as a whale, and walkynge as a swan,' captures a well-fed, self-satisfied, waddling potentate. His wit and mimicry (qualities also possessed by the Summoner) are illustrated by the last line with its punning *eructavit*. But the line is also a piece of dramatic irony, for the suggestion of belching prepares the reader for the coarse climax of the tale.

The crux of the tale is very coarse indeed. Nor does the narrative have the energy and fast-moving plot that redeem the coarseness of *The Miller's Tale*. Chaucer seems bent on giving the nastiness its full weight and not on playing it down. But despite this it is still kept under control by the dramatic framework, and accorded a moral purpose.

The scope of the tale is revealed early, in the fable of the host of friars who dwell in the devil's arse.

> ' "Shewe forth thyn ers, and lat the frere se (1690)
> Where is the nest of freres in this place!"
> And er that half a furlong wey of space,
> Right so as bees out swarmen from an hyve,
> Out of the develes ers ther gonne dryve
> Twenty thousand freres on a route,
> And thurghout helle swarmed al aboute,
> And comen agayn as faste as they may gon,
> And in his ers they crepten everychon.'

The motes of dust in a sun-beam, which was how the Wife of Bath depicted holy friars, have now been transformed into a hellish swarm. The Summoner is matching the Friar's accusation that all summoners are damned, and his retort is vicious. But there is more to the passage than mere scatological abuse. For one thing the passage exemplifies the Summoner himself, his malice suddenly flying forth, then withdrawing again within his unpleasing person. Further, it warns us that the tale will deal with real evil, and of some magnitude. The punishment for the friar devised by his victims is a mere shadow of a greater retribution. Thus, behind the social satire, there is more than a hint of another dimension, of truly eschatological things. A firm sense of an ordained moral order is partially embodied in the poem, and gives greater weight to the social criticism. Compare *The Summoner's Prologue and Tale* with Ezra Pound's fourteenth Canto: Pound's poem is abominable because the links between his opinions and the coarseness are arbitrary; in Chaucer's poem the coarseness loses its power to disgust by being integrated in the larger moral and theological significance.

The framework of the story itself is the testament tale, not uncommon in popular folk literature, wherein good things are bequeathed to friends, and evil things to enemies.[1] The moral structure of *The Summoner's Tale* has to convince the reader that the gift the friar is given is appropriate and deserved, and I believe it succeeds in doing this. In some ways the friar is an attractive rogue, and his manner fascinating, but the note of satire, the slight touches of caricature in his presentation, give distance and objectivity.

> 'A! yif that covent half a quarter otes!   (1963)
> A! yif that covent foure and twenty grotes!
> A! yif that frere a peny, and lat hym go!
> Nay, nay, Thomas, it may no thyng be so!
> What is a ferthyng worth parted in twelve?'

The eloquence here calls such attention to itself that amusement robs it of any power to convince. The last line is also an ironic, and psychological, preparation for the proposed division of Thomas's gift.

More significant than such devices, however, is the clear revelation of the friar's fundamental sin. He speaks God's words for private gain, and empties them of their meaning. He promises rich rewards, and gives no more than vacuous breath. He claims God's mysteries to importune for his own comfort. The sin inherent in these is blasphemy, the kind that not only does dirt on life but does it in the name of the highest things. This sin, by displaying contempt for what is most to be revered, breeds the other sins. Anger, pride, lust, sloth arise from this primal contempt. The best illustration

[1] Bryan and Dempster, *op. cit.* p. 275.

of the friar's evil is the occasion when Thomas's wife mentions her dead child, and with practised ease the friar shifts into exploiting her grief.

> 'Now, sire', quod she, 'but o word er I go.   (1851)
> My child is deed withinne thise wykes two,
> Soone after that ye wente out of this toun.'
>   'His deeth saugh I by revelacioun',
> Seide this frere, 'at hoom in oure dortour.
> I dar wel seyn that, er that half an hour
> After his deeth, I saugh hym born to blisse
> In myn avision, so God me wisse!
> So dide oure sexteyn and oure fermerer,
> That han been trewe freres fifty yeer;
> They may now—God be thanked of his loone!—
> Maken hir jubilee and walke allone.
> And up I roos, and al oure covent eke,
> With many a teere trillyng on my cheke,
> Withouten noyse or clatterynge or belles;
> *Te Deum* was oure song, and nothyng elles,
> Save that to Crist I seyde an orison,
> Thankynge hym of his revelacion.
> For, sire and dame, trusteth me right weel,
> Oure orisons been moore effectueel,
> And moore we seen of Cristes secree thynges,
> Than burel folk, although they weren kynges.'

Here his hypocrisy and inhumanity are inseparable from the blasphemy. All the time the eloquence parodies itself, for the reader undoing what the friar hopes it will do. The friar's artistic touches, as in 'With many a teere trylling on my cheke' and '*Te Deum* was oure song, and nothyng elles' only empha-sise the absence of those feelings they claim for him. The passage invites the reader to suspect that the friar's 'convent' would support him in his lie, and so merit their position on the circumference of the wheel when the time for distribution comes. We might also note the echo of *The Miller's Tale* in the phrase 'Cristes secree thynges'—Nicholas there, like the friar here, also used his claim to know 'Goddes pryvetee' as means for gulling another for his own ends. Again this line leads up to the justice of the friar's reward, for when the enraged Thomas offers his gift:

> 'Now thanne, put in thyn hand doun by my bak',   (2140)
> Seyde this man, 'and grope wel bihynde.
> Bynethe my buttok there shaltow fynde
> A thyng that I have hyd in pryvetee.'

And this may remind us of the devil's 'privitee' the summoner comes to know in *The Friar's Tale*.

The humiliating of the friar is performed in two stages. The first is the crude insult by a justifiably indignant victim. The coarse cunning of the trick at last breaks down the friar's poise and smoothness:

> He looked as it were a wilde boor;   (2160)
> He grynte with his teeth, so was he wrooth.

The second stage shows the friar's public discomfiture when the lord's squire, speaking with a glib and smooth tongue worthy of the friar himself, and clearly expressing what many of the company have thought but dare not say, affirms that all friars are equal in evil, only this particular friar is 'more equal' than the others.

At moments in the course of the tale the drama is so dramatically immediate we may forget that the tale is an expression of the Summoner's malice towards the Friar. But one irony strongly drives this reminder home, and links Friar and Summoner. The friar's sermon has been mainly directed at the sin of anger, but he himself falls into it when the churl makes his churlish gift: so the Summoner's malicious gibe at the Friar serves to remind us with what rage he responded to the Friar's story at his expense:

> This Somonour in his styropes hye stood;   (1665)
> Upon this Frere his herte was so wood
> That lyk an aspen leef he quook for ire.

141

It is as difficult to assess which of the two men is worse, as difficult as equably divide a fart.

The Summoner's Tale does not enforce a theological point as strongly as *The Friar's Tale* may be said to do: yet it touches upon the justice of hell and enacts the moral summed up by the friar's own words:

> The hye God that al this world hath wroght, (1972)
> Seith that the werkman worthy is his hyre.

CHAPTER 7

The Clerk's Tale

AFTER two such rogues as the Friar and the Summoner it is fitting that the next tale should be told by a more worthy representative of the Church: an ecclesiastical student. The Clerk, though warned by the simple Host,

> But precheth nat, as freres doon in Lente,   (12)
> To make us for oure olde synnes wepe,

does relate what is in essence a religious tale, and the integrity of the Clerk's belief rings clear after the false preaching of the other two. In kind *The Clerk's Tale* is similar to *The Man of Law's Tale*, and it pushes further the exploration of needless suffering raised there and in *The Knight's Tale*. But above all it is directly linked to *The Wife of Bath's Prologue and Tale*.

> For trusteth wel, it is an impossible   (688)
> That any clerk wol speke good of wyves,

the Wife of Bath has said. The Clerk's tale is his reply and his charitable revenge. It is difficult to conceive a tale that could more fully answer the Wife of Bath. In her account of herself and her loves, the Wife of Bath stressed that love is the desire to assert one's personality and to dominate one's lover. The Clerk tells a tale showing that love may be the abnegation of personality, the losing of one's self in the self of the beloved. The Wife of Bath has praised uninhibited pleasure. The Clerk preaches the importance of discipline and self-control—the virtue of 'patience.' The Wife of Bath's vision of life is of this world and in this world. The Clerk shows how this world may be subordinated to a higher world. The Clerk, in fact, asserts much that is finest in the medieval Christian tradition.

The Clerk's Tale is essentially a literary tale, yet its wonderful achievement lies in its gentle understanding of human motives and feelings, and in its treatment of different planes of meaning.

143

Griselda is a suffering human being whose virtue is being abused by another; she is at the same time 'Everyman' or 'Every Woman' suffering and enduring the trials and tribulations of life before receiving a Heavenly reward; and she is also the personification of the virtues of meekness, humility, fortitude, fidelity and modesty. At one level, delicately hinted at, Walter stands for fate or cruel misfortune which tests us all; at another level he is a (psychological) study of a man driven to further and further cruelty in the pursuit of gratifying his domination over his beloved; yet he never becomes a totally unsympathetic figure. The success of *The Clerk's Tale* lies in Chaucer's remarkable skill at guiding the responses of the reader, dexterously drawing his attention now to one element, now to another, maintaining all the time his poetic faith.

When the people request Walter to take a wife whom they will choose for him, Walter appears to accede to their demands. He leaves the people with the impression that he has bound himself to their will, but the truth is that he has turned the occasion into an opportunity to marry whom he pleases with their promised consent. This scene shows Walter's dominating masculine intelligence at work, and prepares us for the way in which he will manoeuvre Griselda into marrying him on his own terms. At this stage, though, we admire Walter; and the admiration increases when he chooses Griselda. He has the perspicacity to appreciate her true worth. The biblical imagery with which she is described reveals that she is to be a pearl of infinite price:

> But hye God somtyme senden kan   (206)
> His grace into a litel oxes stalle.

But, like Shakespeare in his treatment of Perdita in *The Winter's Tale*, Chaucer makes the ideal a credible human being in a realistic rural setting.

> And whan she homward cam, she wolde brynge   (225)
> Wortes or othere herbes tymes ofte,
> The whiche she shredde and seeth for hir lyvinge,
> And made hir bed ful hard and nothyng softe.

The Duke's choosing her for wife seems to be an act of grace, but he cleverly manoeuvres her into promising herself completely, in act and thought, to him.

> 'I seye this, be ye redy with good herte   (351)
> To al my lust, and that I frely may,
> As me best thynketh, do yow laughe or smerte,
> And nevere ye to grucche it, nyght ne day?
> And eek whan I sey "ye", ne say nat "nay",
> Neither by word ne frownyng contenance?
> Swere this, and heere I swere oure alliance.'
>
> Wondrynge upon this word, quakynge for drede,
> She seyde, 'Lord, undigne and unworthy
> Am I to thilke honour that ye me beede,
> But as ye wol yourself, right so wol I.
> And heere I swere that nevere willyngly,
> In werk ne thoght, I nyl yow disobeye,
> For to be deed, though me were looth to deye.'

A picture of their ideal life together follows on the marriage, and the wisdom, faithfulness and love of Griselda are portrayed. Then Walter begins to test the strength of his power over her. He does it with a refined intellectual cruelty: the way in which the children are seized from her, the blatant insincerity of his reasons, the cruel behaviour of the sergeant, swell the awfulness of the deed. And later, when Walter pretends to be re-wedding, the callousness with which he dismisses his marriage to her is a calculated cruelty. (Perhaps we might say that the Clerk, coy and still as a maid, would imagine cruelty in just such refined terms.)

Griselda's acceptance of the seizure of her children shocks many people.[1] They feel that Griselda is being inhuman in not protesting. But no criticism of Griselda is presented in the actual lines of the poetry. What the poetry does do is make us feel in these scenes the very religious problem posed by the Lord demanding of Abraham that he sacrifice his only son.[2]

[1] E.g. see Speirs, *op. cit.* p. 152.

[2] Since this was written I have found that Charles Muscatine makes the same point: 'Griselda's deficiency as a mother has been several times deplored; one should on the same basis criticize Abraham's carelessness of Isaac' (*op. cit.* p. 193).

The cruel sergeant is certainly 'that fell sergeant Death' (did Shakespeare get the idea here?) that may visit any family. The death of those we love is the most difficult test of faith. The human anguish is stressed by the poetry, and Chaucer makes us appreciate Griselda's agony of mind by showing the strength of her love for her children. Her mind seizes upon one image that represents to her what death does to her children: the image of their being ravaged by birds and beasts.

> 'Gooth now', quod she, 'and dooth my lordes heeste: (568)
> But o thyng wol I prey yow of youre grace,
> That, but my lord forbad yow, atte leeste
> Burieth this litel body in som place
> That beestes ne no briddes it torace.'
> But he no word to that purpos seye,
> But took the child and wente upon his weye

How this image has haunted her is revealed when her children are restored to her, and in painful joy she utters her mind's dread:

> 'O tendre, o deere, o younge children myne!   (1093)
> Youre woful mooder wende stedfastly
> That crueel houndes or som foul vermyne
> Hadde eten yow...'

She never does complain to Walter of his treatment of her. But when he demands her second child from her, she expresses her feelings and values with an honesty that says more than complaint ever could.

> 'I have', quod she, 'seyd thus, and evere shal: (645)
> I wol no thyng, ne nyl no thyng, certayn,
> But as yow list. Naught greveth me at al,
> Though that my doughter and my sone be slayn,—
> At youre comandement, this is to sayn.
> I have noght had no part of children tweyne
> But first siknesse, and after wo and peyne.
>
> 'Ye been oure lord, dooth with youre owene thyng
> Right as yow list; axeth no reed at me.
> For as I lefte at hoom al my clothyng,

Whan I first cam to yow, right so', quod she
'Lefte I my wyl and al my libertee,
And took youre clothyng; wherfore I yow preye,
Dooth youre plesaunce, I wol youre lust obeye.'

Because she faces so squarely her situation, and shirks none of
the sorrowful difficulties heaped upon her, she holds our admiration. Her feelings are never blunted, her resolution never
blind. She does not complain here, but her straight speech damns
Walter. At the same time as her words make explicit the guilt
of Walter they show her consciousness that our obligations to
ourselves and others are hard burdens we cannot cast off, and
are part of our obligation to God. 'Ye been oure lord, dooth
with youre owene thyng / Right as yow list.' God's necessity
must be obeyed, no matter how strongly tempted we are to
murmur against it. The word 'thyng', however, while it may
describe an individual before the sight of God (and the language of the line suggests we are to think explicitly of God),
makes clear that no man has the right to regard another as
merely an object. In the word we can see how the level of
parable and the level of 'realism' interact with each other.
The Clerk's Tale, even while it is showing how man should
yield himself to God, is also showing how man may be tempted
to assert himself and try to play the role of God. Or to put the
issue another way: the Clerk's criticism of Walter is a cleverly
veiled criticism of 'sovereignty'.

Elizabeth Salter, in her analysis of *The Clerk's Tale*, shows
how Chaucer modified his sources to give greater emphasis
to the pathetic and realistic elements of the tale: 'Chaucer',
she writes, 'is willing to take up and develop further any
slightest hint of adverse criticism where Walter is concerned.
When the Latin and French texts comment, guardedly, upon
Walter's desire to tempt his wife (*Sources and Analogues*,
pp. 310, 311) the English text throws caution to the winds,
and gives us a passage of fervent indignation:

> . . .what neded it   (457)
> Hire for to tempte, and alwey moore and moore,
> Though som men preise it for a subtil wit?

> But as for me, I seye that yvele it sit
> To assaye a wyf whan that it is no nede,
> And putten hire in angwyssh and in drede.'[1]

And she shows how Chaucer also heightens the pathos of Griselda's situation, and dramatises her feelings. She concludes, though, that the effect of these changes pulls the poem apart, as the pathetic realism is at odds with the religious fable. 'When Chaucer was led—it seems, irresistibly—to make a character out of Walter, he lost symbolic authority, either for good or for evil: and this authority is exactly what he needs if he is to justify, or to refuse to justify, his apparently wanton acts of cruelty.'[2] She considers that *The Clerk's Tale* has a confused moral ordering: her accusations, as in her analysis of *The Knight's Tale*, amount to saying that Chaucer is incompetent.[3] I believe she is wrong. I do not think that Chaucer was incapable of deciding upon and abiding by one single set of moral standards for the *Tale*. But to recognise the moral unity of the *Tale* means that we must see how it fits into the pattern developed in the preceding tales.

The Wife of Bath's Prologue emphasised the pro-masculine bias in Christian teaching, particularly on the relationship between the sexes. *The Friar's Tale* and *The Summoner's Tale* revealed how the Church's teaching could be abused and exploited. The significance of Walter's behaviour is most clearly understood if it is regarded in the light of what has gone before. When Walter's people are trying to persuade him to marry, they say:

> 'Boweth youre nekke under that blisful yok   (113)
> Of soveraynetee, noght of servyse,
> Which that men clepe spousaille or wedlock.'

---

[1] *Op. cit.* p. 56.   [2] *Ibid.* p. 59.

[3] Lest it be thought that I am somewhat harshly summarising Elizabeth Salter's viewpoint let me quote a couple of the phrases she uses: 'the trouble originates in an *inability to decide upon and abide by* one single set of moral standards...'; it is interesting that Chaucer *does not seem to recognise the problem* he sets himself...' (my italics). These and a number of other phrases in her book reflect a patronising and belittling attitude improper before a poet of Chaucer's stature and achievements.

And Walter clearly accepts that marriage means 'maistrye' for the husband. Walter's testing of his wife is an expression of this belief, but carried to extreme lengths: he abuses his authority as a husband, and exploits her obligations of 'servyse' to him. Thus in condemning Walter's behaviour the Clerk (and Chaucer clearly endorses his judgment) reinforces the Wife of Bath's attack on Christian wedlock for giving too much power to the husband. But by conceding to her the exploitation of wives by husbands and thus winning her approval, he strengthens his attack on his real target: 'maistrye', the domination and exploitation of any human being by another.

Yet the fact that the teaching of Christianity may be abused or may have some imperfections does not invalidate that teaching. Marriage is not wrong because some husbands, or wives, inflict pain on their spouses. Nor should the defecting of one partner be an excuse for the other to break the vows given. For marriage is always a bond accepted—a contract entered—even though it is never possible at the time to recognise the full consequences of the vows. That Griselda is tricked into swearing such abject obedience makes this point fully. There is high virtue in the humble fulfilment of obligations, perhaps most of all in the face of injustice and unkind treatment. (The same point is made by Henry James in his presentation of Isabel at the end of *Portrait of a Lady*.) Of course this is extremely difficult and perhaps not many have the power to do this, as the Clerk concedes in the epilogue. But it is none the less admirable, and to be emulated if we can.

Furthermore, the fulfilment of personally acquired obligations is linked to the duty of accepting one's lot as a subject of God: the greater is reflected in the lesser. A vow, and the marriage vow in particular, is more than a contract between two people: it is also a promise made to God. Therefore to perform one's duty to another person is at the same time the performance of the highest duty—the keeping of one's truth to the Maker. Injustice and unkindness may have an immediate cause in the other person, but ultimately they exist because of the Divine Will. By Christian belief, and *The Clerk's Tale* embodies this, suffering is not gratuitously visited on people, even when the motives of those agents inflicting it appear gratuitous, but is part of God's plan. 'Behold, happy is the man whom God correcteth: despise not thou the chastening of the Almighty' (Job, v, 17).[1] Or in the Clerk's own words:

> This storie is seyd, nat for that wyves sholde   (1142)
> Folwen Grisilde as in humylitee,
> For it were inportable, though they wolde;
> But for that every wight, in his degree,
> Sholde be constant in adversitee
> As was Grisilde; therfor Petrak writeth
> This storie, which with heigh stile he enditeth.

> For, sith a womman was so pacient
> Unto a mortal man, wel moore us oghte
> Receyven al in gree that God us sent;
> For greet skile is, he preeve that he wroghte.

This is the set of moral standards in the *Tale*, and it can be seen that Chaucer's changes of his sources have been directed towards expressing the moral most forcibly. For example, if Walter is made 'a worthy agent of God's desire to "prove" one of his chosen creatures', as Elizabeth Salter desires,[2] the Clerk's criticism of the abuse of 'sovereignty' in marriage would be lost, and Griselda's command over her personal resentment diminished. Would the Christian myth be strengthened if Pilate were made a nicer man?

The successful interplay of parable and 'realism' in the *Tale* can above all be seen in the character of Griselda. Her love for Walter is very convincingly portrayed. She loves him *because of* himself, but it is also made clear how she loves him *in spite of* himself.

> 'For wiste I that my deeth wolde do yow ese,   (664)
> Right gladly wolde I dyen, yow to plese.

> 'Deth may noght make no comparisoun
> Unto youre love.'

---

[1] Both Charles Muscatine and Elizabeth Salter quote this text.
[2] *Op. cit.* p. 60.

Her love is the love that denies self. It is also a love that recognises and acknowledges the importance of duty. Griselda's love for Walter as a man is united with her dutiful yielding to him as a husband (and feudal lord): neither would exist without the other. The form of marital obedience is filled out with the substance of Griselda's love, and hence we do not feel Griselda's surrender to be abject or resigned. Rather she remains loyal to herself in spirited humility.

Griselda is at once both the object of our admiration and, because her suffering is so needless and undeserved, of our compassion. Indeed, it is by means of the compassion generated in the *Tale* that the Clerk most effectively replies to the Wife of Bath. For the compassion makes us aware of the preciousness of life and of virtue.

> 'The remenant of youre jueles redy be (869)
> Inwith youre chambre, dar I saufly sayn.
> Naked out of my fadres hous', quod she,
> 'I cam, and naked moot I turne agayn.
> Al youre plesance wol I folwen fayn;
> But yet I hope it be nat youre entente
> That I smoklees out of youre paleys wente.

> 'Ye koude nat doon so dishonest a thyng,
> That thilke wombe in which youre children leye
> Sholde biforn the peple, in my walkyng,
> Be seyn al bare; wherfore I yow preye,
> Lat me nat lyk a worm go by the weye.
> Remembre yow, myn owene lord so deere,
> I was youre wyf, though I unworthy weere.'

Griselda's modesty here is not false: it is a genuine respect for herself as woman, as mother, and as Walter's wife. Her very humility emphasises the dignity of life that Walter by his callousness has shoved aside. Through the character of Griselda we are made aware that love is more than the assertion of vitality: it is the recognition of and sacrifice to what is proper and fitting.

At the end of his Tale the Clerk carries home his personal thrust at the Wife of Bath. He has presented an ideal of womanhood in place not only of what the Wife of Bath has said clerks thought women to be, but also in place of what she believes women are. His final irony is to say that Griseldas are few and far between, therefore he will recommend wives to follow the advice of the Wife of Bath!

Yet perhaps it is wrong to talk of *The Clerk's Tale* as being a reply to the Wife of Bath. This implies that what she stands for can be dismissed. But the Wife of Bath exists as much as Griselda. Both are extremes; both represent aspects of love. They are the contraries Blake wrote of in his poem, *The Clod and the Pebble*.

> 'Love seeketh not Itself to please,
> Nor for itself hath any care,
> But for another gives its ease,
> And builds a Heaven in Hell's despair.'
>
> So sung a little Clod of Clay
> Trodden with the cattle's feet,
> But a Pebble of the brook
> Warbled out these metres meet:
>
> 'Love seeketh only Self to please,
> To bind another to Its delight,
> Joys in another's loss of ease,
> And builds a Hell in Heaven's despite.'

CHAPTER 8

The Merchant's Tale

THE Clerk opposed the Wife of Bath not only by setting up a different concept of love but also by setting up a different concept of woman. It is this concept of woman as some 'infinitely suffering, infinitely gentle thing' which brings the Merchant into the fray. With irony the Clerk advised wives of the school of Bath to treat their husbands contemptuously:

'And lat hym care, and wepe, and wrynge, and waille.' (1212)

The Merchant seizes upon this line:

'Wepyng and waylyng, care and oother sorwe (1213)
I knowe ynogh, on even and a-morwe.'

The effect is clearly comic, and probably intentionally so on the Merchant's part (as well as on Chaucer's). His outburst against his wife is not the outburst of a bitterly disappointed husband, but a piece of humorous rhetoric (amusingly taken seriously by the simple Host) which forms a prelude to his ribald, down-to-earth tale. Critics frequently have gone wrong on the tone of this *Tale*. Kittredge, for example, thinks the Merchant is suffering a kind of emotional crisis, and compares the Merchant's cynicism to Iago's;[1] and Holman goes so far as saying it is 'one of the most savagely obscene, angrily embittered, pessimistic, and unsmiling tales in our language'.[2] This is absurd: the *Tale* is very funny though it has its moments of savage satire. The Merchant is certainly only pretending to be personally miserable: it gives him a stance from which to launch his bawdy, smoking-room story. (Of course, mockery

[1] 'Chaucer's Discussion of Marriage' *loc. cit.* pp. 202, 203.
[2] 'Courtly Love in the Merchant's and Franklin's Tale', *ibid.* p. 241.

often has a grain of personal truth.) There is far too much humorous exaggeration in his opening speech for it to be a painful confession.

> 'I have a wyf, the worste that may be;   (1218)
> For thogh the feend to hire ycoupled were,
> She wolde hym overmacche, I dar wel swere.'

This ironical reference to the *Friar's Tale* already is preparing us for the satirical tribute to women's wit and ready tongues demonstrated at the end of the tale.

The Merchant continues the theme of the war between the sexes, but his position is a middle of the way one. His tale backs neither husband nor wife, but shows each abusing the other for his or her own pleasure. The tale rejects an idealistic concept of love or marriage, or rather it reveals how ideal concepts are made use of by the sexual drive. Behind the cynicism of the presentation there is genuine delight in the absurdities of human relations.

The *Tale* is a fabliau, but it employs a remarkable range of stylistic and narrative methods. The effect of this is to widen its satirical attack, and give a serious resonance to the entertainment. Furthermore, it picks up a number of strands from the previous tales. The Clerk's story of how a wife endured with patience her husband's treatment is turned into a story of how a wife foils his domination. The marriage of a young man to an old woman in *The Wife of Bath's Tale* becomes now the marriage of an old man to a young woman, and the account is more realistic. Unlike *The Miller's Tale*, however, where there is a similar situation, the *Tale* does not invite us to side with the wife but rather to see her with the same unillusioned gaze we cast upon the old man. In May's gulling of her husband reappears the Wife of Bath's behaviour to her husbands. There is even an echo of *The Knight's Tale* in the line, 'Lo, pitee renneth soone in gentil herte!'—but now the line has changed its meaning and describes how compassion can be used to disguise sexual desire. Thus in many ways *The Merchant's Tale* parodies much that has gone before.

The conflict between male and female in the *Tale* is pointed and stressed by the conflict between age and youth. The very names, January and May, give the incompatibility of the two people. When January decides to marry he indulges in a false picture of what married life is.

> A wyf! a, Seinte Marie, *benedicite!*   (1337)
> How myghte a man han any adversitee
> That hath a wyf? Certes, I kan nat seye.
> The blisse which that is bitwixe hem tweye
> Ther may no tonge telle, or herte thynke.
> If he be povre, she helpeth hym to swynke;
> She kepeth his good, and wasteth never a deel;
> Al that hire housbonde lust, hire liketh weel;
> She seith nat ones 'nay', whan he seith 'ye'.
> 'Do this', seith he; 'Al redy, sure', seith she.

Here the Merchant is echoing the words of *The Clerk's Tale*. The opening of *The Merchant's Tale* is devoted to presenting the old man's illusions. The two advisers, Placebo and Justinus, help point the absurdity of the old man's thoughts. Placebo is a neat satire on a court flatterer playing on the old man's vanity. Justinus has a more common sense attitude, and recognises that a wife will make demands that the old man will find difficult to satisfy.

> 'By hym that made water, erthe, and air,   (1558)
> The yongeste man that is in all this route
> Is bisy ynough to bryngen it aboute
> To han his wyf allone. Trusteth me,
> Ye shul nat plesen hire fully yeres thre,
> This is to seyn, to doon hire ful plesaunce.
> A wyf axeth ful many an observaunce.
> I prey yow that ye be nat yvele apayd.'

The old man's illusions, however, are not his alone. The praise of marriage in the first part of the *Tale* represents what is commonly said in its favour—the generalisation is obtained by putting this speech in the mouth of the narrator and not in January's mouth. The mockery, though clearly present, is still subdued. When we come to January's own thoughts they

carry to comic excesses the qualities already advanced. Thus
the lines in the preamble,

> 'For wedlok is so esy and so clene,   (1264)
> That in this world it is a paradys.'
> Thus seyde this olde knyght, that was so wys,

become in the speech of January a concern lest the paradise
of matrimony on earth ruins his chances of bliss hereafter.
The joke is carried even further by Justinus' reassurance that
this need not worry him because:

> 'Paraunter she may be youre purgatorie!   (1670)
> She may be Goddes meene and Goddes whippe;
> Thanne shal youre soule up to hevene skippe
> Swifter than dooth an arwe out of a bow.'

Not only is this funny in itself, it also mocks the moral of
The Clerk's Tale.

But the most cutting satire of *The Merchant's Tale* is reserved for the notion that in holy wedlock a man can do no
wrong to his wife.

> 'It is no fors how longe that we pleye;   (1835)
> In trewe wedlok coupled be we tweye;
> And blessed be the yok that we been inne,
> For in oure actes we mowe do no sinne.
> A man may do no synne with his wyf,
> Ne hurt hymselven with his owene knyf...'

The double-edged irony of the last line looks forward to the
retribution that is to catch up with the old man. In the account
of the wedding and the 'sport' that follows, perhaps the most
powerful part of the whole *Tale*, we are shown the self-
centred lust of the old man in action, and the scene is a
grotesque parody of the meaning of marriage. We are shown
the old man's desire growing in the drunken riot of the
wedding-feast, his preparation for love-making by taking aph-
rodisiacs, and the physical repulsiveness of his appearance.

> And Januarie hath fast in armes take   (1821)
> His fresshe May, his paradys, his make.
> He lulleth hire, he kisseth hire ful ofte;

> With thikke brustles of his berd unsofte,
> Lyk to the skyn of houndfyssh, sharp as brere—
> For he was shave al newe in his manere—
> He rubbeth hire about hir tendre face...

And a little later, happy after love-play:

> He was al coltissh, ful of ragerye,   (1847)
> And ful of jargon as a flekked pye.
> The slakke skyn aboute his nekke shaketh,
> Whil that he sang, so chaunteth he and craketh.
> But God woot what that May thoughte in hir herte,
> Whan she hym saugh sittynge in his sherte,
> In his nyghte-cappe, and with his nekke lene;
> She preyseth nat his pleyyng worth a bene.

There is a nightmarish reality about all this. What the wife feels is never directly described, but we have been left in no doubt about the horror of her experience. There is, of course, humour in the account, but it is a savage brand of humour. January's 'rape' of May is ironic even: he thinks he is the sexually dominant partner, but we are made to know that all the sexual vitality is possessed by her; how can Winter pleasure Spring?

In the description of the wedding festivities we are told how Venus

> with hire fyrbrond in hire hand aboute   (1727)
> Daunceth biforn the bryde and all the route.

This picture of inflamed passion forms an introduction to and a contrast with the impotent lust of the old man. But it is also compared with the picture presented by Marcian of the marriage of Mercury and Philology, and the latter is said to be inadequate to describe what happened at January's marriage. That is, the abstract learning of people like the Clerk cannot enable them to understand the sexual passion involved in love and marriage. So *The Merchant's Tale* answers *The Clerk's Tale*.

With the entrance of Damyan into *The Merchant's Tale* the focus swings away from the marital relationsip between male and female to the courtly love relationsip. For Damyan is the courtly lover, and May the mistress he will serve. Initially the poetry reproduces the conventional mode.

> Now wol I speke of woful Damyan,   (1866)
> That langwissheth for love, as ye shul heere;
> Therfore I speke to hym in this manere:
> I seye, 'O sely Damyan, allas!
> Andswere to my demaunde, as in this cas.
> How shaltow to thy lady, fresshe May,
> Telle thy wo? She wole alwey seye nay.
> Eek if thou speke, she wol thy wo biwreye.
> God be thyn helpe! I kan no bettre seye.'
>   This sike Damyan in Venus fyr
> So brenneth that he dyeth for desyr,
> For which he putte his lyf in aventure.

But almost immediately the mockery begins to cast a new light upon it. For just as lust is to be found beneath the ideal of marriage, so too it is to be found beneath the ideal of courtly love. In *The Merchant's Tale* the courtly love tradition too is satirised, and the 'foul rag and bone shop of the heart' out of which it sprung is shown.

Damyan is seized by love at first sight in the true traditional way; and May is said to feel pity in the traditional way.

> This gentil May, fulfilled of pitee   (1995)
> Right of hire hand a lettre made she,
> In which she graunteth hym hire verray grace.

The next line, however, reveals a most unromantic matter-of-factness in her thinking:

> Ther lakketh noght, oonly but day and place...

Many such details help to lay bare the sordid foundation of their romantic love, the most striking perhaps being the little detail of May's destroying Damyan's love-letter by casting it into the privy.

Sordid, I said. This must be qualified immediately. For one aspect of the *Tale* is that sexual desire has its own laws, which take little account of official codes of behaviour. The old man cannot satisfy the sexual needs of the young woman, so she turns to youth to fulfil her. What if the way they take involves deception and a rather absurd courtly tradition of behaviour? Such is life!

But January goes blind and will not let May out of his reach. This is typical of the way Chaucer externalises and makes concrete what is really internal and psychological. The blindness represents simultaneously the old man's lack of self-knowledge, his jealous suspiciousness and ignorant possessiveness.

To some extent there is a reversal of sympathy in the last part of the *Tale*. Our compassion for the wife who has to endure her old husband's embraces and (it is just hinted) perverted desires is alienated by the hard and calculating person she is shown to become. But even more important for bringing round some sympathy for January than his affliction is his changed attitude towards his wife. Where at first he thought of her only as an instrument for his own gratification there comes gradually a recognition of her as a person in her own right, and even a degree of love.

> 'Now wyf', quod he, 'heere nys but thou and I, (2160)
> That art the creature that I best love.
> For by that Lord that sit in hevene above,
> Levere ich hadde to dyen on a knyf,
> Than thee offende, trewe deere wyf!'

The use of the knife-image, by contrast with its previous appearance, emphasises how vulnerable the change in his attitude has made him. Not that his selfishness has fallen away (for example, he cannot bear to think of her marrying again when he is dead), but at least his marital relationship has become a human one. But it is one of the *Tale*'s ironies that, partly no doubt because of his earlier treatment of her, his wife has now become callous and contemptuous towards him.

All the elements of *The Merchant's Tale* are brought together in the scene at the end. The garden in which everything happens is both the garden of the *Romance of the Rose* and the walled garden of marriage.[1] In this garden we find Pluto and Proserpina. The Robinson edition of Chaucer's works has a scholarly note saying that the classical divinities of the lower world are here brought into association with the fairies of northern tradition. But more important is the recognition of the link with the opening of *The Wife of Bath's Tale*, for Pluto and Proserpina represent the male–female dichotomy, and *The Merchant's Tale* is showing both sides of the eternal conflict.

> Pluto, that is kyng of Fayerye,   (2227)
> And many a lady in his compaignye,
> Folwynge his wyf, the queene Proserpyna,
> Which that he ravysshed out of Ethna
> Whil that she gadered floures in the mede—
> In Claudyan ye may the stories rede,
> How in his grisely carte he hire fette—

He attempts to assert his domination over her, and she attempts to foil him. In their conflict is mirrored the January–May conflict. The parallel is strengthened by the fact that Pluto and Proserpina represent the winter and spring months of the year, and by the reminder that Pluto ravished Proserpina.

January entices May into the garden with a lyrical utterance of his feelings which is based on the Song of Solomon. The Biblical origin of the lines, so inappropriate for the situation, points the old man's self-deception about his relationship with his wife.

> 'Rys up, my wyf, my love, my lady free!   (2138)
> The turtles voys is herd, my dowve sweete;
> The wynter is goon with alle his reynes weete.
> Com forth now, with thyn eyen columbyn!
> How fairer been thy brestes than is wyn!
> The gardyn is enclosed al aboute;
> Com forth, my white spouse...'

In the garden January promises three rewards to May for being faithful to him: God's love, her honour, and the inheritance

---

[1] Charles A. Owen, Jr. suggests, rightly I think, that the garden is also linked with the Garden of Eden. There are a number of allusions to Adam and Eve and Paradise in the poem. See 'Crucial Passages in Five of *The Canterbury Tales*', in Wagenknect, *op. cit.* pp. 255–9.

of all his goods. Without hesitation May promises him that she
will never be false, and insinuates that he, as men often are, may
be so. Her mind is not on her husband's rewards but on more
exciting fruits. Pluto, watching, is shocked and repeats some of
the many allegations against women, but Proserpina, like the
Wife of Bath, comes back at him with an aggressive reply.

So to the glorious comedy of the denouement. At the crucial
moment Pluto magically restores the old man's sight; but
Proserpina with even greater magic puts the right answer in
May's mouth:

> 'Out! help! allas! harrow!' he gan to crye, (2366)
> 'O stronge lady stoore, what dostow?'
> And she answerde, 'Sire, what eyleth yow?
> Have pacience and resoun in youre mynde!
> I have yow holpe on bothe youre eyen blynde.
> Up peril of my soule, I shal nat lyen,
> As me was taught, to heele with youre eyen,
> Was no thyng bet, to make yow to see,
> Than strugle with a man upon a tree.
> God woot, I dide it in ful good entente.'
> 'Strugle!' quod he, 'ye, algate in it wente!
> God yeve yow bothe on shames deth to dyen!
> He swyved thee, I saugh it with myne yen,
> And elles be I hanged by the hals!'
> 'Thanne is', quod she, 'my medicyne al fals;
> For certeinly, if that ye myghte se,
> Ye wolde nat seyn thise wordes unto me.
> Ye han som glymsyng, and no parfit sighte.'

No sooner are January's eyes opened to what his wife is up to
behind his back, than her woman's wit persuades him that he
is mistaken, and the joke is made with perfect timing.

The Merchant's Tale is a study in illusion, as May's final
words make explicit:

> 'Beth war, I prey yow; for, by hevene kyng, (2407)
> Ful many a man weneth to seen a thyng,
> And it is al another than it semeth.
> He that mysconceyveth, he mysdemeth.'

Yet this speech is the greatest irony of all, for it is used to persuade January that he never saw her misconduct, and the deception makes him happy. Thus the *Tale* not only mocks positive values, whether they be the idealisms of the Knight and the Clerk, or the joyful expressions of human exuberance of the Miller and the Wife of Bath, but also throws doubt upon man's ability to see things as they are. If the *Tale* has any positives of its own they reside in the clear recognition of people in all their individual fallibility and in the sheer delight at seeing beauty gulling ugliness. Though moments in the *Tale*, particularly the grotesque epithalamion, tug at the reader's compassion, the overall tone of the narration is cynical rather than charitable. The *Tale*, as far as it goes, is a valid comment on life, but we may suspect that its limits are the limits of the Merchant himself, whose interests are materialistic and self-centred, and who himself is caught in the toil of false-seeming.

> His resons he spak ful solempnely,   (*General Prologue*, 274)
> Sownynge alwey th'encrees of his wynnyng.
> He wolde the see were kept for any thyng
> Bitwixe Middelburgh and Orewelle.
> Wel koude he in eshaunge sheeldes selle.
> This worthy man ful wel his wit bisette:
> Ther wiste no wight that he was in dette.

CHAPTER 9

The Squire's Tale

> Or call up him that left half told
> The story of *Cambuscan* bold,
> Of *Camball*, and of *Algarsife*,
> And who had *Canace* to wife,
> That own'd the vertuous Ring and Glass,
> And of the wondrous Hors of Brass,
> On which the *Tartar* King did ride...

Is this a tale that Chaucer never finished, another sad reminder of the incomplete state of the *Canterbury Tales*; or is the tale half-told because Chaucer deliberately made his Franklin interrupt the Squire?[1] No assured answer can be given, but I am inclined to believe the latter. After some 650 lines the Squire pauses to give the plan of what he still has to tell:

> Thus lete I Canacee hir hauk kepyng;   (651)
> I wol namoore as now speke of hir ryng,
> Til it come eft to purpos for to seyn
> How that this faucon gat hire love ageyn
> Repentant, as the storie telleth us,
> By mediacion of Cambalus,
> The kynges sone, of which that I yow tolde.
> But hennesforth I wol my proces holde
> To speken of aventures and of batailles,
> That nevere yet was herd so grete mervailles.
>   First wol I telle yow of Cambyuskan,
> That in his tyme many a citee wan;
> And after wol I speke of Algarsif,
> How that he wan Theodora to his wif,
> For whom ful ofte in greet peril he was,
> Ne hadde he ben holpen by the steede of bras;
> And after wol I speke of Cambalo,

[1] Suggested by Nevill Coghill: *The Poet Chaucer* (Oxford University Press, 1961), p. 167.

That faught in lystes with the brethren two
For Canacee er that he myghte hire wynne.
And ther I lefte I wol ayeyn bigynne.

If the narrative maintained the same pace it has so far had the story would be interminably long. In itself this may be an uncertain argument for suggesting a deliberate interruption: our own age may blind us to the eagerness of other ages to hear lengthy romances. Spenser clearly would not have complained about the length—but then Spenser is Spenser, and his own continuation of the tale is a mere drop in the ocean of *The Faerie Queene* (see Book IV, Cantos II and III). But perhaps the argument might be strengthened by comparing the Squire's technique of story-telling with his father's. The Knight keeps saying how much he could tell if only he had the time to do it—and then usually does tell (for example, the Knight gives the full description of the funeral rites by asserting that he will not do so). This makes a nice ironic contrast between father and son's tales: the one doing what he denies having time to do, the other promising at length what he will do, and then never doing it at all. There are, however, other indications that Chaucer may have intended us to note an ineptness in the Squire's telling particularly by contrast with the Knight's. In my analysis of *The Knight's Tale* I stressed the function and success of this rhetorical device of *occupatio*. But whenever the Squire employs it the effect, far from emphasising the tale's large and heroic (or romantic) realm of discourse, seems to call attention to the speaker himself.

A doghter hadde this worthy kyng also,   (32)
That yongest was, and highte Canacee.
But for to telle yow al hir beautee,
It lyth nat in my tonge, n'yn my konnyng;
I dar nat undertake so heigh a thyng.
Myn Englissh eek is insufficient.
It moste been a rethor excellent,
That koude his colours longynge for that art,
If he sholde hire descryven every part.
I am noon swich, I moot speke as I kan.

164

Not only does the humility here contrast with the brashness of the lines I quoted before (particularly with 'That nevere yet was herd so grete mervailles'), but it seems uneasily balanced between the assumed humility of rhetoric and the personal confession of inadequacy. 'Myn Englissh eek is insufficient' tells us that the Squire because of his education was more at home in French than English—but *occupatio* should function by emphasising that the beauty of the lady is more than any tongue can tell. And the awkwardness of the Squire is made more apparent if his lines are contrasted with the assured disclaimer of the Franklin.

> I lerned nevere rethorik, certeyn; (719)
> Thyng that I speke, it moot be bare and pleyn.
> I sleep nevere on the Mount of Pernaso,
> Ne lerned Marcus Tullius Scithero.
> Colours ne knowe I none, withouten drede,
> But swiche colours as growen in the mede,
> Or elles swiche as men dye or peynte.
> Colours of rethoryk been to me queynte.

Perhaps it is only by seeing how the Squire's *Tale* fits into the pattern of the *Canterbury Tales* that we can appreciate Chaucer's intention. Kittredge was probably right when he wrote, 'But now the Host thinks his companions have surely had enough of marriage. It is time they heard something of love, and with this in view he turns abruptly to the Squire, whom all the Pilgrims have come to know as "a lovyere and a lusty bachiller".'[1] But there is an even stronger reason for feeling that *The Squire's Tale* should succeed *The Merchant's Tale* and be itself followed by *The Franklin's Tale*. Both the other tales deal with the power of illusion, and both in their own way criticise their characters for succumbing to it. Yet what is *The Squire's Tale* but an indulgence in illusion—the illusions of romance? The tale, as it stands, is more about wonders and marvels than about love, and even these seem cherished more for their own sake than for any reality they may embody.

[1] *Op. cit.* p. 208.

Fairy stories, dreams, tales of fantasy often express the depths of man's nature, giving form to ineffable knowledge. *Sir Gawayn and the Grene Knight* is such a tale, but though the entrance of the strange knight in *The Squire's Tale* is similar to the intrusion of the Green Man the similarity stops short at the level of incident. The Squire's knight, and the gifts he brings, have no deeper meanings. The wonder lacks significance. I said of *The Merchant's Tale* that it revealed the 'foul rag-and-bone shop of the heart', but another two lines from Yeats's *The Circus Animals' Desertion* may be said to characterise *The Squire's Tale*:

> Players and painted stage took all my love,
> And not those things they were emblems of.

It is not that Chaucer is incapable of endowing fantasy with symbolic meaning, or of drawing out the significance already inherent in the emblems—his performance as poet shows that. Rather he seems deliberately bent here on emphasising the emptiness of the romance. As elsewhere in the *Canterbury Tales* the tale reflects the sensibility of the narrator, and Chaucer so slants the tale and the poetry that they provide a criticism of the Pilgrim speaking. The undercurrent of humour, and the note of realism in the following passage do more than give variety: they provide a perspective whereby the Squire's romantic notions are unmasked.

> But everemoore hir moste wonder was   (199)
> How that it koude gon, and was of bras;
> It was of Fairye, as the peple semed.
> Diverse folk diversely they demed;
> As many heddes, as many wittes ther been.
> They murmureden as dooth a swarm of been,
> And maden skiles after hir fantasies,
> Rehersynge of thise olde poetries,
> And seyden it was lyk the Pegasee,
> The hors that hadde wynges for to flee;
> Or elles it was the Grekes hors Synon,
> That broghte Troie to destruccion,
> As men moun in thise olde geestes rede…

And sondry doutes thus they jangle and trete,   (220)
As lewed peple demeth comunly
Of thynges that been maad moore subtilly
Than they kan in hir lewednesse comprehende;
They demen gladly to the badder end.

It is an old rhetorical device to gain the reader's 'willing sus-
pension of disbelief' by mocking foolish attempts to rationalise away what is mysterious, but here the device is carried
to such lengths (the whole passage is over seventy lines long),
the portrayal of discussion and dissension rendered so amusing
that the effect is to make the reader critical rather than com-
pliant. He begins to suspect the rhetoric is being parodied,
and that the reactions of the crowd distract from the mystery
the speaker is aiming to achieve. The Squire seems to indulge
too gladly in the romantic wonder, and seems too fond himself
of 'rehersynge of thise olde poetries'. One image particularly
illustrates this. The Squire mocks those who compare the
horse with Synon's, but a little later himself employs the same
parallel.

Swich wondryng was ther on this horse of bras   (305)
That syn the grete sege of Troie was
Theras men wondreden on an hors also,
Ne was ther swich a wondryng as was tho.

The threefold repetition of 'wondering' in four lines betrays
the speaker's striving for an effect—and it is the betrayal not
the effect which catches our attention.

We could consider innumerable examples of the Squire's
rhetoric parodying itself and drawing our attention to the
speaker and not his tale, but let just one more suffice. Trying
to describe the celebrations in the court of Cambuscan the
Squire says,

Heere is the revel and the jolitee   (278)
That is nat able a dul man to devyse.
He moste han knowen love and his servyse,
And been a feestlych man as fressh as May,
That sholde yow devysen swich array.

But these lines echo the description of the Squire himself in the *General Prologue*: the 'lovyere' who is 'as fressh as is the month of May'. Our remembering the earlier lines pricks the rhetoric here, and reveals again the Squire's affected manner of narrating.

With the story of Canacee and the falcon the Squire gets round to a tale of love as he was requested. But while the story may remind us of the *Parlement of Foules*, unlike that poem it has no allegorical meaning: it seems to invite us to take the love-complaint of the falcon on the same plane as we would a tragic human affair. But this it is not possible to do. Inevitably the feeling is that the emotions of betrayed love are being prettified, and that art which thus aims at charm robs agony of reality and significance. Indeed in *The Squire's Tale* Chaucer satirises, good-humouredly though, art for art's sake, and shows how the immature imagination delights in the illusions of fictions and not in its embodied truths. When, for example, the tercel is compared to famous lovers of legend, the effect is to emphasise the unreality of the Squire's narrative and as well reveal his shallow fondness for 'old geestes'.

> 'Anon this tigre, ful of doublenesse, (543)
> Fil on his knees with so devout humblesse,
> With so heigh reverence, and, as by his cheere,
> So lyk a gentil lovere of manere,
> So ravysshed, as it semed, for the joye,
> That nevere Jason ne Parys of Troye—
> Jason? certes, ne noon oother man
> Syn Lameth was, that alderfirst bigan
> To loven two, as writen folk biforn—
> Ne nevere, syn the first man was born,
> Ne koude man, by twenty thousand part,
> Countrefete the sophymes of his art...'

Such exaggeration shows a loss of all common sense, and Chaucer invites us to laugh at the narrator.

Furthermore, Chaucer through his presentation of the tale strongly hints that the Squire wishes life to imitate this kind of art, and that he envisages his own romantic feelings in just such inflated terms. Thus, by his satire, Chaucer suggests how easily art can be a mode of self-deception instead of what it should be, a form of self-understanding.

The mixture of delight and affectation in the Squire's narrative reflects the combination of spontaneity and self-consciousness found in the portrait in the *General Prologue* in lines like

> With lokkes crulle as they were leyd in presse,   (81)

and,

> Embrouded was he, as it were a meede   (89)
> As ful of fresshe floures, whyte and reede.

But the satire, here and in *The Squire's Tale*, is gentle because the affectation and delight in illusion are marks of innocence and youth. The qualities of the Squire can perhaps be summed up in words Keats wrote when he compared human life to a Mansion of many apartments: '. . . We no sooner get into the second Chamber, which I shall call the Chamber of Maiden-Thought, than we become intoxicated with the light and the atmosphere, we see nothing but pleasant wonders, and think of delaying there for ever in delight. . .' There may be more truth in the Merchant's experienced cynicism, than in the Squire's romantic wonder, but it is bought at a sad price. However, Merchant and Squire do not exhaust all the possibilities: with the generous Franklin who speaks next we are shown how experience can live with disillusionment, and truth be lit with wonder.

CHAPTER 10

The Franklin's Tale

CHAUCER seems to endorse some of the tales told by the Pilgrims more than others. Though he sees further than their vision, and gives to their tales significance beyond the speakers' stated intentions, he seems to approve of the values these Pilgrims hold or at least to suggest that the values point in the right direction. The tales told by the Knight and the Miller, for example, despite their immense differences, have Chaucer's support in ways that the tales of the Reeve and the Merchant have not. Chaucer very clearly endorses much of the Franklin's tale. He permits his Franklin to speak with a wisdom that is genial and mature, and while he does suggest limits to the Franklin's awareness he also seeks our approval of his qualities. *The Franklin's Tale* is one of the richest poetically, but much of its resonance arises from the way it embodies incidents and themes from the earlier tales, inviting our reassessment. In particular, the issues of inexplicable suffering, of the values men should live by, and of the overriding duty to see things truthfully and hold to the truth—themes touched upon by most of the tales but especially dramatised by *The Knight's Tale* *The Miller's Tale*, and *The Clerk's Tale*—are explored with fresh insight.

The context of *The Franklin's Tale* is larger than that of the 'marriage debate', but the wisest words on the subject of marriage are assigned to the Franklin. First he rejects 'maistrye' altogether.

> Love wol nat been constreyned by maistrye.   (764)
> Whan maistrie comth, the God of Love anon
> Beteth his wynges, and farwel, he is gon!

Secondly, he combines the Christian ideal of marriage with

the courtly tradition of romantic love—duty and delight united
in one whole.

> Thus hath she take hir servant and hir lord,   (792)
> Servant in love and lord in mariage.
> Thanne was he both in lordshipe and servage.
> Servage? nay, but in lordshipe above,
> Sith he hath bothe his lady and his love;
> His lady, certes, and his wyf also,
> The which that lawe of love acordeth to.

It should also be noted that the cause of this mutual recognition of each's 'otherness' is explicitly said to be brought about
by 'gentilesse'.

Having used the description of Arveragus and Dorigen's
relationship to show what ideal marriage is, the Franklin begins his tale proper. Arveragus has to leave Dorigen for a time,
and his absence causes her to grieve and worry excessively.
Her grief and anxiety seize upon one image to express themselves: the black rocks at the sea's edge. These rocks become
an 'objective correlative' of her fear for her husband's safety,
and her obsession about disaster. They also become symbolic
of all disaster, suffering and evil in life. They are the incompatible elements we cannot account for, the meaningless chaos
that seems to belong nowhere.

> 'Eterne God, that thurgh thy purveiaunce   (865)
> Ledest the world by certein governaunce,
> In ydel, as men seyn, ye no thyng make.
> But, Lord, thise grisly feendly rokkes blake,
> That semen rather a foul confusion
> Of werk than any fair creacion
> Of swich a parfit wys God and a stable,
> Why han ye wroght this werk unreasonable?'

They represent the adversities and cruel misfortunes, such as
Griselda knew, which so try a person's faith. They are also the
unknown elements in ourselves, our unconscious passions,
glimpses of which may frighten and terrify us (this is suggested
by Aurelius's reference to the rocks having come out of their

'owene dirke regione' where 'Pluto dwelleth inne', recalling the explicitly sexual reference to Pluto and Proserpina in *The Merchant's Tale*; furthermore they come to represent for Aurelius the torments of his unslaked desire).

Dorigen is obsessed by these rocks; her fears are presented and criticised as being excessive. They make her unbalanced. She cannot see the harmony and beauty in life. This is shown not only by the difficulty her friends have in comforting her, but also by her obliviousness to the beauty and delight of the garden she is taken to.

> They goon and pleye hem al the longe day. (905)
> And this was on the sixte morwe of May,
> Which May hadde peynted with his softe shoures
> This gardyn ful of leves and of floures;
> And craft of mannes hand so curiously
> Arrayed hadde this gardyn, trewely,
> That nevere was ther gardyn of swich prys,
> But if it were the verray paradys.
> The odour of floures and the fresshe sighte
> Wolde han maked any herte lighte
> That evere was born, but if to greet siknesse,
> Or to greet sorwe, helde it in distresse;
> So ful it was of beautee with plesaunce.
> At after-dyner gonne they to daunce,
> And synge also, save Dorigen allone,
> Which made alwey hir compleint and hir moone,
> For she ne saugh hym on the daunce go
> That was hir housbonde and hir love also.

This garden is clearly linked with the garden of marriage, the garden of the *Romance of the Rose*, and the garden of Eden. It is the place where God's grace and man's endeavours unite in bliss. But Dorigen has withdrawn herself from the dance, and knows not the harmony the dancers know.

Thus, in her state of doubt and dismay, Dorigen is approached by Aurelius. We are not surprised when she answers that she will love him 'best of any man' if he can remove the rocks. We feel that this answer is more than merely a gracious and evasive reply.[1] Obsessed by the horror of the rocks, it seems psychologically right that when searching her mind for an impossible task she should think of removing the rocks: her answer reveals how, inwardly, she is attempting to dispel her fears by wishing them away. But to explain the psychological insight of the incident does not fully satisfy our feeling of its importance. In Dorigen's fears giving rise to this answer, and resulting in her being forced to keep her promise later, we sense a pattern of justice. Aristotle wrote: 'Even matters of chance seem most marvellous if there is an appearance of design as it were in them; as for instance the statue of Mitys at Argos killed the author of Mitys' death by falling down on him when a looker-on at a public spectacle; for incidents like that we think to be not without a meaning. A Plot, therefore, of this sort is necessarily finer than others.'[2] Such a design we are made to feel exists here: Dorigen sinned by her fear, and the punishment comes from the incautious promise her fear led her to make. Behind the actions of life there is an inflexible order with can bring retribution to any who dare deny or rebel against that order.

After Dorigen has given her promise, the attention of the tale focuses upon Aurelius. His situation is a parallel of Dorigen's. Where she fears for the safety of her husband, he is obsessed by his unsatisfied desire. He too now wishes for the removal of the rocks. He prays to Apollo.

> He seyde, 'Appollo, god and governour   (1031)
> Of every plaunte, herbe, tree, and flour,
> That yevest, after thy declinacion,

---

[1] Charles A. Owen, in 'Crucial Passages in Five of *The Canterbury Tales*' suggests that, in *The Franklin's Tale*, there is criticism of some aspects of 'gentillesse' and that it appears at this moment in the narrative. 'But his story is, without his realizing it, a critique of "gentillesse", for it is Dorigen's courteous softening of her refusal that makes the exhibition of gentility at the end necessary. The rocks which suggest the enduring value of gentility also suggest the distinctions which the Franklin in his easy acceptance of the good things of life fails to make' (*loc. cit.* p. 255). This argument goes against the text though, for Dorigen first answers Aurelius quite firmly, and only afterwards, in 'pley' poses the matter of removing the rocks: that is, when she has begun to relax her guard and feels her point has been made.

[2] Aristotle, 'Poetics', in *Introduction to Aristotle* (Modern Library, 1947), p. 637.

To ech of hem his tyme and his seson,
As thyn herberwe chaungeth lowe or heighe,
Lord Phebus, cast thy merciable eighe
On wrecche Aurelie, which that am but lorn...

'Youre blisful suster, Lucina the sheene, (1045)
That of the see is chief goddesse and queene
(Though Neptunus have deitee in the see
Yet emperisse aboven hym is she),
Ye knowen wel, lord, that right as hir desir
Is to be quyked and lightned of youre fir,
For which she folweth yow ful bisily,
Right so the see desireth naturelly
To folwen hire, as she that is goddesse
Bothe in the see and ryveres moore and lesse.
Wherfore, lord Phebus, this is my requeste—
Do this miracle, or do myn herte breste—
That now next at this opposicion
Which in the signe shal be of the Leon,
As preieth hire so greet a flood to brynge
That fyve fadme at the leeste it oversprynge
The hyeste rokke in Armorik Briteyne;
And lat this flood endure yeres tweyne.
Thanne certes to my lade may I seye,
"Holdeth youre heste, the rokkes been aweye."'

Here the poetry affirms the essential order and harmony of the universe. All elements give to each other and take from each other, dancing together. Naturally there can be no answer to Aurelius' prayer, for it, like Dorigen's anxiety, is an unacceptance of the divine order of things that must be endured: 'To ech of hem his tyme and his seson'.

In despair Aurelius turns to wish-fantasies, and illusions. His brother, out of pity for his state, tells him of the powers of magicians.

'My brother shal be warisshed hastily; (1138)
For I am siker that ther be sciences
By whiche men make diverse apparences,
Swiche as thise subtile tregetoures pleye.
Ful ofte at feestes have I wel herd seye

> That tregetours, withinne an halle large,
> Have maad come in a water and a barge,
> And in the halle rowen up and doun.
> Somtyme hath semed come a grym leoun;
> And somtyme floures sprynge as in a mede;
> Somtyme a vyne, and grapes white and rede;
> Somtyme a castel, al of lym and stoon...'

This passage, in its rich colouring and vitality of images, gives the power and attractiveness of illusions. 'Humankind cannot bear very much reality.' But when Aurelius himself visits the magician and is shown the magician's powers, the illusions he sees are all expressions of his own lust and cruelty.

> He shewed hym, er he wente to sopeer,   (1189)
> Forestes, parkes ful of wilde deer;
> Ther saugh he hertes with hir hornes hye,
> The gretteste that evere were seyn with ye.
> He saugh of hem an hondred slayn with houndes,
> And somme with arwes bled of bittre woundes.
> He saugh, whan voyded were thise wilde deer,
> Thise fauconers upon a fair ryver,
> That with hir haukes han the heron slayn.

The magician asks a thousand pounds for making the rocks *seem* to disappear. Aurelius replies,

> 'Fy on a thousand pound!   (1227)
> This world, which that men seye is round,
> I wolde it yeve, if I were lord of it.'

So men sell the whole rich reality that is—for fantasies, for deceptions. The moral is made explicit by the Franklin's own comment a little earlier,

> For hooly chirches feith in oure bileve   (1133)
> Ne suffreth noon illusioun us to greve.

Dorigen, whose husband has returned safely, proving all her fears to have been unnecessary, is now trapped by the promise her lack of faith led her to make. Aurelius demands that she fulfil her vow to love him best, as he has done what she wished. (Aurelius is now in the position of a husband who demands his bond of his wife: cf. Walter, and January.)

In Arveragus' absence Dorigen meditates suicide, recalling a long list of examples of women who killed themselves rather than face dishonour. This passage answers those who despise women and think them incapable of virtue; it is also a rebuke to the Wife of Bath for what she has said of her own sex. Dramatically, it represents Dorigen's fearful attempt to talk herself into doing what she feels she ought to do. But when Arveragus returns and learns what has happened he takes it with fortitude and makes no attempt to shirk reality. He speaks with calm wisdom.

> 'Is ther oght elles, Dorigen, but this?' (1469)
> 'Nay, nay', quod she, 'God helpe me so as wys!
> This is to muche, and it were Goddes wille.'
> 'Ye, wyf', quod he, 'lat slepen that is stille.
> It may be wel, paraventure, yet to day.
> Ye shul youre trouthe holden, by my fay!
> For God so wisly have mercy upon me,
> I hadde wel levere ystiked for to be
> For verray love which that I to yow have,
> But if ye sholde youre trouthe kepe and save.
> Trouthe is the hyeste thyng that man may kepe.'

'Truth' here seems to include not only that she should honour her bond (like Griselda), but seems also to refer back to the whole indulgence in wishful-thinking and illusion in her and Aurelius: one must be truthful to oneself and accept one's situation. One must not shirk things as they are—perhaps this is the bond to God which must be honoured.

On her way to the garden, the place whose beauty must now be marred because of her earlier weakness, Dorigen meets Aurelius, and tells him she is going

> 'Unto the garden, as my housbonde bad, (1512)
> My trouthe for to holde, allas! allas!'

Aurelius is overcome by this:

> And in his herte he caughte of this greet routhe (1520)
> Considerynge the beste on every syde,
> That fro his lust were hym levere abyde

176

Than doon so heigh a cherlyssh wrecchednesse
Agayns franchise and alle gentillesse;
For which in fewe wordes seyde he thus:
  'Madame, seyth to youre lord Arveragus,
That sith I se his grete gentillesse
To yow, and eek I se wel youre distresse,
That him were levere han shame (and that were routhe)
Than ye to me sholde breke thus youre trouthe,
I have wel levere evere to suffre wo
Than I departe the love bitwix yow two.'

By releasing her from her promise he shows that he too can act with 'gentillesse'. And he in turn is then released from his promise to pay the magician a sum that would beggar him. All act with 'gentillesse'.

The Franklin's Tale does not resolve all the thematic conflicts that have arisen; what it does is to reaffirm, more directly than other *Tales*, some of the moral values most worth cherishing. In truth and 'gentillesse' men may learn that denial of self which is the highest fulfilment of self. Concluding his tale the Franklin asks:

> Lordynges, this question, thanne, wholde I aske now,   (1621)
> Which was the mooste fre, as thynketh yow?

The question expects no reply: it merely reminds us, in the word 'fre', that he receives most who also gives most.

We can see how the Franklin's own qualities should lead him to moralise the way he does. His generosity, which can earn him the title of 'Saint Julian' in his own country, perhaps his ambition to make his family a noble one, which causes him so to envy the Knight for the good manners of his son, are in keeping with his praise of magnanimity and 'gentillesse'. But in him these qualities are secular and worldly wise:

> For he was Epicurus owene son,   (336)
> That heeld opinioun that pleyn delit
> Was verray felicitee parfit.

His tolerance, admirable as it is, seems inclined to look for the cheerful view of things. All in his tale behave with generosity

—but what, one wonders, if they had not? What if Aurelius had not been moved to compassion by Dorigen's words? Isn't there the suggestion that the Franklin himself does not care to gaze too fully on 'thise grisly feendly rokkes blake'? And it is not only the sombre side but perhaps the larger frame of things he turns away from. For what the *Tale* asserts, beyond the Franklin's own consciousness of it, is the divine order of the universe which incorporates a 'fearful symmetry'. And finally even truth, generosity and 'gentillesse' are incomplete if they remain only secular qualities—ultimately, and this I believe to be Chaucer's vision, they should be religious virtues, man's grateful (but always imperfect) response to the Creator's bounty.

CHAPTER 11

The Physician's Tale

AFTER the complex ironies of the 'Marriage Debate' group of tales, *The Physician's Tale* represents a turn to didactic simplicity and moral earnestness. On literary grounds there are good reasons for believing it should follow *The Franklin's Tale*. Dorigen, in her predicament, had said,

> 'Hath ther nat many a noble wyf er this,   (1364)
> And many a mayde, yslayn hirself, allas!
> Rather than with hir body doon trespas?'

and recalled a list of noble women who chose death before unchastity. The tale of Virginia follows the same pattern: we may surmise that this incident in the story related by the Franklin led the Physician to choose the tale he tells. But his story rebukes the Franklin. Arveragus had advised his wife to keep her promise to Aurelius, and the Franklin in narrating this seemed to put truth above chastity. This shocks the Physician, and his tale asserts the cardinal importance of chastity.

The Franklin had protested his ignorance of the 'colours of rethoryk', though he related his tale with great skill, and much of his tale's charm lies in the cunning story-telling. The Physician, however, goes out of his way to emphasise that his tale is not a fable but a 'historial thyng notable'. He appears to have a puritan distrust of fiction. Only Nature can paint and shape human creatures, he asserts in words that echo and reprove the Franklin's modest disclaimer.

> For Nature hath with sovereyn diligence   (9)
> Yformed hire in so greet excellence,
> As though she wolde seyn, 'Lo! I, Nature,
> Thus kan I forme and peynte a creature,
> Whan that me list; who kan me countrefete?
> Pigmalion noght, though he ay forge and bete...

'For He that is the formere principal (19)
Hath maked me his vicaire general,
To forme and peynten erthely creaturis
Right as me list, and ech thyng in my cure is
Under the moone, that may wane and waxe;
And for my werk right no thyng wol I axe;
My lord and I been ful of oon accord.
I made hire to the worshipe of my lord;
So do I alle myne othere creatures,
What colour that they han, or what figures.'

And the Physician seems to be making his own tale to the worship of his somewhat severe God.

The innocent shall suffer and the wicked shall be punished. The harsh morality of *The Physician's Tale* shocks after the genial optimism of the Franklin. Perhaps it should also be read as a bitter corrective to *The Man of Law's Tale* and *The Clerk's Tale*. Like Constance and Griselda, Virginia is a model of Christian virtues (though the story has a non-Christian origin), but unlike them no miracle or change of heart in her persecutor saves her. Her end is described with brutal bluntness.

Hir fader, with ful sorweful herte and wil, (254)
Hir heed of smoot, and by the top it hente,
And to the juge he gan it to presente.

The Physician does not doubt the rightness of the father's action. Virginius' cruelty is a kindness that saves her from far worse iniquity.

'For love, and nat for hate, thou most be deed.' (225)

Indeed, had he acquiesced in his daughter's defilement his sin would have been almost as great as that of the false judge who entrapped them. For his duty as father and guardian was to protect and ensure his daughter's innocence.

The kind of mind that believes this, that sees in a father's murdering his daughter a benign responsibility, will also advocate strict discipline for children and stringent rectitude of behaviour in parents. The Franklin's easy prodigality, or the

Wife of Bath's exuberant advice to wives, must fill him with horror. The Physician, whose tale reveals his rigid moral principles, halts his narrative, now and then, explicitly to preach against licence and latitude. He condemns feasts, revels and dances as things which may corrupt children. He asserts that the most pestilential form of treason is that which betrays innocence, and he urges parents to guard their own actions.

> Ye fadres and ye moodres eek also, (93)
> Though ye han children, be it oon or mo,
> Youre is the charge of al hir surveiaunce,
> Whil that they been under youre governaunce.
> Beth war, that by ensample of youre lyvynge,
> Or by youre necligence in chastisynge,
> That they ne perisse; for I dar wel seye,
> If that they doon, ye shul it deere abeye.
> Under a shepherde softe and necligent
> The wolf hath many a sheep and lamb torent.

The image employed in the last two lines may suggest a touch of fanaticism in the speaker. Perhaps it is also fanaticism which makes him address 'maistresses...That lordes doghtres han in governaunce' when no such governesses seem to be present among the Canterbury Pilgrims, for when a man is possessed by an obsession the same worn phrases are flung out. At any rate, this seems to me a better explanation of the lines than the suggestion[1] that here Chaucer intervened and was himself addressing the court circle to whom he read his poems. Chaucer may have been willing to permit the passage to call to his audience's mind the scandal attaching to John of Gaunt's family, but that these lines represent his own sentiments on the upbringing of children seems unlikely from what we know of Chaucer from his other writings. It is far more probable that these lines dramatically portray the character of the Physician.

Yet I must admit I find the character of the narrator of *The Physician's Tale* at odds with the character presented in the *General Prologue*. Usually the characters described in the

[1] See, for example, Coghill, *op. cit.* pp. 173-4.

General Prologue are identifiably the same as the pilgrims who tell the stories: but with the Physician this is not so. The Physician in the *General Prologue* is a professional man, interested in the lore of his craft and the wealth his specialised knowledge brings: 'His studie was but litel on the Bible.' But here the narrator is a bigot with a strong religious and anti-sexual bias. Perhaps these characteristics are not utterly incompatible, but we do not expect to find them in the same person. Here again we have to account for the difficulty by reminding ourselves that the *Canterbury Tales* was unfinished. Perhaps Chaucer wished for a tale like this of Virginia to fit into his pattern, saddled it on the Physician and never got around to altering the earlier portrait. But let us hold back from pursuing speculation further.

The crux of the Physician's tale is Virginius's announcement to his daughter that he must kill her, and her reception of it. The scene is Chaucer's own, and does not derive from his sources. The pathos is not played up, and the psychological drama is scarcely sketched. Virginia speaks with all the model virtue of a paragon. The scene would seem to exemplify the Physician's moral. Yet it is strangely disturbing.

> 'Goode fader, shal I dye? (235)
> Is ther no grace, is ther no remedye?'
> 'No, certes, deere doghter myn', quod he.
> 'Thanne yif me leyser, fader myn', quod she,
> 'My deeth for to compleyne a litel space;
> For, pardee, Jepte yaf his doghter grace
> For to compleyne, er he hir slow, allas!
> And, God it woot, no thyng was hir trespas,
> But for she ran hir fader first to see,
> To welcome hym with greet solempnitee.'
> And with that word she fil aswowne anon,
> And after, whan hir swownyng is agon,
> She riseth up, and to hir fader sayde,
> 'Blissed be God that I shal dye a mayde!
> Yif me my deeth, er that I have a shame;
> Dooth with youre child youre wyl, a Goddes name!'

Perhaps Virginia's inhuman resignation before her fate causes the uneasiness. Perhaps it is the reference to Jephthah and his daughter which is unsettling. She at least bewailed her virginity, her father at least rent his clothes with anguish, though they felt themselves bound by his vow to give a human sacrifice. Perhaps it is the feeling that a god of love and grace would not welcome such sacrifice: that the Physician's god, like Jephthah's, is a harsh and cruel deity. The Physician is calling upon his audience to admire Virginius and his daughter, and to confirm the values they hold. But the effect of the passage defeats his intention. For it sufficiently evokes the awfulness of Virginia's predicament, and challenges the humanity of her father's action, to make the reader feel that the Physician's moralising is glib and callous. His conception of virtue is too cold-blooded for acceptance. And when the reader comes to the final stated moral of the tale, he may well wonder how a story which dealt with undeserved and innocent suffering could illustrate the punishment of sin:

> Heere may men seen how synne hath his merite. (277)
> Beth war, for no man woot whom God wol smyte
> In no degree, ne in which manere wyse
> The worm of conscience may agryse
> Of wikked lyf, though it so pryvee be
> That no man woot therof but God and he...
> Forsaketh synne, er synne yow forsake. (286)

The suicide of Apius hardly balances the fate of Virginia, and the Physician's satisfaction at the deserts of wickedness seems to blind him to concern for the victims.

Again I am arguing that Chaucer is dramatising his pilgrim's spiritual vision, and asking the reader to recognise its defects. It is not that Chaucer chose an unsuitable tale for his talents, and botched his rendering. He has presented the convictions of the Physician, with accuracy but also with justice, evoking from the sensitive reader no more sympathy than those bigotries deserve.

As elsewhere, Chaucer points what he is doing by showing the warm and human reactions of the Host: he may have missed the story-teller's moral ('Hire beautee was hire deth, I dar wel sayn') but he has a generous heart and his sympathies finally flow in the right direction:

'My herte is lost for pitee of this mayde.' (317)

Even in his swearing he expresses an unconscious wisdom, for he swears by Christ's 'nayles and by blood' which calls to mind that Christ sacrificed himself for others and did not demand human sacrifice from them. Perhaps too, in the Host's jocular references to the Physician's 'urynals', 'jurdones', 'galiones' and other paraphernalia of his trade, Chaucer wished to draw a connection between the Physician's cold-blooded morality and the reputed callousness of his profession.

CHAPTER 12

The Pardoner's Prologue and Tale

Heere may men seen how synne hath his merite,

the Physician had said, somewhat complacently. *The Pardoner's Tale* demonstrates, in a way that is both more startling and more true, the rewards of sin. The Pardoner is a complete scoundrel, perhaps the most vicious of all the pilgrims, and proud of it. In the *Prologue* he boasts of his vices, and in his tale displays the cunning of his tongue.

> Thus spitte I out my venym under hewe   (421)
> Of hoolynesse, to semen hooly and trewe.

His hypocrisy masks a boundless contempt for those he dupes, and he exults in his own motives.

> For myn entente is nat but for to wynne,   (403)
> And nothyng for correccioun of synne.
> I rekke nevere, whan that they been beryed,
> Though that hir soules goon a-blakeberyed.

For his contempt and pride he has ample justification: people are only too eager to swallow his medicine-man lies, and he earns a good living. The *General Prologue* tells us that in a day he could earn more money than a parson could get in two months from his own parishioners. In every way he is a successful trickster, and without doubt derives great pleasure from it. Thus, at one level, *The Pardoner's Prologue and Tale* may be read as a cynical refutation of the Physician's moralising. The wicked may flourish and enjoy themselves, and others may still think them holy and respect them.

But the *Prologue* and *Tale* also discover the Pardoner's true character. Usually, as the Physician has said, a man's wickedness is a secret he shares only with God; here the Pardoner exhibits himself without his usual reserve. For a brief space we are invited, as it were, to understand an evil man with much the same understanding as his God has of him. Each nuance, each twisted look, each shuffling step and surreptitious snatch, are lit up for our inspection. More is shown indeed than the Pardoner thinks he is revealing. For the poetry, by catching just the right tone of the speaker's voice, publishes the motive concealed behind motive. For example, when the Pardoner is boasting how easy it is to gull the crowd, and to persuade them that his relic has marvellous properties which can transmute the water of any well, he says:

> And, sires, also it heeleth jalousie;   (366)
> For though a man be falle in jalous rage,
> Lat maken with this water his potage,
> And nevere shal he moore his wyf mystriste,
> Though he the soothe of hir defaute wiste,
> Al had she taken prestes two or thre.

The Pardoner knows that guilt undermines judgment, and many a wife, worried that her husband may discover she has had a lover, will in desperation try his remedy. But in the last line there is a nudging snigger. Wife, priests, and auditors are all drawn as accomplices into the guilty circle. It pleases the Pardoner to think that others are also hypocrites, and he offers to share the joke with them. It is an unintended revelation of how the Pardoner perceives mankind as commonly corrupt.

In boasting to his fellow-pilgrims what a cunning rogue he is, the Pardoner actually confesses to the very nature of his roguery, and portrays what he is to an extent he can never imagine. Why does he so betray himself? John Speirs suggests that such a question is irrelevant, and says that criticism should recognise Chaucer's use of a poetic convention here. *The Pardoner's Prologue* 'consists, as he drinks, of his "confession" —a "confession" of the same order as that of the Wife of Bath. The "confession" should simply be accepted as a convention like those soliloquies in Elizabethan plays in which the villain comes to the front of the stage and, taking the audience entirely into his confidence, unmasks himself ("I am determined to prove a villain"). The consideration that the rogue is here apparently giving away to his fellow-pilgrims the secrets he lives by will only intervene when we refuse (incapacitated, perhaps, by modern "naturalistic" conventions) to accept the convention... Even by "naturalistic" expectations the phenomenon is not outrageously improbable. In an excess of exhibitionism, glorying and confident in his invincible roguery, his tongue loosened by drink, the Pardoner is conceivable as sufficiently carried away to boast incautiously as well as impudently. But such considerations are hardly relevant ones here.'[1] I think they are very relevant, for if they are ignored much of the irony here will be missed. There is the obvious irony of his cleverness overreaching itself, resulting in the Host's abusing him when he says he will begin by shriving him first as the 'moost envoluped in synne'. But there are more subtle ironies than this in the *Prologue and Tale*. The Pardoner's 'confession' is quite unlike the Wife of Bath's. She is expounding the woes and joys of marriage, giving advice to wives, and justifying her life by attacking the restrictive doctrines of the Church. But the Pardoner is not attempting to justify himself. He is not putting forward excuses, but is expounding his own cleverness.

> 'What, trowe ye, that whiles I may preche,   (439)
> And wynne gold and silver for I teche,
> That I wol lyve in poverte wilfully?
> Nay, nay, I thoghte it nevere, trewely!...
>
> 'I wol have moneie, wolle, chese, and whete,   (448)
> Al were it yeven of the povereste page,
> Or of the povereste wydwe in a village,
> Al sholde hir children sterve for famyne.'

The evil is expressed with a disconcerting yet winning honesty. It is as though the years of hypocrisy have created in him an urge to proclaim publicly intentions and tricks he normally conceals.

[1] Speirs, *op. cit.* p. 169.

Related to this is perhaps another facet of the matter. The
Pardoner seems totally without conscience or fear of retribution. Yet he never seems to doubt the doctrine of damnation.
When he says that he does not care if others' souls 'goon a-
blakeberyed' he is accepting the holy truths he exploits for
his own avarice. But these doctrines, for all his skill at clothing
them in impressive words, never come alive to him. He never
grasps imaginatively the reality of his own perdition. When
he describes the portrait of sin he seems at the same time to be
mentally preening himself. Thus, when he says,

> 'O dronke man, disfigured is thy face,   (551)
> Sour is thy breeth, foul artow to embrace,
> And thurgh thy dronke nose semeth the soun
> As though thou seydest ay "Sampsoun, Sampsoun!"'

we may feel that he is in his own mind contrasting such ugliness with his own effeminate grace, and contrasting the ugly
snoring sound of a drunk with his own treble. But we, who
know he himself is drunk, and remember that there is something
very distasteful about his whole appearance, are all the more
conscious of his blindness to his own spiritual condition. Indeed, so ridiculous, so extreme, does his crassness seem to be
that we feel it almost borders on madness:

Swiche glarynge eyen hadde he as an hare. (*General Prologue*, 684)

If this image suggests something of the intensity with which
he gazes at those he intends to gull, it also suggests an intensity
deficient in basic human traits of consciousness. From this we
turn to his boastfulness, his avarice and other vices almost with
relief, for they are by contrast so human. But the Pardoner's
complacency, his blankness about a crucial part of his own
self, his disregard of his own spiritual peril, create a powerful
tone of irony throughout the poem.

The tale he tells itself embodies similar contrasts: the
apparent fortune of the three rioters (their finding the gold)
results in their killing one another; they seek death but have
carried death inside themselves. But, we might say, where the

Prologue is a psychological study of an evil man, *The Pardoner's Tale* explores the nature of evil more objectively, relating it to other fundamentals of the human condition. (Of course, there is the further irony here: the tale, possibly one the Pardoner has learnt by heart, reveals truths he is quite incapable of comprehending.) The tale is one which has always caught the popular imagination, and doubtless this popularity derives from the story's cathartic dramatisation of elemental anxieties. In Chaucer's version the poetry makes these profounder significances all the more felt.

The rioters devote themselves to pleasure and, like the Pardoner himself, are contemptuous of all but their own satisfaction.

> They daunce and pleyen at dees bothe day and nyght, (467)
> And eten also and drynken over hir myght,
> Thurgh which they doon the devel sacrifise
> Withinne that develes temple, in cursed wise,
> By superfluytee abhomynable.
> Hir othes been so grete and so dampnable
> That it is grisly for to heere hem swere.
> Oure blissed Lordes body they totere,
> Hem thoughte that Jewes rente hym noght ynough;
> And ech of hem at otheres synne lough.

The Pardoner's sermonising on their wickedness delays the commencement of the story proper, builds up expectation and, I think, also in reaction makes us more sympathetic towards the rioters even while we acknowledge their sinfulness. Their habits are an extreme example of trivial pursuits, but there is a bit of a rioter in all of us, and who has not felt his life to be no more than a selfish search for unsatisfactory pleasure? In such moods death seems a terrible threat, the ultimate, irrevocable spoil-sport:

> 'He was, pardee, an old felawe of youres; (672)
> And sodeynly he was yslayn to-nyght,
> Fordronke, as he sat on his bench upright.
> Ther cam a privee theef, men clepeth Deeth...'

Here *The Pardoner's Tale* links up with earlier tales which touched on death: we may think back on Arcite's dying just at the moment when he seemed to have won his love, or on the Wife of Bath sadly reflecting that her love-making must have an end, or on the Reeve bitterly complaining that his life was being drawn away uselessly. The attitudes people adopt towards death derive from what they would make of their lives.

Though we recognise the futile presumption of challenging death, do we not feel briefly a sneaking admiration for the aggressive response of the rioters?

> 'Herkneth, felawes, we thre been al ones;   (696)
> Lat ech of us holde up his hande til oother,
> And ech of us bicomen otheres brother,
> And we wol sleen this false traytour Deeth.
> He shal be slayn, he that so manye sleeth.'

This passage well illustrates the balance of parable and 'realism' in the *Tale*: we concede the possibility of seeking such a person as Death even while recognising that this is the boast of men besotted by drink.

Shortly after setting out, the three rioters meet the figure of an old man. This episode has given rise to some controversy among critics,[1] and the old man has variously been interpreted as an allegorical figure of Age and even Death himself. But more relevant is how the poetry here manipulates the reader's responses.

> This olde man gan looke in his visage,   (720)
> And seyde thus: 'For I ne kan nat fynde
> A man, though that I walked into Ynde,
> Neither in citee ne in no village,
> That wolde chaunge his youthe for myn age;
> And therfore moot I han myn age stille,
> As longe tyme as it is Goddes wille.
> Ne Deeth, allas! ne wol nat han my lyf.

---

[1] For example, see Raymond Preston, *Chaucer* (Sheed and Ward, 1952), p. 235, and Speirs, *op. cit.* p. 176.

Thus walke I, lyk a resteless kaityf,
And on the ground, which is my moodres gate,
I knokke with my staf, both erly and late,
And seye "Leeve mooder, leet me in!
Lo how I vanysshe, flessh, and blood, and skyn!
Allas! whan shul my bones been at reste?
Mooder, with yow wolde I chaunge my cheste
That in my chambre longe tyme hath be,
Ye, for an heyre clowte to wrappe in me!"
But yet to me she wol nat do that grace,
For which ful pale and welked is my face.'

In *Gulliver's Travels*, to show what an awful gift immortality
could be, Swift drew the terrible picture of the Struldbrugs.
But the feeling evoked by this passage is a grim pathos. Look,
it says, what a sadly unwanted gift too-long life is. Not only
does the poetry portray the yearning of the old man for rest,
but the imagery probes further, suggesting that death is a returning to the womb and part of the cycle of birth and recreation. 'I knokke with my staf, both erly and late', sketches
the tired traveller, friendless and alone, shut out from the place
he loves, calling for notice early in the morning and late in the
evening; the staff also gives a picture of the old man, bent with
age, supported by a prop whose every rap upon the ground is
an impatient demand for death. Compassion is urged upon the
reader, but the limits of compassion are wryly noted: no one
would voluntarily change places with the old man. Though to
this we may come: the poetry enforces the sobering reflection.
Ironies pervade the passage. The old man, his desire frustrated,
wanders 'lyk a resteless kaityf': the phrase compares him to
the three restless rioters. The old man wishes to exchange the
chest of his possessions for a shroud of hair-cloth: in effect
the rioters will exchange the heap of gold they find for shrouds.
But the real importance of the passage lies in the way it changes
the concept of death. Earlier, death had been described to the
reader with some effect as a 'privee theef', now it is appreciated
as something which may be benevolent and desired. Life too,
we apprehend, may be experienced as a 'superfluytee abhomyn-

able', and Death is God-given, and not without kindness and purpose. Death has an ordained role, and to rebel against this is the ultimate in human pride and egoism.

As the tale proceeds we are given a third picture of Death— he comes to the three rioters as just retribution. Doubtless part of our pleasure at seeing the rioters destroy themselves comes from the satisfaction of seeing the arrogant brought to book; we have a vested interest in seeing others conform to mortality. But in the main our satisfaction is a moral one. Men so avaricious, so contemptuous of other lives, so besotted with their own acquisition, do not deserve to live. Their terrible callousness is pointed by the irony of the repeated words 'brother' or 'friend', and the poetry catches the very tone of cold calculation:

> And preyde hym that he hym wolde selle   (853)
> Som poyson, that he myghte his rattes quelle;
> And eek ther was a polcat in his hawe,
> That, as he seyde, his capouns hadde yslawe,
> And fayn he wolde wreke hym, if he myghte,
> On vermyn that destroyed hym by nyghte.

The youngest of the rioters is clearly producing all these reasons for his purchase partly from nervous excitement, partly from a scornful joke with himself at his fellows. They reciprocate his contempt:

> 'Now lat us sitte and drynke, and make us merie,   (883)
> And afterward we wol his body berie.'

With their mutually inflicted deaths the pattern of the tale is completed, but the grim awe that pattern evokes makes us feel that something of a divine design has been mirrored here. The existence of death has been vindicated.

Then with a shock we are flung back again into the Pardoner's rhetoric. The confidence of his manner, his hypocrisy, seem more surprising than ever after this moral: his exuberance inexplicable. Where lies the truth? Are the wages of sin death, as the tale informs us? Or are the wicked buoyantly unrepentant? The Pardoner's return to glib confidence seems more than ever crass and spiritually suicidal. But he is incorrigibly himself.

Yet, in his display of himself as well as in the moral of his story, the Pardoner turns his audience against the sins he practises while he denounces them. Thus we have demonstrated to us the truth of the Pardoner's boast:

> I preche of no thyng but for coveityse.   (424)
> Therfore my theme is yet, and evere was,
> *Radix malorum est Cupiditas.*
> Thus kan I preche agayn that same vice
> Which that I use, and that is avarice.
> But though myself be gilty in that synne,
> Yet kan I maken oother folk to twynne
> From avarice, and soore to repente.
> But that is nat my principal entente...

In *The Pardoner's Prologue and Tale* Chaucer pushes further the unmasking of evil ecclesiastics that he began with *The Friar's Tale* and *The Summoner's Tale*: his *Prologue and Tale* is a piece of social satire on Pardoners and their corruption, a psychological study of an individual scoundrel, and an exploration of the nature of evil; and like the other two *Tales* it celebrates the divine Will which manifests itself even through a man's venal intentions. The outburst of the Host at the end of the *Tale* shows how one simple man at any rate has taken personal offence at the Pardoner's wickedness and his attempt to gull the people.

Yet the *Tale* does not end with the Host's indignation, but with the pilgrims laughing and the Knight reconciling the Host and the Pardoner.

> But right anon the worthy Knight began,   (960)
> Whan that he saugh that al the peple lough,
> 'Namoore of this, for it is right ynough!
> Sire Pardoner, be glad and myrie of cheere;
> And ye, sire Hoost, that been to me so deere,
> I prey yow that ye kisse the Pardoner.

> And Pardoner, I prey thee, drawe thee near,
> And, as we diden, lat us laughe and pleye.'
> Anon they kiste, and riden forth hir weye.

Why this ending? It is not intended to show obtuseness in the Knight, nor is it a sign of moral shirking on Chaucer's part. Rather it affirms the transcendent rightness of gaiety, good spirits and tolerance. Without renouncing the moral perceptions implicit in the *Prologue and Tale* nor repudiating the judgment on the Pardoner which he has elicited from the reader (the Host surely erred in being too vehement), Chaucer rejoices in God's creatures. Even in a man like the Pardoner, he is saying in effect, there is a wonderful crooked beauty. Indeed, on reflection, much of the delight of the *Prologue and Tale* arises from fascination with the Pardoner's very being, and again and again the poetry has celebrated it. A sudden turn in the verse, or an unexpected image arising (as below with the image of the dove) casts splendour upon the man.

> I stonde lyk a clerk in my pulpet, (391)
> And whan the lewed peple is doun yset,
> I preche so as ye han herd bifoore,
> And telle an hundred false japes moore.
> Thanne peyne I me to strecche forth the nekke,
> And est and west upon the peple I bekke,
> As dooth a dowve sittynge on a berne.
> Myne handes and my tonge goon so yerne
> That it is joye to se my bisynesse.

Even the Pardoner is part of the glory of Creation.

CHAPTER 13

The Shipman's Tale

CLEARLY *The Shipman's Tale* was not originally intended for the Shipman, but was to be told by a woman:

> The sely housbonde, algate he moot paye,   (11)
> He moot us clothe, and he moot us arraye,
> Al for his owene worshipe richely,
> In which array we daunce jolily.

The obvious surmise is that the narrator was the Wife of Bath. The sentiments of the *Tale* accord with her character, and the plot of a wife getting money out of her lover—an ecclesiastic— and talking her husband round into letting her keep the money demonstrates just such wiles as the Wife of Bath advocates for other wives, and suggests that the *Tale* was to fit into the 'marriage debate'. Perhaps Chaucer replaced this story with that of the knight and the old woman because he felt that a tale qualifying the Wife of Bath's demand for 'maistrye' would come more ironically from her mouth. There is also reason to believe, I think, that *The Shipman's Tale* was intended to stand before *The Physician's Tale*, for the occasion for his outburst on the upbringing of children seems to be provided by the lines,

> A mayde child cam in hire compaignye,   (95)
> Which as hir list she may governe and gye,
> For yet under the yerde was the mayde.

The Physician would be offended by the notion of such a scheming woman as this being a guide and model to an innocent child.

Why Chaucer later gave the tale to the Shipman we do not know. Did he feel that the cynicism of the tale would be appropriate to one of whom he had said, 'Of nyce conscience took he no keep'? Would he have left the tale with the Shipman, or given it to someone else or back to the Wife of Bath as her second tale? We do not know. Clearly the tale had not been completely revised, for the first-person identification with a woman narrator has been left. The linking passage between *The Shipman's Tale* and *The Prioress's Tale* suggests that he had contemplated leaving the tale (revised?) with the Shipman. But whether in the final placing of the tales *The Prioress's Tale* was to have come before, or after, *The Physician's Tale* with which it seems to have some links, again we do not know. So long as these issues are borne in mind they should not trouble us too much when analysing *The Shipman's Tale* itself.

The *Tale* is light-heartedly cynical. Though Master John and the wife cheat each other and the husband, no harm comes of it and everybody gets off happily with some reward. The monk enjoys the wife with the aid of the husband's money, the wife retains the money after all, and the husband is satisfied to receive her repayment in bed. Has the *Tale* any moral? Well, wives are out for what they can get, and men are happy to make love, and perhaps a little licence seasons married life. The real zest of the *Tale* comes from the witty account of the characters, and the neat permutations of the plot. It has the dance-like gaiety, though not perhaps the intricacy, of a Molière farce.

A handsome and virile monk, a fair and clothes-conscious wife, a cuckold poring over his accounts—the characters may seem from stock. But they are more subtly drawn than appears at first sight. An air of luxury and wealth hangs over them. Though the merchant is worried about his prosperity, and can even mention the dodge of going on a pilgrimage to escape creditors (is this why the Merchant of the *General Prologue* is going to Canterbury?), he lives well and spends freely. The monk is of some eminence in his order, and can so freely afford gifts that the servants are as glad of his coming 'As fowel is fayn whan that the sonne up riseth.' The wife is sociable, and delights in revelry and expense. Theirs is a privileged existence,

and their manners and talk have the easy sophistication that
accompanies such a life.

> 'O deere cosyn myn, daun John', she sayde,   (98)
> 'What eyleth yow so rathe for to ryse?'
>   'Nece', quod he, 'it oghte ynough suffise
> Fyve houres for to slepen upon a nyght,
> But it were for an old appalled wight,
> As been thise wedded men, that lye and dare
> As in a fourme sit a wery hare,
> Were al forstraught with houndes grete and smale.
> But deere nece, why be ye so pale?
> I trowe, certens, that oure goode man
> Hath yow laboured sith the nyght bigan,
> That yow were nede to resten hastily.'
> And with that word he lough ful murily,
> And of his owene thought he wax al reed.

The guilty blush at the end is comic because it is so out of
keeping with the liberties of the speech: the monk's private
imaginings have obviously been much bolder than his words.
The mocking of husbands, with its casual suggestion that he
himself is younger and more energetic, the undercurrent of a
sexual taunt in his expressed concern that she is weary, convey
his dangerous charm. Clearly he feels no unease in flirting with
the wife of his sworn brother. Not that the bond of their
friendship amounts to much: the amity between the monk and
the merchant has its foundations in pleasure. The small hypocrisy of claimed blood-kinship points to a shallow intimacy,
despite their larger assertions.

> And for as muchel as this goode man   (33)
> And eek this monk, of which that I bigan,
> Were bothe two yborn in o village,
> The monk hym claymeth as for cosynage;
> And he agayn, he seith nat ones nay,
> But was as glad therof as fowel of day;
> For to his herte it was greet plesaunce.
> Thus been they knyt with eterne alliaunce . . .

Life, friendship and dalliance come as easy and pleasantly to
this class of persons as day to the fowls of the air, and on the
whole they give as little thought to the morrow.

Particularly interesting to watch is the question of money as
it arises in their relationships. The merchant shuts himself up
to work out his accounts, so that no one should actually know
how rich he is. Though he has quite a hoard stored up (and
is shortly to make another killing) he speaks to his wife about
the dangers of bankruptcy.

> 'For of us chapmen, also God me save,   (226)
> And by that lord that clepid is Seint Yve
> Scarsly amonges twelve tweye shul thryve
> Continuelly, lastynge unto oure age...
> For everemoore we moote stonde in drede
> Of hap and fortune in oure chapmanhede.'

The merchant is generous, spends on his wife freely enough,
and offers the loan to the monk just as freely.

> 'My gold is youres, whan that it yow leste,   (284)
> And nat only my gold, but my chaffare.
> Take what yow list, God shilde that ye spare.'

Since the reader knows by this stage that the monk intends to
'take' the merchant's wife the second line acquires an ironic
meaning. But I wonder if a *double entendre* does not underlie
many of the references to money. When the merchant explains
why he would like the money back, he says:

> 'But o thyng is, ye knowe it wel ynogh,   (287)
> Of chapmen, that hir moneie is hir plogh.
> We may creaunce whil we have a name;
> But goldlees for to be, it is no game.'

In its context here has not the comparison of money to a
plough something of a sexual association? If this seems a far-
fetched interpretation there can be no doubt about the ending
of the poem. But of that more in a moment. After the merchant's
return from Bruges he needs to borrow some money. He goes
to see Master John but, he emphasises this to himself, not to
reclaim the money he lent; and he is quite upset when the monk

raises the matter and claims to have returned the money to the
wife. As the merchant reports the matter to his wife later:

> '...ye han maad a manere straungenesse   (386)
> Bitwixen me and my cosyn daun John.
> Ye sholde han warned me, er I had gon,
> That he yow hadde an hundred frankes payed
> By redy token; and heeld hym yvele apayed,
> For that I to hym spak of chevyssaunce;
> Me semed so, as by his contenaunce.
> But nathelees, by God, oure hevene kyng,
> I thoughte nat to axen hym no thyng.'

This niceness of the merchant's over the loan, twice emphasised,
is somewhat strange. What causes his attitude? He seems to
feel that friendship and money matters should be kept apart,
and feels slightly guilty that he had the ulterior motive of
recovering his money when he went to see his 'cousin'. Yet
his love-making with his wife is clearly celebrating his profit-
able deal in Paris. Money, for the merchant, seems intimately
bound up with his manhood. As though he would no more
demand money off a friend than he would, out of modesty,
before the monk call into doubt his own virility. In the
marriage bed, however, successful trading seems to imbue him
with sexual energy.

What of the wife? She is the most interestingly drawn of
the three. When she complains to the monk of the woe of her
married life (in a tone that precludes the reader from taking
her seriously) she confesses to little interest in the act of love.

> 'In al the reawme of France is ther no wyf   (116)
> That lasse lust hath to that sory pley.'

Yet she contradicts herself soon afterwards when she mentions
the six things a wife expects of a husband.

> 'And wel ye woot that wommen naturelly   (173)
> Desiren thynges sixe as wel as I:
> They wolde that hir housbondes sholde be
> Hardy, and wise, and riche, and therto free,
> And buxom unto his wyf, and fressh abedde.'

When she tells the monk she needs a hundred francs before Sunday or she will be ruined, does she really need the money or is it simply an excuse so that she can give herself to the monk? Since we are shortly afterwards informed that her husband never will let the silver in her purse fail, it clearly seems to be an excuse. But is it the money, or pleasure of the monk she desires? Both, and in her mind there seems to be little distinction. She is not selling herself for money: rather she seems to think that a woman is entitled to extort the financial and the sexual gift from a man, and that the two gifts are interchangeable. The situation is virtually repeated later with her husband. Having been told the money the monk gave her is the repayment of his loan he asks why his wife did not mention it. But the wife sticks to the money by saying that she will amply repay him in another coinage.

> 'I wol answere yow shortly to the poynt.   (412)
> Ye han mo slakkere dettours than am I!
> For I wol paye yow wel and redily
> Fro day to day, and if so be I faille,
> I am youre wyf; score it upon my taille,
> And I shal paye as soone as ever I may.
> For by my trouthe, I have on myn array,
> And nat on wast, bistowed every deel;
> And for I have bistowed it so weel
> For youre honour, for Goddes sake, I seye,
> As be nat wrooth, but lat us laughe and pleye.
> Ye shal my joly body have to wedde.'

Money and sex are one and the same. She differs from her husband in quite consciously thinking so. Of course, in turn the money is spent on finely clothing her that she may please her husband the more. The money has been spent 'nat on wast': the attitude of mind is certainly the Wife of Bath's.

In this particular sophisticated comedy of adultery no harm has been done. The monk is not out of pocket, as the husband paid for his adventure; the husband does not lose, because his money stays with his wife (to whom he probably would have given it anyway) and for being cuckolded he is rewarded with his wife's greater amorousness; the wife gets the money, enjoys a lover and has her husband's spousal attentions. The eternal triangle has been set on a graph whose axes of reference intersect a fourth point: money. In many ways, the *Tale* with the wife striking a bargain with a third person in her husband's absence mirrors the plot of *The Franklin's Tale*. But there the fourth point was—truth. Doubtless the two stories were intended to be juxtaposed.

Wealthy people in privileged positions often confuse love and money, yet dwell in amoral happiness. Such a life is just what one would expect the Wife of Bath to praise, for she is a rising bourgeois with aspirations above her station. Her social pride was described in the *General Prologue*:

> In al the parisshe wif ne was ther noon   (449)
> That to the offrynge bifore hire sholde goon.

And the prayer that concludes the *Tale*, with its conjoined monetary and sexual pun, quite typifies the Wife of Bath with her devotion to wealth and love:

> Thus endeth now my tale, and God us sende   (433)
> Taillynge ynough unto oure lyves ende. Amen.

CHAPTER 14

The Prioress's Tale

When Madame Eglentyne tells her tale she comes to speak for the religious consciousness of the folk. She becomes as anonymous as her story, which expresses cruelty, and also tenderness and adoration honouring the Mother and the Child. Now the fourteenth century was a period of astonishing spiritual vitality, in mysticism the classical moment of Christendom. Richard Rolle and Walter Hilton and Lady Julian of Norwich and the author of the *Cloud of Unknowing* in England. John Tauler and the Friends of God, Gerard Groote and Blessed Henry Suso and John Ruysbroeck *doctor ecstaticus*, and St Brigid of Sweden and St Catherine of Siena abroad; and St Vincent Ferrer, the great Dominican preachers, converted Jews instead of killing them. But *The Prioress's Tale* is not a presentation of exceptional religious consciousness; it is an exceptional presentation of the mind of the people...(Chaucer) respected the folk imagination; he purified it; he expressed it as it had never been expressed before.[1]

There is much truth in Raymond Preston's comment: the *Tale* does contain the credulous wonder and naive bigotry of Christianised folk-belief. As such it is received by the company of pilgrims, who for a short moment are held by silent awe when the story is done:

> Whan said was al this miracle, every man   (691)
> As sobre was that wonder was to se.

Tales such as this stirred the common mind, and Chaucer has captured the pathos and ecstasy inherent in the legend. But Chaucer was capable of sophistication as well as innocence. With his dramatic skill he draws the reader into the heart of medieval belief, and at the same time, by means of one or two slight touches, he invites an objective appraisal. Experience this belief, he says in effect, but remember it is only *belief*, the

---

[1] Preston, *op. cit.* p. 207.

sensibility of one woman fed by popular feelings: understand, sympathise, but recognise the human limitation.

The invocation to the Virgin Mary which precedes the *Tale* sets the tone of religious sincerity.

> 'O Lord, oure Lord, thy name how merveillous   (453)
> Is in this large world ysprad', quod she;
> 'For noght oonly thy laude precious
> Parfourned is by men of dignitee,
> But by the mouth of children thy bountee
> Parfourned is, for on the brest soukynge
> Somtyme shewen they thy heriying.
>
> Wherfore in laude, as I best kan or may,
> Of thee and of the white lylye flour
> Which that the bar, and is mayde alway,
> To telle a storie I wol do my labour...'

The last two lines of the first stanza are a paraphrase of lines in Psalm 8 ('Out of the mouths of babes and sucklings...'), and the paradox they express falls into place among the other holy paradoxes mentioned in the invocation—the virgin mother, the burning bush—and prepares us for the miracle of the *Tale*. The lines assert the mystery of God. All things praise Him in being, and the need or satisfaction of a child at the breast may more truly express the marvel of the Creator than the wisest spoken eulogy. This notion is subtly reversed when it reappears in the closing stanza of the invocation.

> 'My konnyng is so wayk, o blisful Queene,   (481)
> For to declare thy grete worthynesse
> That I ne may the weighte nat susteene;
> But as a child of twelf month oold, or lesse,
> That kan unnethes any word expresse,
> Right so fare I, and therfore I yow preye,
> Gydeth my song that I shal of yow seye.'

The Prioress, in genuine humility, confesses she is as ignorant as a child. But because of what has gone before we are invited to accept what she has to say as a witness perhaps all the more true because it is so innocent.

The Prioress is not a wholly anonymous story-teller. In particular there are two moments when we are specially reminded that she is telling the story. Once when she says,

> This abbot, which that was an hooly man,   (642)
> As monkes been—or elles oghte be—

a simple objection to the presentation of the monk in *The Shipman's Tale* (and perhaps to the Monk riding in her company). The other is more significant. After the murder of the child she gives a visionary account of what becomes of his soul.

> I seye that in a wardrobe they hym threwe   (572)
> Where as thise Jewes purgen hire entraille.
> O cursed folk of Herodes al newe,
> What may youre yvel entente yow availle?
> Mordre wol out, certeyn, it wol nat faille,
> And namely ther th'onour of God shal sprede;
> The blood out crieth on youre cursed dede.

> O martir, sowded to virginitee,
> Now maystow syngen, folwynge evere in oon
> The white Lamb celestial—quod she—
> Of which the grete evaungelist, Seint John,
> In Pathmos wroote, which seith that they that goon
> Biforn this Lamb, and synge a song al newe,
> That nevere, flesshly, wommen they ne knewe.

The poetry soars from the disgust of the privy and the horror of the murder to the joy and serenity of the 'white Lamb celestial'. Yet at the moment almost of ecstasy Chaucer chose to include that *quod she*. It is surely not (*pace* F. N. Robinson[1]) a trifling oversight, but a deliberate touch. It is not disturbing enough to break the mood, but just sufficient to cause a fleeting reflection: this is the Prioress's vision, drawn from the Bible, but is it really true? We only know this world though we have beliefs about the next. The interjection produces, on a slighter scale, the honest doubt of the lines from *The Knight's Tale*:

> His spirit chaunged hous and wente ther,   (2809)
> As I cam nevere, I kan nat tellen wher.

[1] Robinson, *op. cit.* p. 839.

This hint of a question in *The Prioress's Tale*, far from weakening her religious vision, strengthens it. The more we recognise the human limitation, the more we must concede the mystery of God. Maybe the Prioress, for all her simplicity and conventional piety, is guided in her song by Mary; and, like the child in her story, a 'greyn' has been laid upon her tongue.

The parallels between the Prioress and the little child of her story are important, and give added authenticity and relevance to the *Tale*. Both are moved to sing praise of Christ's mother. The ignorance of the child is emphasised. He is seven years of age (Chaucer's own addition to his sources) and, hearing his elder schoolfellows singing *Alma redemptoris*, yearns to sing it too. The stanzas describing this, wholly Chaucer's own invention, not only fill out the tale with humanity, they also enrich the theme.

> Noght wiste he what this Latyn was to seye,   (523)
> For he so yong and tendre was of age.
> But on a day his felawe gan he preye
> T'expounden hym this song in his langage,
> Or telle hym why this song was in usage;
> This preyde he hym to construe and declare
> Ful often tyme upon his knowes bare.
>
> His felawe, which that elder was than he,
> Answerde hym thus: 'This song, I have herd sye,
> Was maked of our blisful Lady free,
> Hire to salue, and eek hire for to preye
> To been oure help and socour whan we deye.
> I kan namoore expounde in this mateere;
> I lerne song, I kan but smal grammeere.'

The children's earnestness is captured with charm, their ignorance of the Latin tongue depicted with amusement. Yet worship is more than wit, and their unformed minds have grasped the core of the song's meaning. So too the Prioress's account of the miracle touches truths deeper than theology.

Despite the occasional scriptural references and proverbial sayings, the overall tone of the Prioress in the tale is itself childlike. Perhaps there is a Chaucerian irony in this which accords with the description of her in the *General Prologue*. There she is depicted as a woman with many genteel affectations: the way she sings, speaks French, eats, keeps pets, wears her clothes, all point to someone anxious to appear well-bred and in the courtly fashion.

> And peyned hire to countrefete cheere   (139)
> Of court, and to been estatlich of manere,
> And to ben holden digne of reverence.

The gentle satire on the courtly lady of the Rose in the nun's attire has been ably commented upon,[1] but we should not forget the simple girl behind the courtly mannerisms. The important thing is not only that she kept pets, against ecclesiastic injunction but perhaps in accordance with fashion, but also that she wept when they died or were beaten. Sentimental? I wonder. Perhaps slightly. But I suspect Chaucer rated highly the gift of feeling sympathy, and there is tribute as well as mockery in his saying, 'And al was conscience and tendre herte'. The description of the Prioress culminates in the account of her brooch with the crowned A and the inscription *Amor vincit omnia*. Doubtless a touch of worldly vanity disguising itself behind a religious motto. But is there not a further significance which generates a more profound irony? Behind the nun who plays at being a courtly lady is there not a country girl with a naive and loving heart? Even her name, Eglentyne, symbolises the ambiguity of her character: a rose which is the emblem of courtly love, but it is also a wild rose that invokes purity and rural innocence. At any rate, when she comes to tell her tale the simple country girl speaks and not merely the affected lady or dignified prioress. And the tale she tells turns out to be one of the most genuinely religious of all the tales.

Doubtless 'conscience' and her 'tendre herte' guide her choice of story. In its cheerful piety *The Prioress's Tale* contrasts with the amoral cynicism of the preceding *Tale* originally intended probably for the Wife of Bath. But also it should be

[1] For example, Speirs, *op. cit.* pp. 104–7.

compared with *The Physician's Tale*. Both treat of a plot by wicked people directed at an innocent and young person, and both show the wicked being found out. In *The Physician's Tale* the young girl is killed by her father to prevent her degradation. In *The Prioress's Tale* the child is murdered and his body degraded (the casting of it into the privy) but the innocent spirit is unquenched: miraculously the child sings on his praise of the Virgin till in decorum the priest removes the grain placed on his tongue and his spirit passes on to a greater realm. Perhaps the tale borders on being naive and sentimental. But the tone triumphantly holds it from falling over. The child-like innocence of the narration fuses with the simplicity of the child's version at the climax of the poem.

> 'This welle of mercy, Cristes mooder sweete, (656)
> I loved alwey, as after my konnynge;
> And whan that I my lyf sholde forlete,
> To me she cam, and bad me for to synge
> This anthem verraily in my deyynge,
> As ye han herd, and whan that I hadde songe,
> Me thoghte she leyde a greyn upon my tonge.

> 'Wherfore I synge, and synge I moot certeyn,
> In honour of that blisful Mayden free,
> Til fro my tonge of taken is the greyn;
> And after that thus seyde she to me:
> "My litel child, now wol I fecche thee,
> Whan that the greyn is fro thy tonge ytake.
> Be nat agast, I wol thee nat forsake."'

The tone of the Virgin's speech is so right, in its balance of kindness, motherliness and mercy, that it suspends disbelief. These are, of course, qualities dear to the Prioress, but then no one can but love 'after his konnynge', and the true flight of that love is Heaven's gift. Chaucer's achievement in this poem is to make us feel that the Prioress's story wells up from the purest and most tender part of her being, undistorted by her minor vanities; and to make us wonder whether, in the glorification of miraculous charity, she speaks better than she knows.

In the foreword to his translation of the poem[1] Wordsworth wrote, 'The fierce bigotry of the Prioress forms a fine background for her tender-hearted sympathies with the Mother and Child.' Bigotry lies more in the folk-origins of the story than in the Prioress herself. But we may suspect that the sentimental side of her nature, which makes her dwell on the innocence of the child so tenderly, betrays her into accepting the darkened evil of the Jews unquestioningly: sentimentality is frequently the companion of indifference and prejudice. In *The Prioress's Tale*, by intertwining what is admirable with what is bigoted, Chaucer portrays the human imperfection to be found even at the heart of worship and wonder.

[1] William Wordsworth, *Poetical Works* (Oxford University Press, 1956), p. 432.

CHAPTER 15

The Tales of Sir Thopas and Melibeus

No character in the *Canterbury Tales* is more enveloped in irony than the author. As Chaucer portrays himself, this pilgrim is a man of singular stupidity and naïvety. If some lines in the *General Prologue* are to be credited, he is easily taken in by the most obvious rascals. He thinks that the Pardoner is 'in chirche a noble ecclesiaste', and when the Monk sets out his notion of what monks should be and what they should feel free to do the author merely murmurs that 'his opinion was good'.[1] Chaucer the pilgrim disclaims all responsibility for the invention or bawdry of the tales, saying that he merely tried to repeat what was said as closely as he could; and he apologises for not being able to set the Pilgrims down in their proper degree because, 'My wit is short, ye may well understonde'. Naturally the reader finds all this amusing, and enjoys the piquant trick of Chaucer belittling his own shrewdness and artistry. (It must have had even more point for the audience to whom Chaucer read his own poetry: to see the author before them assuming an air of contrite stupidity.)

When the Host calls upon Chaucer the Pilgrim to tell a tale the same trick, as we would expect, is exploited further. There is delight in observing the Host, whom after all Chaucer did invent (whatever models he may have had), condescendingly joke about the author's own appearance.

> 'He in the waast is shape as well as I;   (700)
> This were a popet in an arm t'enbrace
> For any womman, smal and fair of face.
> He semeth elvyssh by his contenaunce,
> For unto no wight dooth he daliaunce.'

[1] Of course in both these cases we may *also* detect the scathing irony, not of Chaucer the stupid pilgrim, but of Chaucer the wily poet who leaves us in no doubt of his condemnation of these characters.

The last couplet is particularly rich in comic irony. Chaucer, who has led us to believe that he has sociably talked to all the Pilgrims, and been accepted as one of their company, is here portrayed by the Host as something of an outsider—a figure who is so remote within himself that he seems to come from a different realm. That the Host is apparently unaware of Chaucer's poetic vocation makes all the more pungent the mockery of poets for the withdrawn manner they notoriously affect. The reference to elves in the passage prepares us for the *Tale of Sir Thopas* with its unreal world that the Host will find so objectionable. It is a nice touch too that the Host will finally interrupt Chaucer for being an incompetent versifier, and abuse him for his foolishness.

The *Tale of Sir Thopas* fits neatly into the joke. So authentic is the burlesque of romances that we can well believe that Chaucer the pilgrim is unaware how bathetic his doggerel is, and the Host's interruption comes none too soon. If the *Tale* is slightly boring for the modern reader for whom the romances parodied are quite dead, this is the risk any burlesque runs which accurately takes off the vices of tenth-rate literature which is soon lost in the whirligig of fashion. There is sufficient absurdity in the verse, however, for it still to have some life of its own:

> His sadel was of rewel boon,   (878)
> His brydel as the sonne shoon,
> Or as the moone light.

The point of *Sir Thopas* is quickly got. But what are we to make of the prose tale that follows it?

The *Tale of Melibeus* is an enormous bore, and the bane of commentators. Some critics merely mutter a soothing nothing before it and hastily pass on to the next tale;[1] others more openly confess their bafflement or exasperation.[2] The critics

[1] For example, see Speirs, *op. cit.* pp. 181–2; or Coghill, who appears to be having his cake and eating it, *op. cit.* p. 153.
[2] W. P. Ker is the most outspoken and interesting commentator: 'The *Tale of Melibeus* is perhaps the worst example that could be found of all the intellectual and literary vices of the Middle Ages—bathos, forced allegory,

who deal with it are split between those who regard the *Tale of Melibeus* as another burlesque or painful leg-pull,[1] and those who regard it as a seriously intended piece of moralising quite in keeping with the dull homiletics of the time. Let me immediately confess that I am as baffled by it as any of them. Perhaps the best way of expressing the mixed responses this work arouses in me is to give a fictitious biographical account of how Chaucer might have written *Melibeus*.

I imagine that one day Chaucer was approached by an acquaintance who had a low regard for poetry, art or genuine thought, but who wished at times to be informed on matters of fashionable interest. This acquaintance had heard discussed a treatise on consolation and advice, and desired to read it. Having little French or Latin he turned to Chaucer who, while his versifying might not amount to much, was clearly literate and reputed to be a good translator. Chaucer had heard of this work, thought a discussion of prudent forgiveness might be worth studying, and agreed to make the translation. When he came to work on it, however, he found it to be quite preposterous.

A man called Melibeus returns home to find that foes have attacked and wounded his daughter in five different parts of her body. Desiring revenge, he calls for counsel. First he hearkens to flatterers (his name means 'a man that drynketh hony'), but his wife soon sets him right. Most of the tale in fact consists of the debate between Melibeus and Dame Prudence in which not only does she do most of the talking but what she says is invariably right, and recognised to be so by

spiritless and interminable moralising. Contented acquiescence in this exhausted air is not what one would expect from Chaucer, and sometimes one is tempted to think that the *Tale of Melibeus* is a mischievous companion of the *Rime of Sir Thopas*, and meant to parody a worse kind of "drasty speech". But that suggestion is desperate, and there is nothing for it but to believe that Chaucer found some interest in the debate of Melibeus and his wife Prudence.' See 'Chaucer' in *English Prose*, vol. I, *Fourteenth to Sixteenth Centuries*, ed. Henry Craik (Macmillan, 1893), pp. 40–3.

[1] See Ker above; also Paull F. Baum, *Chaucer, A Critical Appreciation* (Duke University Press, 1958), pp. 79–81; and G. G. Coulton, *Chaucer and his England* (London, 1927), p. 157.

her husband. But all this is not to be read too literally, as the tale is really an allegory: Melibeus' daughter is his heart; the three foes are the flesh, the fiend, and the world; the five wounds are the five senses through which the foes enter; and Dame Prudence is the wiser part of Melibeus' reason. She counsels reconciliation rather than revenge. Through her timely intervention, Melibeus forgives the three foes and takes them to his grace, as he trusts God will do to all men. What happens to the daughter is not made clear, but doubtless she recovers.

Perhaps such a tale could have made a powerful piece of didactic writing: but this, Chaucer soon found, was not the case here. To succeed, the conventions holding the tale together would have to be skilfully controlled. Instead reality and symbol, humanity and preaching were ineptly juxtaposed. But even more disastrous than this and what most struck Chaucer with his sensitive feeling for language, was the tale's ridiculous overabundance of proverbs. But he had agreed to translate it, and he began by trying to make the best of a bad job. Some parts of it, whole paragraphs even, he could render lucidly and forcefully.

Up roos tho oon of thise olde wise, and with his hand made contenaunce that men sholde holden hem stille and yeven hym audience./'Lordynges,' quod he, 'ther is ful many a man that crieth "Werre! werre!" that woot ful litel what werre amounteth./Werre at his bigynnyng hath so greet an entryng and so large, that every wight may entre whan hym liketh, and lightly fynde werre;/but certes, what ende that shal therof bifalle, it is nat light to know./For soothly, whan that werre is ones bigonne, ther is ful many a child unborn of his mooder that shal sterve yong by cause of thilke werre, or elles lyve in sorwe and dye in wrecchednesse./And therfore, er that any werre bigynne, men moste have greet conseil and greet deliberacion.'/And whan this olde man wende to enforcen his tale by resons, wel ny alle atones bigonne they to rise for to breken his tale, and beden hym ful ofte his wordes for to abregge./For soothly, he that precheth to hem that listeth nat heeren his wordes, his sermon hem anoieth./For Jhesus Syrak seith that 'musik in wepyng is noyous thyng'; this is to seyn: as muche availleth to speken bifore folk to which his speche anoyeth, as it is to synge biforn hym that wepeth./And whan this wise man saught that hym wanted audience, al shamefast he sette hym doun agayn./For Salomon seith: 'Ther as thou ne mayst have noon audience, enforce thee nat to speke.'/'I see wel', quod this wise man, 'that the commune proverbe is sooth, that "good conseil wanteth whan it is moste nede".'/

But the material as a whole defeated serious adaptation. Chaucer realised that as it stood it was a monument to misguided purpose and inept craftsmanship. Hence he was all the more amused to find that his patron, who so despised Chaucer's finest poetry, praised this work and its translator.

In time a mischievous idea took root in Chaucer's mind. Why not incorporate it in the *Canterbury Tales* as the tale he himself tells? What could more fittingly illustrate the fumblings of the uninspired *litterateur* he was portraying himself to be? What could more mockingly settle the score with those in his audience wanting in all literary judgment, particularly as they would not even recognise any mockery at all? Furthermore, some of the arguments in the tale would fit in quite well with themes in *Canterbury Tales*. *The Physician's Tale* deals with a father whose daughter is wronged, and *The Prioress's Tale* touches upon the vengeance wrought upon the Jews for killing the little child. At least *Melibeus* will draw people into reconsidering the rightness of vengeance. The unreal debate between husband and wife in *Melibeus* could also be used to good effect by contrasting it with the Wife of Bath's monologues directed at her husbands. To bring this out Chaucer deliberately develops the argument on the merits of women, and lets Dame Prudence at one stage use the very same words as the Wife of Bath.

'And as to youre fourthe resoun, ther ye seyn that the janglerie of womman kan hyde thynges that they wot noght, as who seith that a womman kan nat hyde that she wood;/sire, thise wordes been understonde of wommen that been jangleresses and wikked;/of which wommen men seyn that thre thynges dryven a man out of his hous, that is to seyn, smoke, droppyng of reyn, and wikked wyves;/and of swich wommen seith Salomon that "it were bettre dwelle in desert than with a womman that is riotous"./And sire, by youre leve, that am nat I . . .'

The sweet eloquence(!) of Dame Prudence also can cause the Host to contrast her with his own wife, and so introduce a touch of comedy not unrelated to the 'marriage debate'.[1]

Chaucer further hoped, I surmise, by including this tale to make the perceptive reader appreciate a writer's difficulty in organising his material. For a writer, one of his crucial problems is how to direct and control his reader's responses, and one of the important methods he has at his disposal is the employment of recognised *conventions*. He has to eschew matter alien to the convention he selects, or so modify it that it will not conflict with the basic unfolding of his subject. Where he mixes two or more conventions he has to be even more careful, lest the shift from one to another leads the reader to misapprehend the tone or purport of parts of the work. Since Chaucer himself was in the habit of juggling with many conventions in one work, he must have been particularly aware of the risks entailed. Where a writer, through ineptitude or bad craftsmanship, muddles his conventions, the reader is disconcerted to find extraneous and contradictory notions entering into his reading, and he doubts the writer's argument even while it is unfolding. Perhaps Chaucer, recognising that this is exactly what the inept construction of *Melibeus* resulted in, attempted to turn it into good use by making it a model of how *not* to present an argument. Thus he deliberately permitted the 'naturalism' in *Melibeus* clumsily to jostle the allegory, and encouraged the human situation of marital discussion to throw off-balance the allegorical debate. To illustrate this briefly: when Melibeus weeps at the injury to his daughter, Dame Prudence remembers Ovid in the 'Remedie of Love' saying, 'He is a fool that distourbeth the mooder to wepen in the deeth of hire child . . .'; she lets her husband weep a little while before attempting to stop him. The slight shock

[1] See especially R. A. Pratt, 'The Order of the Canterbury Tales', *PMLA*, LXVI (1951), 1158–9 and n. 34.

of seeing that Dame Prudence is treating her husband as though he were the weak woman permits an element of comic reality to upset the earnestness of the allegorical situation.

Further, a writer must know when to prune and avoid excess. A literary device overdone loses its effectiveness. But Chaucer makes no attempt to stop the flow of proverbs in *Melibeus*: on the contrary he lets them pile up till the effect is preposterous, and the reader, now impatient with proverbs and their shifting uses, grows completely sceptical of their application. Only a blockhead could write so badly, and that is exactly how Chaucer wished to portray himself as a pilgrim. Once again Chaucer may have been parodying one of his own characteristics, namely his habit of ringing changes on common proverbs: we need only think of the variety of uses to which he puts the proverbial phrase, 'Taketh the fruyt, and lat the chaf be stille,' in the *Canterbury Tales* to recognise this possibility.

Of course Chaucer realised that if he was to use *Melibeus* as a demonstration of inept authorship, the reader would have to be forewarned, and also provided with some writing which would establish a standard for contrast. These two safeguards he took. First, before commencing *Melibeus* he has himself say:

> Therfore, lordynges alle, I yow biseeche,   (953)
> If that yow thynke I varie as in my speche,
> As thus, *though that I telle somwhat moore*
> *Of proverbes than ye han herd bifoore*
> Comprehended in this litel tretys heere,
> To enforce with th' effect of my mateere,
> And though I nat the same wordes seye
> As ye han herd, yet to yow alle I preye
> Blameth me nat; for, as in my sentence,
> Shul ye nowher fynden difference
> Fro the sentence of this tretys lyte
> After the which this murye tale I write.

The inappropriateness, which soon becomes apparent, of the descriptions *little* and *merry*, and the emphasis on more proverbs than his audience had heard before, as well as the suggestion that they may be misquoted without change of meaning, all prepare the reader to approach the tale with some scepticism. When the tale is told the Host, who so damned *Sir Thopas*, is apparently impressed (this itself is comic), but Chaucer has him break out into a rich account of his own wife. The energy and human warmth of this speech shows up the unreality of *Melibeus* by providing, the illusion is so complete, the touchstone of life itself.

> 'I hadde levere than a barel ale   (1893)
> That Goodelief, my wyf, hadde herd this tale!
> For she nys no thyng of swich pacience
> As was this Melibeus wyf Prudence.
> By Goddes bones! whan I bete my knaves,
> She bryngeth me forth the grete clobbed staves,
> And crieth, "Slee the dogges everichoon,
> And brek hem, bothe bak and every boon!"
>   'And if that any neighebor of myne
> Wol nat in chirche to my wyf enclyne,
> Or be so hardy to hire to trespace,
> Whan she comth hoom she rampeth in my face,
> And crieth, "False coward, wrek thy wyf!
> By corpus bones, I wol have thy knyf,
> And thou shalt have my distaf and go spynne!"
> Fro day to nyght right thus she wol bigynne.
> "Allas!" she seith, "that evere I was shape
> To wedden a milksop, or a coward ape,
> That wol been overlad with every wight!
> Thou darst nat stonden by thy wyves right!"'

How clogged and clumsy the language of *Melibeus* is seen to be beside this passage whose life, of course, is achieved by a craftsmanship so skilful that it almost conceals itself. Here language prickles with bodily sensation. The weight and the ugly, knobby surface of the staves are felt in the sound and rhythm of 'bryngeth me forth the grete clobbed staves', just as the explosive alliteration of 'And brek hem, both bak and every boon!' gives the wife's commanding fury and also the sensation of being struck by a cudgel. This is the real Chaucer of economic vitality: *Melibeus* is merely his caricature of himself as a stodgy and tedious adapter. Perhaps his very desire to distinguish his false shadow from his real art betrayed him into dragging out *Melibeus* so interminably.

In this chapter, partly by means of the suppositious account of how Chaucer came to write and include the tale, I have tried to present my mixed responses to this work with its earnestness of theme and its un-Chaucerian dullness of performance. But whatever its purpose, *Melibeus* to my mind is not a success. I cannot be grateful for its inclusion in the *Canterbury Tales*. One critic has remarked of Chaucer's work, 'No doubt Chaucer nodded like all other artists, but I think he did not often snore'.[1] Whether he did or not here is debatable, but (to twist the 'sentence') I suspect many a reader faced with this tale has snored.

[1] G. G. Sedgewick, 'The Progress of Chaucer's Pardoner, 1880–1940', reprinted in *Chaucer Criticism*, vol. 1, ed. Richard Schoek and Jerome Taylor (University of Notre Dame Press, 1960), p. 202.

CHAPTER 16

The Monk's Tale

MOST of the Canterbury tales demonstrate different modes of story-telling, but in certain tales Chaucer apparently intended to make the literary form itself a chief focus of attention. In *The Squire's Tale*, *The Tale of Sir Thopas*, *The Tale of Melibeus*, and now in *The Monk's Tale*, the narrators are presented as falling short of their intentions, and Chaucer employs this incompetence to burlesque the literary form itself. The vices the tellers display point to the temptations inherent in those kinds of tales: the Squire loses himself in the intricate unrealities of romance; *Sir Thopas* jingles meaninglessly, and *Melibeus* knots himself into a tangle of accumulated proverbs. The Monk produces a series of mechanical 'tragedies' in which human interest surrenders to the inevitable 'fall' of the plot. Only in *The Nun's Priest's Tale* does parody co-exist with the speaker's masterly performance, but there the tale rises far above mere burlesque.

That the Monk should choose tragedy as his subject is surprising. Clearly someone as vigorous and virile as the Monk should tell a full-blooded story celebrating the natural man, a story as gay as his bridle bells

> Gynglen in a whistlyng wynd als cleere   (170)
> And eek as loude as dooth the chapel belle.

That he does not we owe to the banter of the Host. Harry Bailly, having confessed his shameful subordination to his brawny wife, attempts to ease his own humiliation by humbling someone else. He picks the Monk who, though apparently a man's man, is vowed to celibacy. The Host's jocular address is openly sexual.

> 'I pray to God, yeve hym confusioun   (1943)
> That first thee broghte unto religioun!
> Thou woldest han been a tredefowel aright...'

> 'God yeve me sorwe, but, and I were a pope, (1950)
> Nat oonly thou, but every myghty man,
> Though he were shorn ful hye upon his pan,
> Sholde have a wyf; for al the world is lorn!
> Religioun hath take up al the corn
> Of tredyng, and we borel men been shrympes.'

If the Monk denies these imputations he belittles his own virility; if he admits them he confesses his own disregard for his vows. That these comments get under the Monk's skin is suggested by the Host's apology (with the sting in its tail):

> 'But be nat wrooth, my lord, though that I pleye. (1963)
> Ful ofte in game a sooth I have herd seye!'

Perhaps too the Host is hoping to taunt the Monk into an autobiographical account of 'the natural vigour of the venial sin'. But the Monk does not rise to the bait. When he speaks, his words are mild enough, and he apparently ignores completely these digs at him. He manifests the same patience he displayed during *The Shipman's Tale* with its portrayal of a seducing monk, and the same silent disregard he gave the Prioress's remark that monks are holy men or *should be*. However, to avoid any more personal comments, he first offers to tell the life of Saint Edward, but then begins with another neutral subject.

> 'Or ellis, first, tragedies wol I telle, (1971)
> Of whiche I have an hundred in my celle.'

Since—we know this from the description of him in the *General Prologue*—the Monk never spends much time in his cell but is usually off elsewhere hunting, or in the stables, or on pilgrimage, naturally his knowledge of the books in his cell is superficial. Like most people with scant regard for literature, he carries with him little more than the outline of the plot. With tragedy, the plot is apparently always very simple.

> 'Tragedie is to seyn a certeyn storie, (1973)
> As olde bookes maken us memorie,

> Of hym that stood in greet prosperitee,
> And is yfallen out of heigh degree
> Into myserie, and endeth wrecchedly.'

He also remembers learning that they are usually in metre.

> 'And they ben versified communely   (1978)
> Of six feet, which men clepen *exametron*,
> In prose eek been endited many oon,
> And eek in meetre, in many a sondry wyse.
> Lo, this declaryng oghte ynogh suffise.'

These lines in their tone perfectly catch the Monk's unimaginativeness and lack of interest. Perhaps if the Monk had been in a position favourable to a hunting story, the tale he would then have told would have soared or pranced with a subject dear to his heart. Instead we get cold fare.

Commenting on the series of 'tragedies' delivered by the Monk (with the exception of the tale of Ugolino), R. K. Root writes: 'A discussion of the literary merit of the "tragedies" must resemble the famous chapter on the snakes of Ireland. With few exceptions they have no literary merit. Apart from the unspeakable monotony of the series, the dry epitomising character of the individual narrations, and the inevitable recurring moral make them intolerable.'[1] This is true if we look at them merely as the Monk's narration. But if we see behind the Monk the mocking figure of Chaucer, we may recognise the skill with which the series has been organised to point the mindless repetition of (almost) meaningless incident.

The first few tragedies particularly reveal the Monk's inadequacies as story-teller. In stanza 1 the near identity of the rhymes gives the verse a heavy sing-song which is (deliberately on Chaucer's part) clumsy and inappropriate:

> I wol biwaille, in manere of tragedie,   (1991)
> The harm of hem that stoode in heigh degree,
> And fillen so that ther nas no remedie
> To brynge hem out of hir adversitee.
> For certein, whan that Fortune list to flee...

[1] R. K. Root, *The Poetry of Chaucer* (Peter Smith, 1957).

The Monk then despatches, in a stanza each, Lucifer ('though he an angel were') and Adam (driven out 'To labour, and to helle, and to meschaunce'—as though all these were much on a par). After this the sequence of tales is jumbled, the tragedies inexplicably leaping backwards and forwards from Biblical to classical themes, suggesting the Monk's own confusion ('Have me excused of myn ignoraunce'). Nor do the tales always have the same moral: though the Monk's introduction warns men not to trust in Fortune, sometimes the fall is due not to the fickle goddess but to the punishment of God. No attempt is made to reconcile these explanations. The tragedy of Sampson is even accounted for by saying that he told his counsel to his wife, and the moral (in contrast to *Melibeus*) warns husbands not to take wives into their confidence! With Hercules it looks as if Deianira will be blamed for his fall, but, unexpectedly, Fortune is once again the cause.

Chaucer must have realised that if the tales were not to be utterly monotonous there would have to be some variation, and some tales would have to come near to being genuine tragedies. Thus gradually the tales are filled out with more detail, and approach art. For example, though Cenobia does not die, her changes of fortune elicit more interest than the earlier tragedies. But it is only with the Ugolino story that the poetry becomes dramatic and generates proper compassion. With it, the deepest seriousness of *The Monk's Tale* is reached. Ugolino is followed by some grotesque villains, whose tragedies can hardly touch us. Then come Alexander and Julius Caesar, who are both described as knights ('He was of knyghthod and of fredom flour'). This, as much as the boredom spread by the Monk, seems to be the cause of the Knight's breaking in, and affirming his preference for stories of achievement, success and joy. But boredom beyond the limits of his tolerance plays its part, as his opening exclamation shows.

'Hoo!' quod the Knyght, 'good sire, namoore of this!   (2767)
That ye han seyd is right ynough, ywis,
And muchel moore; for litel hevynesse
Is right ynough to muche folk, I gesse.

I seye for me, it is a greet disese,
Wheras men hath been in greet welthe and ese,
To heeren of hire sodeyn fal, allas!
And the contrarie is joye and greet solas,
As whan a man hath been in povre estaat,
And clymbeth up and wexeth fortunat,
And there abideth in prosperitee.
Swich thyng is gladsom, as it thynketh me,
And of swich thyng were goodly for to telle.'

The Knight's protest is almost as simple-minded as the Monk's definition of tragedy, for it also puts the whole emphasis on the events and none on their presentation. But the Knight's own tale had more to it than this: though the tale ended with the felicity of Palamon and Emilye, it portrayed the tragedy of Arcite and the disruptive power of Fortune more forcefully than anything in the Monk's tale. Thus the Knight's remarks here suggest he never fully appreciated the darker undertones of his own tale (though, of course, Chaucer did). What the Knight has said is an invitation for a happy tale to follow the Monk's attempts, and soon the Nun's Priest accepts the challenge. But the Knight's words also keep in the forefront of the reader's mind the question of literary form, and stress the inadequacy of the Monk's performance.

Some critics have suggested that the 'tragedies' here derive from an early attempt on Chaucer's part to construct such a sequence.[1] Even if this were true, in my opinion he has re-shaped and recast the material to place it in the Canterbury debate. Furthermore, it would be quite in character for Chaucer to mock his own immature efforts, and laugh at his earlier respect for pedantic literary definitions.

The tragedy of Ugolino, as I suggested earlier, seems the one exception in the series, for this tale alone seems to have much of Chaucer's mature quality in its writing. The version derives from Dante. Was Chaucer paying a subtle tribute to 'the master' here by suggesting that even a person as unimaginative as the Monk found himself inspired when he repeated the

[1] E.g. Root, *ibid.* pp. 206–7.

Italian poet's tale? At any rate, though Chaucer's version is the inferior, it is worth comparing in some detail with the original. Doing so also has the advantage of setting some verse of Chaucer's beside poetry excelling in that 'high seriousness' which Matthew Arnold once criticised Chaucer for lacking.[1]

Pathos is the key-note of Chaucer's rendering, as the verse immediately announces:

> Off the Erl Hugelyn of Pyze the langour   (2407)
> Ther may no tonge telle for pitee.

While this pathos never descends into the cloying or senti-mental, still, in order to attain it, Chaucer softens the details provided by Dante, excluding the further reaches of com-passion with the further reaches of horror. Thus Chaucer says explicitly that the prisoners have been kept half-starved, while in the *Inferno* the reader is forced, with apprehension, to deduce this from the children's uneasy sleep. Upon the door of the tower being locked (actually nailed up) Chaucer tells us what Ugolino is thinking, and describes him as weeping for himself.

> And in his herte anon ther fil a thoght   (2427)
> That they for hunger wolde doon hym dyen.
> 'Allas!' quod he, 'allas, that I was wroght!'
> Therwith the teeris fillen from his yen.

In Dante, Ugolino is not credited with mere self-concern, and we are forced to conceive the terrible despair which numbs him as he apprehends what is to be done to them.

> ...I looked into the faces of my sons, without uttering a word.
> I did not weep: so stony grew I with in; they wept; and my little Anselm said: 'Thou lookest so, father, what ails thee?'[2]

Much of Chaucer's pathos is generated through his presenta-tion of the children (as in 'it was greet crueltee / Swiche briddes

---

[1] Matthew Arnold, *Essays in Criticism: Second Series* (Macmillan, 1941), pp. 23–4.
[2] The quotations from *The Divine Comedy* are taken from the Carlyle–Wicksteed translation (Modern Library, 1932).

for to putte in swich a cage!'—ll. 3210–11); here he expands
the child's speech, emphasising the innocence and simplicity.

> 'Fader, why do ye wepe? (2432)
> Whanne wol the gayler bryngen oure potage?
> Is ther no morsel breed that ye do kepe?
> I am so hungry that I may nat slepe.
> Now wolde God that I myghte slepen evere!
> Thanne sholde nat hunger in my wombe crepe;
> Ther is no thyng, save breed, that me were levere.'

Though the passage contains one very fine stroke—the child
feeling hunger moving like some animal in his *womb* (the
associations this word evokes bring an awful irony in)—the
repetition of information and the dwelling on the querulous
pleading of the child for bread tone down the horror, and distract from the pain and desperation the prisoners experience.
While the child's death in Chaucer, when it comes, is touching,
there is too much sweetness and decorum in the description
for the full agony to be comprehended.

> Thus day by day this child bigan to crye, (2439)
> Til in his fadres barm adoun it lay,
> And seyde, 'Farewel, fader, I moot dye!'
> And kiste his fader, and dyde the same day.

Chaucer brings out the love shared between father and sons,
but plays down the extremities of their situation. When the
father, on the death of the youngest child, bites his arms for
woe (the word 'wo' is repeated three times with diminishing
effect) the other children thinking his act is a gesture of
hunger offer themselves sacrificially to him in words which
carry strong sacramental overtones.

> (They) seyde, 'Fader, do nat so, allas! (2449)
> But rather ete the flessh upon us two.
> Oure flessh thou yaf us, take oure flessh us fro,
> And ete ynogh.'

When finally the remaining sons die they also do so peacefully,
in the comfort of their father's lap—'They leyde hem in his
lappe adoun and deyde.'

The greater intensity in Dante's version is partly accounted for by the first person narrative, which makes us imagine the scene as Ugolino suffered it; but more than that, it arises because Dante has grasped more of the total terribleness, and shows it starkly. He has portrayed the love of father and sons, but he also dramatises the bitterness, the helplessness, the anguish and the physical torment. At first the children weep, then with time they pass beyond this relief and their countenances grow like their father's. It is when he sees this he bites both his hands. The children misunderstand his action (it is easier to see why here than in Chaucer) and offer themselves as food. It is an act of desperate misery as much as sacrificial love. Both are futile. The Biblical echoes in the children's speech, and in Gaddo's cry later, have a more unsettling function than in Chaucer, for they call to mind God's (apparent) forsaking of man and of His own Son. There is no decorum in the deaths by starvation. Ugolino is reduced to crawling, almost sub-humanly, over the dead bodies, crazedly refusing to accept that they are dead. Finally it is not the utmost of feeling which kills him but mere famine, as though spiritual torment were ultimately subordinate to physical. (Of course, in the plan of the *Inferno* this is ironically shown not to be so: for 'eternity' Ugolino relives the anguish, his punishment in hell being to experience what callous treachery and man's cruelty to man really mean.)

'When a small ray was sent into the doleful prison, and I discerned in their four faces the aspect of my own,

I bit on both my hands for grief. And they, thinking that I did it from desire of eating, of a sudden rose up,

and said: "Father, it will give us much less pain, if thou wilt eat of us: thou didst put upon us this miserable flesh, and do thou strip it off."

Then I calmed myself, in order not to make them more unhappy; that day and the next we all were mute. Ah, hard earth! why didst thou not open?

When we had come to the fourth day, Gaddo threw himself stretched out at my feet, saying: "My father! why don't you help me?"

There he died; and even as thou seest me, saw I the three fall one by one, between the fifth day and the sixth: whence I betook me,

already blind, to groping over each, and for three days called them, after they were dead; then fasting had more power than grief.'

I have restricted my analysis of Dante's passage to what it shares with Chaucer's version: the dramatic portrayal of human anguish. Even in this limited regard the Dante is immeasurably superior to the Chaucer. But it would be unjust to Dante not to touch upon his profounder purposes in this passage. For eternity, Dante makes us imagine, Ugolino gnaws at the skull of Ruggieri. Christina van Heyningen, writing on this passage, goes to the heart of the matter.

I have chosen this passage because of the horror and savagely exultant cruelty in it. Dante means us to accept these unspeakable punishments as just, and coming from the Christian God of Love. In my opinion he succeeds, and he succeeds only by the way he chooses and organises his details. It is art that makes us feel only what he wants us to feel and nothing else, and that is how we know what he means by Virtue and the Justice of God...Our senses shudder; but Dante does not let them off. The detail is so exact that they can't escape. Dante forces us to feel the full horror of the punishment (of Ruggieri). Then comes the story; and when the story is over, he returns to the punishment...But something has happened to us. When the story is over, we don't mind about the physical torture—we rather welcome it as a relief. For Dante's point is that all this physical horror is weak, it is nothing at all, compared with the moral horror of what Ruggieri has done. This is what he wants us to realise. In the *Inferno* he wants us to understand to the marrow of our bones the evil of evil...The style (of the part depicting the suffering of Ugolino and his children) is almost stony: only a hard style could contain pity and anger so strong. The effect is almost as if no words were being used—as if what is described is happening and 'speaks for itself'...The tortures in the ninth circle of Hell are felt to be as nothing compared with the horror of Ruggieri's sin. Ugolino does not even feel Hell. All he is aware of even here (where Dante feared that the mere passing through might wither up his tongue) is the cruelty of Ruggieri...there is nothing worse than moral evil...The episode is tragic because the beauty and power in it balance the horror. The beauty and power are in Ugolino. He could not so ignore Hell and so hate Ruggieri, Dante has made us realise, were he not capable of feeling, with even greater intensity, love and compassion. Love and compassion could not have been revealed with such power but by evil. The 'tragic joy' we feel is like that of a woman who had been through the last war's three occupations of Poland, and who said, 'I would not have been without the experience'. It comes from having seen the beauty of life put to the severest test that could be imagined, and seen it survive.[1]

Dante's passage belongs to that realm where the skill of craftsmanship is wholly subordinate to an imagination which can completely incorporate the extreme spasms of the human spirit. It is a realm Chaucer does not reach: his version of Ugolino remains 'literary'—skilful, tactful, sensitive, but imprisoned in the decorums of art, eschewing the heights and the depths of human experience.

Of course, *Hugelyn of Pyze* is not Chaucer at his best: indeed, may have been largely intended to draw attention to the poet of Italy whose supremacy Chaucer recognised—'Fro point to point, nat o word wol he faille.' Comparison is unfair. I chose to make it because we now come to one of Chaucer's finest tales, The *Nun's Priest's*, and perhaps by recognising some of Chaucer's limitations here, and by glancing at a work of 'high seriousness', we may the better appreciate the unique achievement of Chaucer at the height of his powers. Naturally there can be no question of comparing the story of the cock and the fox with the visions of Dante: just as it is impossible to compare the perfection of Mozart's Clarinet Quintet with the greatness of Bach's *St Matthew Passion*.

[1] See Christina van Heyningen, *Clarissa, Poetry and Morals* (University of Natal Press, 1963), pp. 222–6.

CHAPTER 17

The Nun's Priest's Tale

'FUL ofte in game a sooth I have herd seye,' the Host has remarked to the Monk: *The Nun's Priest's Tale* is a comedy reverberating with cosmic truth. The superb quality of the *Tale* has frequently been acknowledged.[1] In this tale Chaucer's exploitation of mixed modes of writing is carried to its uttermost, and no other work he wrote is so rich in juxtaposition of styles and rhetorical devices. Medieval rhetoric was more concerned with ornamentation than with the structure of poetic argument: it taught how to 'pad' rather than how to create.[2] Chaucer's genius led him to realise how this rhetoric could be wholly integrated in a work. As I have suggested before, Chaucer employed the mixture of styles in order to reveal the multi-dimensional character of his subject so that we might see in, through, below and beyond. The many styles are held together by the framework of a mock-heroic poem, but the poem's intention goes far beyond the small bounds of parody.

Furthermore, crowded as the poem is, the meaning becomes even greater if we recognise how the *Tale* echoes, renews and raises themes dealt with in the other stories. Certainly the *Tale* burlesques 'tragedye' as the Monk conceived it. Courtly love, marriage and the relation between man and woman, dramatically debated in so many of the tales, are here presented in fuller perspective. Many of the religious and metaphysical problems posed elsewhere are also touched upon: the limitation of human wisdom, the dangers of self-delusion and false doctrine, the significance of dreams, and the controversies over free will

---

[1] See, for example, Kittredge, *Chaucer and his Poetry* (Harvard University Press, 1915); more recently, Speirs, *op. cit.* or T. W. Craik, *The Comic Tales of Chaucer* (Methuen, 1964).

[2] See Paull F. Baum, *Chaucer: A Critical Appreciation* (Duke University Press, 1958), p. 182; also J. M. Manly, 'Chaucer and the Rhetoricians', reprinted in Schoek and Taylor, *op. cit.* I, 268–90.

and necessity. Yet the seriousness of the thought never s.
into solemnity, nor does the fun ever evaporate into frivolit,
Above all, the poem celebrates joy and truth, and extols the
bounty of God. 'Ah, take the game and let the ernest go'—in
The Nun's Priest's Tale the breach is healed: 'ernest' and
'game' become one.

After the Monk declines to tell a hunting story in place of
his painful tragedies with the words, 'I have no lust to pleye',
the Host turns to the Nun's Priest. Hitherto we have had no
description of this pilgrim, and the Host's address provides our
first impression.

> 'Com neer, thou preest, com hyder, thou sir John!   (2810)
> Telle us swich thyng as may oure hertes glade.
> Be blithe, though thou ryde upon a jade.
> What thogh thyn hors be bothe foul and lene?
> If he wol serve thee, rekke nat a bene.
> Looke that thyn herte be murie everemo.'

The Host, of course, is contrasting the Nun's Priest's appearance with the Monk's; and there is a parallel ironic contrast
between their tales. The vigorous man of flesh tells (unfelt)
tales of disaster: his opposite displays a merry heart indeed.
But perhaps the lines have profounder overtones. The image
of the beast that bears man easily becomes the symbol of the
flesh that carries his spirit,[1] and the contrast between 'murie
herte' and the jade 'foul and lene' brings up this symbolic
meaning. Thus we may feel, delicately suggested in these lines,
something of the affirmation Yeats made in *Sailing to Byzan-
tium* when he wrote,

> An aged man is but a paltry thing,
> A tattered coat upon a stick, unless
> Soul clap its hands and sing, and louder sing
> For every tatter in its mortal dress.

Certainly, as I shall try to show, such symbolic meaning is in
keeping with the methods and meaning of the *Tale* itself.

[1] For example, see Shakespeare's sonnet, 'How heavy do I journey on the
way'.

The *Tale* opens soberly with the picture of the poor widow, growing old and living a simple life on her smallholding. Sickness and age are lightly pencilled in, that we may appreciate the health and blessing of her life, and yet remember the course of mortality. The poetry at first relies upon simple statement:

> In pacience ladde a ful symple lyf,   (2826)
> For litel was hir catel and hir rente.
> By housbondrie of swich as God hire sente
> She foond hirself and eek hir doghtren two.

From the sheep having a name we can infer the care and love with which the family keep their few possessions. Soon the tone of the poetry grows more complex:

> Ful sooty was hir bour and eek hir halle,   (2832)
> In which she eet ful many a sklendre meel.
> Of poynaunt sauce hir neded never a deel.
> No deyntee morsel passed thurgh hir throte;
> Hir diete was accordant to hir cote.
> Repleccion ne made hire nevere sik;
> Attemptre diete was al hir phisik,
> And exercise, and hertes suffisaunce.
> The goute lette hire nothyng for to daunce,
> N'apoplexie shente nat hir heed . . .

By means of the references to 'bour' and 'halle', 'gout' and 'apoplexie' the widow is contrasted with the wealthy spendthrift—for mankind has always known the false morality of 'conspicuous consumption'. She escapes the ills of such 'good' living. Thus in the first paragraph of the poem the bedrock principles of life are established: simple content even before the prospect, which none can escape, of sickness and mortality; squander and waste are despised. Not only does this opening establish the moral ground of the poem, it also provides a 'realistic' frame in which the fantasies that follow may take their proper place.

The sheep named Malle prepares us for the cock called Chantecleer. But this cock, in the glory of his being, seems wealthier and more privileged than his mistress. No noble was more self-satisfied. His chief talent, and the near cause of his destruction later, is mentioned immediately.

> His voys was murier than the murie organ   (2851)
> On messe-dayes that in the chirche gon.

(This comparison assumes that worship is a natural and joyous thing.) As the poetry proceeds Chantecleer's pride, and the beauty of his appearance, are both evoked. Most superb of all in the poetry is the energy with which it celebrates the very existence of such a fabulous beast as a cock. Man could no more have imagined a cock than, as D. H. Lawrence says, he could have imagined 'the redness of a red geranium'.[1]

> His coomb was redder than the fyn coral,   (2859)
> And batailled as it were a castel wal;
> His byle was blak, and as the jeet it shoon;
> Lyk asure were his legges and his toon;
> His nayles whitter than the lilye flour,
> And lyk the burned gold was his colour.

Our delight is made up of laughter *and* wonder. The cock has been meticulously observed, and in close-up too: by comparing his comb to a 'castel wal' the poetry makes the cock tower up before us, so that we have, as it were, a diminutive, hen-eyed view of him. We can appreciate how the very magnificence of his being—of the very life of him—abounds with temptation: how easy for such a creature to swell with pride at its own existence. Further, we are made to feel that, while he is a cock, he is also more than a cock: in the glory of his armour he is some knight, some proud chevalier. Such associations having been established, the poetry can easily slip into the humorous and explicit depiction of farmyard affairs in terms of courtly love and chivalric customs. Pertelote is accorded the virtues of a beautiful lady: the comedy illuminates

---

[1] D. H. Lawrence, *The Complete Poems* (Heinemann, 1957), III, 131–2.

both realms, depicting the genteel demeanour hens display and at the same time mocking human modes of behaviour.

> Curteys she was, discreet, and debonaire,　　(2871)
> And compaignable, and bar hyrself so faire,
> Sin thilke day that she was seven nyght oold,
> That trewely she hath the herte in hoold
> Of Chauntecleer, loken in every lith...

Constantly the poetry celebrates the joy of each creature's existence, even while evoking our delight in the fanciful conjoining of disparate realms.

> He loved hire so that wel was hym therwith.　　(2876)
> But swich a joye was it to here hem synge,
> Whan that the bryghte sonne gan to sprynge,
> In sweete accord, 'My lief is faren in londe!'
> For thilke tyme, as I have understonde,
> Beestes and briddes koude speke and synge.

By the time we reach the last two lines we have fully suspended all disbelief in this pristine world.

Similar delight in the wonders of God's creation, with all its unique creatures, is generated by Chauntecleer's description of the beast in his dream: here the account functions like riddle poetry (though the riddle is an easy one) which flakes off the hard shell of custom by its teasing challenge:

> 'I saugh a beest　　(2899)
> Was lyk an hound, and wolde han maad areest
> Upon my body, and wolde han had me deed.
> His colour was bitwixe yelow and reed,
> And tipped was his tayl and bothe his eeris
> With blak, unlyk the remenant of his heeris;
> His snowte smal, with glowynge eyen tweye.
> Yet of his look for feere almoost I deye.'

With this vision the long debate on dreams commences.

Pertelote soon turns out in her speech to be far from 'curteys', 'discreet' or 'debonaire', and addresses her spouse like any hennish housewife. Perhaps many ladies of courtly love were as far from the ideal in their lovers minds as Pertelote. Despite her desire that a husband should have certain 'romantic' acquirements, she has a practical, indeed a grossly literal, mind. For her, dreams only signify bodily disorders. Loudly proclaiming this conviction she sets out to nag, rather than nurse, her husband back to health.

> 'Certes this dreem, which ye han met to-nyght,   (2926)
> Cometh of the greet superfluytee
> Of youre rede colera, pardee,
> Which causeth folk to dreden in hir dremes
> Of arwes, and of fyr with rede lemes,
> Of rede beestes, that they wol hem byte,
> Of contek, and of whelpes, grete and lyte...
>
> 'Lo Catoun, which that was so wys a man,   (2940)
> Seyde he nat thus, "Ne do no fors of dremes?"
> Now sire', quod she, 'whan we flee fro the bemes,
> For Goddes love, as taak som laxatyf.'

Throughout this speech the voices of lady and hen are marvellously mingled, and the timing—as in the sudden conclusion of Cato's wisdom in 'taak som laxatyf'—superbly deft. Yet, through this portrayal of Pertelote's hen-sureness, a larger picture of the folly human reason may commit is beginning to emerge. For one of the attributes of well-handled mock-heroic poetry is that the laughter reaches out in both directions: if a hen seems more absurd for being able to quote Cato, or practise courtly love, the reverse also happens and Cato or courtly love come under humorous scrutiny.

Chauntecleer, in his turn, speaks with all the conceit of masculine superiority: he adopts a courteous tone towards his spouse which scarcely masks his contempt. He knows, or claims to know, greater authorities than she has mentioned. To prove his point about dreams, that they may significantly foretell the future, he illustrates his argument by recounting several stories. These *exempla*, however, are in quite a different key from the rest of *The Nun's Priest's Tale*. The first, particularly, is quite long and is sombre and serious. Are they digressions which are too drawn-out and could they be omitted without loss? Have they an integral function in the whole work?

Their most obvious function can be described by quoting one of the basic mottoes of the theatre: 'Make them laugh, make them weep, make them wait.' An audience demands variety and enjoys suspense. It is well known that comedy is more effective if the laughter is played off against touches of sadness, or even sentimentality, which is why comedians often strive for pathos to salt their humour. Also, as Chaucer well knew, there is a right way of holding up a story, so that the audience are all the more prepared and receptive when the action at last becomes fast and furious. But in addition to these reasons I think there are more important justifications for the inclusion of the *exempla*. Though the general tone of the *Tale* is playful, at times wholly fanciful, the import of the work is quite serious. Indeed, as we gradually come to realise, the whole tale is itself an *exemplum* told by a most skilful preacher who knows how to sweeten his message. But lest he be taken too lightly, his hearers must for a moment or so be enticed into a sombre and more reflective mood. The *exempla* can make them realise that the fall from security to disaster may be more than a joke, and that the world is sinister as well as delightful.

What is true of the Nun's Priest holds even more for the narrator behind him, and speaking through him. For Chaucer, perhaps more than in any other tale, is here endorsing the narration of his pilgrim. *The Nun's Priest's Tale* acquires greater resonance if we recognise in it, and especially in the *exempla*, cross-references to other tales. The accounts of accident, murder and carnage in the *exempla* gain force if they call to mind similar events in other places. Perhaps it may be far-fetched to see, in the detail of the murder of the traveller taking place in 'an oxes stalle', a reference to *The Clerk's Tale*. But the explicit echoes of *The Prioress's Tale* are surely deliberate: the little child who was flung in a pit of excrement finds a parallel in the murdered man being concealed in a dung cart.

The moral derived from the discovery of the corpse too has its origin in *The Prioress's Tale*:

> O blisful God, that art so just and trewe (3050)
> Lo, how that thou biwreyest mordre alway!
> Mordre wol out, that se we day by day.
> Mordre is so wlatsom and abhomynable
> To God, that is so just and resonable,
> That he ne wol nat suffre it heled be,
> Though it abyde a yeer, or two, or thre.

A link with *The Pardoner's Tale* may be felt in the line, 'My gold caused my mordre, sooth to sayn', though the Nun's Priest preaches with quite a different object in view from that of the Pardoner. In the second *exemplum* the reference to shipwreck may recall *The Man of Law's Tale* (perhaps also *The Franklin's Tale* with its terrible rocks inviting shipwrecks). The life of 'Seint Kenelm' may again suggest *The Prioress's Tale*.

Certainly all these references are slight. But they are sufficient I think to colour the *exempla* with feelings carried over from other sections of the *Canterbury Tales*. Similarly, how much weight the reader will give to the reference to Hector will depend on what associations of tragic suffering he brings from his memory of the Grecian story.[1]

> 'Lo heere Andromacha, Ectores wyf, (3141)
> That day that Ector sholde lese his lyf,
> She dremed on the same nyght biforn
> How that the lyf of Ector sholde be lorn,
> If thilke day he wente into bataille.
> She warned hym, but it myghte nat availle;
> He wente for to fighte natheles,
> But he was slayn anon of Achilles.'

This passage, with its reference back to all the classic 'tragedies' of *The Monk's Tale*, further provides the transition

---

[1] Though we should remember that Homer's *Iliad* was unknown to the medieval West except through the late condensation, the 'Ilias Latina'. See J. S. P. Tatlock, *The Mind and Art of Chaucer* (Syracuse University Press, 1950), pp. 36-7.

across again into parody and the mock-heroic style. The dark possibilities are left behind, the tension relaxes, and full comedy returns.

'Shortly I seye, as for conclusioun, (3151)
That I shal han of this avisioun
Adversitee; and I seye forthermoor,
That I ne telle of laxatyves no stoor,
For they been venymous, I woot it weel;
I hem diffye, I love hem never a deel!'

Suddenly we realise that all Chauntecleer's arguments about dreams amount to no more than a rationalisation of his simple repugnance towards laxatives! The comedy takes another amusing twist when Chauntecleer, after all he has said about the importance of dreams, explains why he disregards the warning of his own dream:

'Ye been so scarlet reed aboute youre yen. (3161)
It maketh al my drede for to dyen;
For al so siker as *In principio*,
Mulier est hominis confusio,—
Madame, the sentence of this Latyn is,
"Womman is mannes joye and al his blis."
For whan I feel a-nyght your softe syde,
Al be it that I may nat on yow ryde,
For that oure perche is maad so narwe, allas!
I am so ful of joye and of solas,
That I diffye bothe sweven and dreem.'

This is the world of *The Wife of Bath's Prologue* with its skirmishing male and female (only made more ridiculous by the reminder that it takes place in the hen-house): but here the husband gets the better of his wife by concealing his contempt behind learning and flattery. He justifies what he was going to do anyway with as ready a tongue as May of *The Merchant's Tale* possessed. Upon the conclusion of this speech Chauntecleer flies down from his perch, struts about the yard, pecks corn, chucks to the hens, 'feathers and treads' Pertelote, and completely forgets the foreboding of his dream. The tale pauses here for a moment, on Chauntecleer smug and secure:

> Thus roial, as a prince is in his halle,   (3184)
> Leve I this Chauntecleer in his pasture.

The lines that begin the next forward movement of the story have great resonance and beauty:

> Whan that the month in which the world bigan,   (3187)
> That highte March, whan God first maked man,
> Was compleet, and passed were also,
> Syn March bigan, thritty dayes and two,
> Bifel that Chauntecleer in al his pryde...

T. W. Craik says of them: 'Chaucer's way of reckoning the fatal date from "the month in which the world bigan / That highte March, whan God first maked man" naturally puzzles modern readers, who may be tempted to find hidden meanings. But Chaucer is simply counting from the beginning of the medieval calendar, in which March was the first month.'[1] Poetry, however, means more than any literal paraphrase; and when lines are memorable we suspect that they are crammed with meaning. Thus, for example, Cleopatra's lines, 'Give me some music,—music, moody food, / Of us that trade in love', is not simply a stage-direction: it is a marvellous revelation of her whole being at that moment. Similarly with Chaucer's poetry here: we are made to feel that the event described took place, not merely on a certain calendar day, but near the beginning of time when the world still possessed much of its pristine wonder, when indeed 'Beestes and briddes koude speke and synge'—a time when the major events of existence, the Creation, the Temptation and the Fall, seem as fresh as childhood impressions. In this world of primal vision, the careful accuracy of the poetry emphasises, on a certain day Chauntecleer walked in his garden.

---

[1] Craik, *op. cit.* p. 82.

But T. W. Craik is quite right to murmur against too moralistic or too allegorical interpretations of *The Nun's Priest's Tale*. To build an elaborate philosophical superstructure upon the comedy would crush it; just as the opposite error of seeing nothing more in the poem than trivial but superbly timed humour would ignore the poetic richness. *The Nun's Priest's Tale* is undoubtedly one of Chaucer's finest achievements: but how to demonstrate this without misrepresentation? Perhaps something of the poem's achievement may be sketched by adopting an oblique approach. Let us then briefly digress to consider what qualities often appear in poetry of high order.

Though they did not use his terminology, long before Freud poets and writers on poetry discussed the importance of the two principles he called the reality principle and the pleasure principle.[1] Indeed, so important has been the emphasis on these principles, whether the writer sets up one in opposition to the other, or whether like Keats in his phrase 'Beauty is truth, truth beauty' he affirms their identity, that we must believe they are fundamental indeed. Some literature seems to belong fairly purely to one or the other of the two principles. The pleasure principle expresses itself in many ways. At its lowest reaches are whimsy, or fancy, or simply sensuous indulgence (perhaps much of Keats's early poetry is an example of the last). At its highest poetry belonging to the pleasure principle celebrates 'life's own self-delight'[2]—the joyous dance of sense, imagination and intellect linked together. On the other hand, the reality principle manifests itself in works which are mainly didactic or in which the harsher truths are faced: among these I would put Dr Johnson's *Rasselas* or some of the plays of Ibsen. Naturally this division is one of degree: the starkest truth in art must be expressed with some pleasure

---

[1] For a very interesting discussion of the importance of Freud's work to literary criticism see Lionel Trilling, *Freud and the Crisis of Our Culture*, Beacon Press (Boston, 1955).

[2] W. B. Yeats, 'Meditations in Time of Civil War', *The Collected Poems* (Macmillan, 1950), p. 225.

or we could not bear to witness it; the most frivolous playing implies some recognition of things as they are, if only in the writer's struggle with language which will communicate.

But in the greatest works of art we often feel that Keats is right, and that in the fusion and reconciliation of pleasure and 'reality' we cannot separate truth from beauty. Frequently the two principles seem opposed, and it is only by a powerful act of integration the writer achieves unity. To clarify what I have said, and to demonstrate it more specifically, I should like to glance briefly at two poems which take this victory as their very subject.

The first is *Lapis Lazuli* by W. B. Yeats. Here Yeats shows how the human spirit must arise above the joy-emptied anxiety about the world—the neurotic obsession with daily reality or the desperate concern over international crises—which make the gaiety of 'palette and fiddle-bow' seem irresponsible. Far from being irresponsible, the truest art expresses 'tragic joy' which is the very source and product of truth and creation. Ostensibly the poem justifies all joy as part of the process by which man creates and builds what is constantly being destroyed, but that joy which the poem rates most highly, and which the poetry itself exemplifies, is the joy which still arises after the protagonist has faced the worst disaster and dread can do. The 'hysterical women' who demand that something 'drastic' be done express their own surrender to helplessness and self-pity: they cannot face what they fear. Opposed to them stand the great tragic figures, images of man's ability to triumph even in disaster—

> ...Hamlet and Lear are gay;
> Gaiety transfiguring all that dread.

Briefly yet powerfully the third section of the poem conjures up civilisations that have been destroyed: yet their achievements are not utterly lost, for the same joy that created them can do it again—just as Yeats's own imagination can reproduce in poetry the marvellous handiwork of Callimachus. The closing section of the poem describes a small Chinese carving which, in its 'Every accidental crack or dent', witnesses to the disasters and tribulations of centuries. The wise men carved here, like the object itself, have gazed on 'all that tragic scene', yet they still assert indestructible joy:

> Their eyes mid many wrinkles, their eyes,
> Their ancient, glittering eyes, are gay.

The second poem also takes the image of an old man as a symbol of joy achieved through harsh adversity: Wordsworth's *Resolution and Independence*. The poem begins with a lovely invocation of the pleasures of a common day:

> There was a roaring in the wind all night;
> The rain came heavily and fell in floods;
> But now the sun is rising calm and bright;
> The birds are singing in the distant woods;
> Over his own sweet voice the Stock-dove broods;
> The Jay makes answer as the Magpie chatters;
> And all the air is filled with pleasant noise of waters.
>
> All things that love the sun are out of doors;
> The sky rejoices in the morning's birth;
> The grass is bright with rain-drops;—on the moors
> The hare is running races in her mirth;
> And with her feet she from the plashy earth
> Raises a mist; that, glittering in the sun,
> Runs with her all the way, wherever she doth run.

But a sudden change of mood, which mirrors the insecurity man is subject to, and is partly a consequence of man's ability to contemplate the future and remind himself of harsh possibilities, obliterates this pleasure.

> But, as it sometimes chanceth, from the might
> Of joy in minds that can no further go,
> As high as we have mounted in delight
> In our dejection do we sink as low;
> To me that morning did it happen so;
> And fears and fancies thick upon me came;
> Dim sadness—and blind thoughts, I knew not, nor could name.

The traveller in the poem broods upon 'Solitude, pain of heart, distress, and poverty', upon his own selfish and irresponsible mode of existence, and on poets whose lives began 'in gladness' but ended in dejection and insanity. From the despair of these contemplations he is rescued by the advent of the old man. The stranger seems the very product of all that hardship, age, toil, uncertainty and suffering can do to a man. Life, and any pleasure it can hold, must long since have shrunk and withered. But this is not so, as the poetry forcibly makes us apprehend. In a precarious world, following an uncertain occupation, the Leech-gatherer abides, undefeated and undejected. Further, he possesses an overwhelming, an awe-inspiring, mysterious vitality accompanied by a cheer and vigour of mind which manifest his joy in his continuing existence.

Both poems, for all the many differences, admonish us to face reality in its harshest aspect and still be aware of the power in ourselves to rejoice. And here too we may find their kinship with *The Nun's Priest's Tale*. Following, as it does, *The Monk's Tale* with its morbid accumulation of disasters, it sets out to affirm joy: not by denying the harshness of reality, but by mocking morbidity that we may the better know truth as well as pleasure. There are some lines even which are remarkably similar in tone to Wordsworth's: for example, with the stanzas from *Resolution and Independence* quoted above compare a passage such as this:

> 'Herkneth thise blisful briddes how they synge,   (3201)
> And se the fresshe floures how they sprynge;
> Ful is myn herte of revel and solas!'
> But sodeynly hym fil a sorweful cas,
> For evere the latter ende of joye is wo.
> God woot that worldly joye is soone ago...

Yet the Nun's Priest is talking of 'worldly joye'. His tale while dramatising the destruction of joy, whether through the fall of a cock or through the murder of an innocent traveller, sets all within a Christian framework. The joy of this world often is no more than false vanity which overrates itself, as Chauntecleer prides himself on his voice, his appearance, his learning, his virility. Such joy must inevitably know defeat, unless it can be converted into a better joy. The beauty of this world, of the creatures in it, must be understood to mirror only as in a glass darkly the greater beauty of the Creation and God's abiding purpose, and each creature must humbly recognise his own littleness. So Chauntecleer, like any cock, is a miracle of nature—but he is also only a cock trying to behave like Sir Lancelot. The dialectic whereby the principles of pleasure and reality are transcended in a new unity in the *Tale* is patterned on Christian beliefs.

The *Nun's Priest's Tale* does not set out its argument in philosophical form. Indeed, even by associating it with the terminology Freud employed I am dangerously near making overexplicit what is naturally implicit in the poetry. Abstract notions may hinder more than they help, confusing the mind which can know truth more easily through the subtleties of art. Philosophy—which attempts to peg and systematise experience in intellectual terms—is also a human vanity which may, like the anxiety of the hysterical women in Yeats's poem, stifle the most vital responses. Indeed the *Tale* itself warns us of the treacherous paths of philosophic pursuings. The Nun's Priest says:

> But what that God forwoot moot nedes bee,　　(3234)
> After the opinioun of certein clerkis.
> Witness on hym that any parfit clerk is,
> That in scole is greet altercacioun
> In this mateere, and greet disputisoun,
> And hath been of an hundred thousand men.
> But I ne kan nat bulte it to the bren,
> As kan the hooly doctour Augustyn,
> Or Boece, or the Bisshop Bradwardyn,
> Wheither that Goddes worthy forwityng
> Streyneth me nedely for to doon a thyng,—
> 'Nedely' clepe I symple necessitee;
> Or elles, if free choys be graunted me
> To do that same thyng, or do it noght,

> Though God forwoot it er that I was wrought;
> Or if his wityng streyneth never a deel
> But by necessitee condicioneel.
> I wol nat han to do of swich mateere;
> My tale is of a cok, as ye may heere...

The speaker himself is humble: he has struggled to comprehend Augustine and Boethius and Thomas Bradwardine (as we know Chaucer did), but he falls back on the simple truth he knows. The humility is not incompatible with an irony which suggests that the wisest know no more than farmyard truths could tell, and that much philosophy is as vain as the strutting of a cock. In simple things, in a fable which will delight a child, there may be more wisdom than in the most erudite arguments. So put aside philosophy, and see things with the innocent and open eye of childhood. For one of the prime aims of the *Tale* is to cast out vanity by making apparent, for all to see, the cockiness of mankind.

Pride and 'overanxious care'[1] are equally forms of vanity: both overrate trivial things at the expense of abiding truths. Chauntecleer's strutting and Pertelote's tongue-wagging comically portray the folly of self-centredness. But while through them the *Tale* unmasks mankind's false pretensions, it does so by making us enjoy the facts of life. A cock *is* a marvellous creature, his arrogance as enjoyable as the red of his comb—provided we do not take it too seriously. The greater the *Tale's* flights of fancy, the greater the human achievements brought in by the burlesque style, the more the mockery deflates it all and ties us to simple reality. 'My tale is of a cok, as ye may heere...' We are all like cocks or hens, and need to see ourselves truly.

Nothing escapes the comedy of the *Tale*: even the narrator himself becomes an object of it.

> Wommannes conseil broghte us first to wo,   (3257)
> And made Adam from Paradys to go,
> Ther as he was ful myrie and wel at ese.

---

[1] See Wordsworth, 'Mutability' in *Poetical Works* (Oxford University Press, 1936), p. 353.

But for I noot to whom it myght displese,
If I conseil of wommen wolde blame,
Passe over, for I seyde it in my game.
Rede auctours, where they trete of swich mateere,
And what they seyn of wommen ye may heere.
Thise been the cokkes wordes, and nat myne;
I kan noon harm of no womman divyne.

Did the Nun's Priest really say the first words only in joke?
The hasty, and untrue, explanation that they are the cock's
words suggest not. For a moment the Nun's Priest fell into
the moralising phraseology of a sermon—he is a preacher after
all, and perhaps like many other clerics inclined to be a misogy-
nist—till the firm reaction of the Wife of Bath or the milder
glance of the Prioress whom he serves taught him caution, and
he began to make excuses for what he had said. His reference to
'auctors' shows that even he can be misled by the vanity of
relying on written authorities.

All the elements of the *Tale* are brought together in the
climax. The entry of the fox is preceded by a brief description
of the complacent joy of the birds.

> Faire in the soond, to bathe hire myrily,   (3267)
> Lith Pertelote, and alle hire sustres by,
> Agayn the sonne, and Chauntecleer so free
> Soong murier than the mermayde in the see;
> For Phisiologus seith sikerly
> How that they syngen wel and myrily.

The comparison of Chauntecleer's song to that of the mer-
maids refers to the Sirens whose song, in the medieval Latin
bestiary, symbolises deceitful worldly pleasures, and is generally renowned for the sweet temptation that lured men to
their doom. Its aptness here, on the brink of Chauntecleer's
letting his own voice bring about his capture, is obvious. But
more subtle is the way the couplet referring to Physiologus,
with its mock pedantic tone, satirises learned men who see only
the praise made of the Sirens' song and ignore the moral
which warns of its danger.

When Chauntecleer sees the fox he starts up in fear. The natural and intuitive responses with which God has gifted all his creatures is truer than the rationalisations their own intelligence produce.

> (He) cride anon, 'Cok! cok!' and up he sterte (3277)
> As man that was affrayed in his herte.
> For natureelly a beest desireth flee
> Fro his contrarie, if he may it see,
> Though he never erst hadde seyn it with his ye.

The flattery of the fox is nicely exaggerated so that the folly of Chauntecleer may be all the more comic: the references to *devil* and *angel* are part of the burlesque, but they also enlarge our notion of pride by bringing in the pattern of Lucifer's downfall.

> 'Now, certes, I were worse than a feend, (3286)
> If I to yow wolde harm or vileynye!
> I am nat come youre conseil for t'espye,
> But trewely, the cause of my comynge
> Was oonly for to herkne how that ye synge.
> For trewely, ye have as myrie a stevene
> As any aungel hath that is in hevene.'

When the fox comes to describe the singing of Chauntecleer's father, the poetry captures all the concentration and energy a cock puts into his crowing: and further, through this, portrays the very essence of forgetful single-mindedness in any activity.

> 'He wolde so peyne hym that with bothe his yen (3305)
> He moste wynke, so loude he wolde cryen,
> And stonden on his tiptoon therwithal,
> And strecche forth his nekke long and smal.
> And eek he was of swich discrecioun
> That ther nas no man in no regioun
> That hym in song or wisedom myghte passe.'

(These lines may remind us of the Pardoner who also stretched forth his neck like a bird when he put himself heart and soul into preaching for gain: among the Pilgrims he undid himself by being carried away by his own power of speech.) The crowning irony, however, in the fox's address is that he should win Chauntecleer round by praising 'wisedom and discrecioun': this irony also connects up with the criticism earlier in the poem of the vanity of human wisdom with its theories about free will and determinism, and about the nature of dreams.

To some extent I suspect this section of the tale can be read as the Nun's Priest's attack on false preachers such as the Pardoner, the Friar and perhaps even the Monk. Certainly the Nun's Priest falls once more into the hortatory note of a sermon.

> Allas! ye lordes, many a fals flatour   (3325)
> Is in youre courtes, and many a losengeour,
> That plesen yow wel moore, by my feith,
> Than he that soothfastnesse unto yow seith.

The remarkable thing is how the Nun's Priest's own sermonising 'soothfastnesse' succeeds in being at the same time intensely pleasurable. The brief didactic comments interspersed like this dramatically hold the action up for a moment, increasing our excitement and expectation. The fox's seizing Chauntecleer while his eyes are closed in song, and bearing him away, is immediately followed by a long series of rhetorical exclamations.

> O destinee, that mayst nat been eschewed!   (3338)
> Allas, that Chauntecleer fleigh fro the bemes!
> Allas, his wyf ne roghte nat of dremes!
> And on a Friday fil al this meschaunce.
> O Venus, that art goddesse of plesaunce,
> Syn that thy servant was this Chauntecleer,
> And in thy servyce dide al his poweer,
> Moore for delit than world to multiplye,
> Why woldestow suffre hym on thy day to dye?

In these and the following lines a multitude of targets are being sniped at. The instructions of medieval treatises on rhetoric are burlesqued to show the artificiality of their practice; again the poetry is satirising the unreality of human learning. The references to destiny and the gods call to mind the mention of the deities in *The Knight's Tale*,[1] and mock man for ascribing to the intervention of the gods the consequences of his own foolishness. The poetry even briefly side-swipes the morality of the Wife of Bath who also serves Venus 'moore for delit than world to multiplye'.

But as the mock-heroic tone grows in preposterousness, the images become wider and more serious in their reference to human carnage.

> But sovereynly dame Pertelote shrighte, (3362)
> Ful louder than dide Hasdrubales wyf,
> Whan that hir housbonde hadde lost his lyf,
> And that the Romayns hadde brend Cartage.
> She was so ful of torment and of rage
> That wilfully into the fyr she sterte,
> And brende hirselven with a stedefast herte.
>   O woful hennes, right so criden ye,
> As, whan that Nero brende the citee
> Of Rome, cryden senatoures wyves
> For that hir husbondes losten alle hir lyves,—
> Withouten gilt this Nero hath hem slayn.

The comparisons certainly make the hens' outcry all the funnier. But this is done without making the renowned disasters of history themselves seem preposterous and merely hysterical expressions of human anguish. The poetry dwells just sufficiently on Hasdrubal's wife for her sacrifice to be felt as an act of heroic courage. Yet such a sombre touch does not halt the exuberance of the passage: rather, we feel, here is high comedy which celebrates the pleasure and variety of life, and can in its joyful exultation incorporate even pain and suffering as occasions for laughter and blessing. Rejoicing goes hand in hand with clearsightedness.

The full climax of the poem comes in a wonderful outbreak of energy with the account of the farmyard uproar. The poetry

[1] Even Craik, who is bent on a very literal interpretation keeping close to the narrative techniques of *The Nun's Priest's Tale*, recognises the parallel: 'The gods, it seems, are as involved in Chauntecleer's destiny as they are in the fates of Palamon and Arcite' (*op. ci* . p. 85).

continues to leap backwards and forwards between specific and actual farmyard incidents, and events of greater dimension.

> This sely wydwe and eek hir doghtres two   (3375)
> Herden thise hennes crie and maken wo,
> And out at dores stirten they anon,
> And syen the fox toward the grove gon,
> And bar upon his bak the cok away,
> And cryden, 'Out! harrow! and weylaway!
> Ha! ha! the fox!' and after hym they ran,
> And eek with staves many another man.
> Ran Colle oure dogge, and Talbot, and Gerland,
> And Malkyn, with a distaf in hir hand;
> Ran cow and calf, and eek the verray hogges,
> So fered for the berkyng of the dogges
> And shoutyng of the men and wommen eeke,
> They ronne so hem thoughte hir herte breeke.
> They yolleden as feendes doon in helle;
> The dokes cryden as men wolde hem quelle;
> The gees for feere flowen over the trees;
> Out of the hyve cam the swarm of bees.
> So hydous was the noyse, a, *benedicitee!*
> Certes, he Jakke Straw and his meynee
> Ne made nevere shoutes half so shrille
> Whan that they wolden any Flemyng kille,
> As thilkke day was maad upon the fox.
> Of bras they broghten bemes, and of box,
> Of horn, of boon, in whiche they blewe and powped,
> And therwithal they skriked and they howped.
> It semed as that hevene sholde falle.

The poetry makes us feel that we ourselves are present at the uproar ('Ran Colle *oure* dogge'), and the sound of the last lines particularly renders the din and excitement of the participants. Yet for Chaucer's contemporaries the attempted insurrection of the Peasant's Revolt of 1381 must still have been raw in memory. Many of those involved must have felt that indeed all order was being confounded, and that 'hevene sholde falle'. Worry about security and fear of disaster must have oppressed many, just as today riot and rumours of riot (particularly in Africa) blight the hopes of men. Yet, reading this passage, accumulated tension or vestiges of anxiety are blown away by the gusto of the poetry. All the fierce anguish and chaos of human experience, set against the unconquerable order of the heavens, can no more disturb the balance of existence than can a farmyard scare. By making us see not only human pride but also human dread and hysteria in this story of a cock, the poetry temporarily exorcises our sub-merged fears, gaily establishing perspective and sanity.

The final twist of the story, embodying the poem's other major theme, is Chauntecleer's escape from the fox by tricking him in turn with flattery. Even the tempter himself is vain and easily outwitted. Chauntecleer's rejection of the fox's bland-ishments and the fox's reply express the counter lesson of the tale—truth is attained by the humility of self-awareness.

> 'Thou shalt namoore, thurgh they flaterye,   (3429)
> Do me to synge and wynke with myn ye;
> For he that wynketh whan he sholde see,
> Al wilfully, God lat him nevere thee!'

Or, as *The Canon's Yeoman's Tale*, which shares with this the observation that much human wisdom is mere vanity, puts the moral:

> He that semeth the wiseste, by Jhesus   (967)
> Is moost fool, whan it cometh to the preef.

The comedy of *The Nun's Priest's Tale*, by bringing the cock's pride and complacency to the test, has shown the foolishness of human conceit, and restored through mirth the joy of self-knowledge. The final prayer of the poem suggests that in this *exemplum*, for that is what the most captivating of all preachers has given us, there is a final lesson which we might apply to our own improvement—though with the equivocal way the poetry states it, clearly we shall have to find for ourselves what is fruit, what is chaff.

> But ye that holden this tale a folye,   (3438)
> As of a fox, or of a cok and hen,
> Taketh the moralite, goode men.

For seint Paul seith that al that writen is,
To oure doctrine it is ywrite, ywis;
Taketh the fruyt, and lat the chaf be stille.
Now, goode God, if that it be thy wille,
As seith my lord, so make us alle goode men,
And brynge us to his heighe blisse! Amen.

When the story is completed the Host expresses his delight, and begins to chaff the Nun's Priest in much the same way as he had the Monk—for the Nun's Priest, despite his appearance, has shown himself to be virile indeed. This is a humorous reversal of the joke made about the Monk's probable venery. The likening of the Nun's Priest to a bird also humorously turns the point of the tale on its narrator. But perhaps in these lines we may detect a similar symbolic undercurrent. Just as in the *Prologue to the Nun's Priest's Tale* we felt in the portrayal of the Nun's Priest astride an old jade an image of the spirit riding the worn body, perhaps now in the piercing sharpness of the sparrow-hawk's eyes we detect similar poetic intention. Something at any rate of the tale's clearsightedness, confident vigour and noble wisdom seem reflected in the new portrait of the Nun's Priest:

'See, whiche braunes hath this gentil preest,   (3455)
So gret a nekke, and swich a large breest!
He loketh as a sperhauk with his yen;
Him nedeth nat his colour for to dyen
With brasile, ne with greyn of Portyngale.
Now, sire, faire falle yow for youre tale!'

CHAPTER 18

The Second Nun's Tale

It is generally supposed that *The Second Nun's Prologue and Tale* were composed earlier, and were incorporated into the *Canterbury Tales* without revision. The reference to the narrator as an 'unworthy sone of Eve' (l. 62), and the later line 'Yet preye I yow that reden that I write' seem inappropriate to the situation of a nun speaking to fellow-pilgrims.[1] Robinson refer to the *Tale's* 'immaturity of style' when discussing the date of its composition.[2] Scholars tend to assume that Chaucer's use of stanzas and a certain formality of style are certain evidence of an earlier period of writing, and that once he had begun to write freely within the couplet form he could not employ his earlier manner. Such a line of reasoning is clearly fallacious: many good writers are capable of changing their styles, and for certain effects may revert to an earlier style they had once used. A poet as deliberate and self-aware in the employment of styles as Chaucer everywhere shows himself to be could certainly slip from one to another. *The Nun's Priest's Tale*, for example, is accepted as one of Chaucer's maturest works, and correctly so, yet it contains rhetorical devices to an extent more typical of his early poems and unknown in his later ones. Arguments about date of composition must be approached with scepticism. The important question is not when was this or that tale written, but how did Chaucer intend to fit it into the *Canter-*

---

[1] Actually there is no need to assume that only a man could refer to himself as a 'sone of Eve'. W. B. Gardner, in 'Chaucer's "Unworthy Sone of Eve"' (University of Texas *Studies in English*, XXVI, 77–83), shows that Chaucer was merely using a word-pattern from the *Salve Regina* which he knew every Religious actually used every day of her life in reciting the Divine Office: 'Hail, quene, modir of merci, oure liyf, oure setnesse & oure hope, hail! to thee we crien, exciled sones of eue.' Hence the phrase is quite appropriate for the second Nun.

[2] Robinson, *op. cit.* p. 862.

bury Tales? Is a tale merely stuck in, or is there some principle of organic unity at work?

Much of the drama of the *Canterbury Tales* is achieved by conflict and contrast between speakers so that one pilgrim often seems to debate against another in the story he tells. The Miller opposes the Knight, the Reeve the Miller, the Clerk the Wife of Bath, the Merchant the Clerk, and so on. *The Second Nun's Tale* and *The Canon's Yeoman's Tale* are similarly bound together—but with one difference that gives a new twist to the debate: the speakers themselves are unaware of the contrast and are not consciously in conflict. The Nun cannot foresee the arrival of the Canon's Yeoman, and he is unaware of the tale that was told just before he arrived. The subject which links the two tales, and provides the grounds for contrast, is that of *industry*. The Nun, picking up one of the proverbs of *Melibeus*, says that the vice of idleness can only be cured by its contrary—

> That is to seyn, by leveful bisynesse,   (5)
> Wel oghten we to doon al oure entente,
> Lest that the feend thurgh ydelnesse us hente.

Ironically the confession of the Canon's Yeoman will show that it is precisely by misplaced industry that men can fall into foul pursuits and a hellish state of being. The Second Nun's notion of industry is, of course, quite different from that exemplified by the alchemists: for her it is employment in revealing, amid the dross of this world, the golden truth of the eternal world; for deluded men like the Canon and his Yeoman it is the futile attempt to transmute dross into gold, one base form of matter into another falsely evaluated by the world.

The Second Nun has devoted her time to translating the legend of Saint Cecilia—whose life and martyrdom exemplify those qualities the Nun herself can only faintly copy by her vows of chastity, her hours of devotion, her industry at translating the legend. Hence the appropriateness of the suggestion that her tale is unlike those of the other pilgrims: theirs can be spontaneously spoken, hers must reflect devoted hours of preparation. It is easy to suppose that even on a pilgrimage she would carry her manuscript with her, and deliver her story as she had written it down. The Second Nun's telling of her story is a form of unworldly activity, and this seems to be emphasised by the tale's carefully wrought style.

The style is remote and unworldly, elevated by verbal paradoxes and intellectual incantation. It belongs to a tradition of devotional poetry—psalms and hymns, and the writings of mystics. Above all it is indebted to the rarefied structures of Dante's *Paradiso*.

> Thow Mayde and Mooder, doghter of thy Sone, (36)
> Thow welle of mercy, synful soules cure,
> In whom that God for bountee chees to wone,
> Thow humble, and heigh over every creature,
> Thow nobledest so ferforth oure nature,
> That no desdeyn the Makere hadde of kynde
> His Sone in blood and flessh to clothe and wynde.

I can see nothing 'immature' in verse like this. While it cannot perhaps match the elegant elation of the passage of Dante on which it is based (*figlia del tuo Figlio*),[1] it has a fine poetic organisation of its own. The way in which the alliteration and movement knit or contrast key words is remarkable. For example, how the *d* sound binds the attributes of Mary ('May*d*e and Moo*d*er, *d*oghter of thy Sone') and contrasts her with the softer and stronger word 'Sone'; in the next line the mercy with which she graces mankind springs forth in the open and easy movement of 'Thow welle of mercy', then visits and pauses on each troubled being in the slower pace of '*s*ynful *s*oules cure', and the *s* alliteration here harks back to the forceful 'Sone' of the previous line, reminding us that the sacrifice which is the source of all grace belongs to Christ. Or again in the second last line of the stanza how the alliteration binding '*d*es*d*eyn' and 'ha*dd*e' is contradicted by the unifying of God with man by the *k* alliteration of 'Makere' and 'kynde'. Or how in the last line the phrase 'clothe and wynde' suggests the care of God wrapping his Son in blood and flesh, while at

[1] See St Bernard's prayer at the beginning of Canto XXXIII of Dante's *Paradiso*.

the same time emphasising the temporal and mortal nature of the human body (clothes can be discarded: 'wynde' brings in the association of winding sheets as well as swaddling garments).

The effect of techniques such as this is to transform the nature of language: words and phrases acquire a mystical significance over and above their literal denotation. The world of ordinary meanings splits apart like a husk to reveal the realm of Divine truths. The extended interpretation of the meaning of Saint Cecilia's name, which follows the *Invocacio ad Mariam,* carries even further the notion of language being magical in nature, and filled with analogues of transcendental things.

> First wolde I yow the name of Seint Cecilie (85)
> Expowne, as men may in hir storie see.
> It is to seye in Englissh 'hevenes lilie,'
> For pure chaastnesse of virginitee;
> Or, for she whitnesse hadde of honestee,
> And grene of conscience, and of good fame
> The soote savour, 'lilie' was hir name.
>
> Or Cecilie is to seye 'the wey to blynde,'
> For she ensample was by good techynge;
> Or elles Cecile, as I writen fynde,
> Is joyned, by a manere conjoynynge
> Of 'hevene' and 'Lia'; and heere, in figurynge,
> The 'hevene' is set for thoght of hoolynesse,
> And 'Lia' for hire lastynge bisyness...

We are led to accept that the noise and gabble of speech conceal a pattern of significance which can be elucidated by proper meditation. Hidden in the wastes of the contingent can be sought and found the eternal which gives all meaning. In this way the opening sections of the poem prepare us for the legend that is to follow which in theme and action portrays the incarnation of the divine in the world of flux. The blindness of mankind, the venial and venal follies he is sunk in (displayed by the pride of Chantecleer or the obsession of the alchemists in *The Canon's Yeoman's Tale,* and particularly by the arrogance of Almachius in this tale) are set off against the light-filled and light-revealing qualities of the martyr. The poem's style mirrors its intention.

The difference between *appearance* and *being* is established almost immediately in the way Cecilia is presented.

> Under hir robe of gold, that sat ful faire,   (132)
> Hadde next hire flessh yclad hire in an haire.
>
> And whil the organs maden melodie,
> To God allone in herte thus sang she . . .

The importance of 'sang' here is that it emphasises that Cecilia's asceticism is not morbid self-laceration, but a joyful abnegation of the false pleasures of this world—not a losing, but a winning. Similarly her desire to preserve her chastity is not contrary to the meaning of marriage: her chastity recreates marriage so that husband and wife achieve a love which fulfils both partners, a love which is also paradoxically more fruitful. Pope Urban's words to Valerian describe the spiritual significance of her action.

> The teeris from his eyen leet he falle.   (190)
> 'Almyghty Lord, O Jhesu Crist', quod he,
> 'Sower of chaast conseil, hierde of us alle,
> The fruyt of thilke seed of chastitee
> That thou hast sowe in Cecile, taak to thee!
> Lo, lyk a bisy bee, withouten gile,
> Thee serveth ay thyn owene thral Cecile.'

I suppose literally the last line means that Cecilia serves her Lord all the time, but because of the inverted sentence structure the line also suggests that God ('Sower of chaast conseil, hierde of us alle') also has all the time looked after his own thrall. Her virtuous industry then images God's. And the 'fruitfulness' of her chaste love manifests itself in the many conversions she wins.

Shortly after Valerian has been converted an angel miraculously appears before him. I suggested in the chapter on *The Man of Law's Tale* that in that story the miracles seemed a kind of wishful thinking, an easy answer to the problem of unmerited suffering and disaster in life. In *The Prioress's Tale*, on the other hand the miracle became acceptable because through it the Prioress gave expression to her genuine and child-like (in the best sense) religious compassion. Here the miraculous appearance of the angel is not a trick to satisfy credulous readers ('Give us a sign, o Lord'), but is another symbol used to embody the poem's theme—the existence of a divine realm behind the world of mere appearance. In particular, the angel is present to bestow the key image of the poem: the invisible coronets of roses and lilies. The actual appearance of the angel is passed over almost matter-of-factly, and the casual tone gives greater credence to and emphasises more the wonder of his gift.

> Valerian gooth hoom and fynt Cecilie   (218)
> Withinne his chambre with an angel stonde.
> This angel hadde of roses and of lilie
> Corones two, the which he bar in honde;
> And first to Cecile, as I understonde,
> He yaf that oon, and after gan he take
> That oother to Valerian, hir make.
>
> 'With body clene and with unwemmed thoght
> Keepeth ay wel thise corones', quod he;
> 'Fro paradys to yow have I hem broght,
> Ne nevere mo ne shal they roten bee,
> Ne lese hir soote savour, trusteth me;
> Ne nevere wight shal seen hem with his ye,
> But he be chaast and hate vileynye.'

They are the rewards whose existence the 'world-besotted' can never know. A few stanzas later, by using the common experience of smelling hidden flowers and being overwhelmed by their absent but pervading presence, the poetry enacts the deeply personal sense of being on the threshold of wonderful discovery. When Valerian's brother arrives he says,

> 'I wondre, this tyme of the year,   (246)
> Whennes that soote savour cometh so
> Of rose and lilies that I smelle heer.

For though I hadde hem in myne handes two,
The savour myghte in me no depper go.
The sweete smel that in my herte I fynde
Hath chaunged me al in another kynde.'

The bloom of flowers in the wrong season of the year signifies
the contrast between the eternal and the passing; just as the
line 'The savour myghte in me no depper go', acquiring its
poetic intensity from the sensation of being internally possessed
by a scent whose source is at once unknown and everywhere,
dramatises in physical analogy the workings of the Holy
Spirit. Furthermore, experiences of such vivid sensuousness as
this break the usual boundaries of our conceptually arranged
world, and confute our notions of what is real and unreal.
Because of this, Valerian's reply to Tiburce's question possesses greater authority.

> Tiburce answerde, 'Seistow this to me   (260)
> In soothnesse, or in dream I herkne this?'
> 'In dremes', quod Valerian, 'han we be
> Unto this tyme, brother myn, ywis.
> But now at erst in trouthe oure dwellyng is.'

The poetry carries part of its meaning 'alive into the heart'
by evoking sensuous experiences: but part of the meaning is
enforced in another way through the rich associations that
have grown round the symbols of crowns and flowers. The
coronets here represent the crowns of victory, and also the
crowns of marriage: the way of denial has its own rewards,
and here is the true nuptial love which not only weds wife and
husband but weds Cecilia to other like souls, and above all
weds the earthly to the divine. The lily, traditional symbol
of purity, is the reward and sign of their chastity; the rose,
traditional symbol of martyrdom, signifies the end they
have chosen in their beginning.[1] The deaths they die, we
thus realise, are more than the accidental outcome of their

[1] See Robinson's note on ll. 220 ff.

circumstances: their deaths are their ultimate renunciation of the falseness of the world.

The living savour of the flowers is opposed by the dead stone of the pagan idols.

> Tho shewed hym Cecile al open and pleyn   (284)
> That alle ydoles nys but a thyng in veyn,
> For they been dombe, and therto they been deve,
> And charged hym his ydoles for to leve.

The clash between 'coronet' (the Biblical crown of life) and 'stone' is dramatically represented by the conflict between Cecilia and Almachius. When Tiburce and Valerian are brought before this traditional Herod-like figure, Almachius curtly condemns them with stony inhumanity.

> 'Whoso wol nat sacrifise,   (365)
> Swape of his heed; this my sentence heer.'

His cruelty is contrasted to the undismayed faith of Cecilia in her speech, which follows almost immediately, with its significant use of 'coronet' to describe the immortality the condemned will now win.

> 'Now, Cristes owene knyghtes leeve and deere,   (383)
> Cast alle awey the werkes of derknesse,
> And armeth yow in armure of brightnesse.
>
> 'Ye han for soothe ydoon a greet bataille,
> Youre cours is doon, youre feith han ye conserved.
> Gooth to the corone of lif that may nat faille;
> The rightful Juge, which that ye han served,
> Shal yeve it yow, as ye han it deserved.'

The subsidiary images in this passage are worth noting for the way they prevent Cecilia's words from seeming fanatical or inhumane. The introduction of 'knyghtes' and 'bataille' reminds us of the courage of men of arms: if for lesser victories soldiers will surrender their lives, how more justified would be the sacrifice of this mortal existence for the greater glory of

life eternal. 'The werkes of derknesse' represent both the ignorant blindness of this world, as well as the evil which has
ensnared the captives; 'the armure of brightnesse' represents
their glittering impregnability—their pride in their own truth
and grace—and also perhaps suggests their dissolution and
merging in God's light. Finally, there is the distinction between the false and the true judge—between Almachius and
God, between the temporal realm and the eternal.

The 'fruitfulness' of Cecilia appears in the way she inspires
and converts the officers of Almachius, even though they pay
for their conversion with their lives. But the price of life everlasting is always death in this world—this is the doctrine of
the poem, and every element of the action embodies it.

The climax of the poem comes with Cecilia confronting
Almachius, and expressing through her fearless contempt of
the tyrant her total casting off of worldly things. The dramatic
speech here is more 'naturalistic' than most of the tale, yet it
is still transfigured with symbolic meanings. Like any tyrant,
Almachius makes foolishly arrogant claims.

> 'Han noght oure myghty princes to me yiven,   (470)
> Ye, bothe power and auctoritee
> To maken folk to dyen or to lyven?
> Why spekestow so proudly thanne to me?'

But these words (and Cecilia's reply) are richer if we recognise
in them the boasts of the flesh whom the soul, knowing that
only God can grant life everlasting, must put down.

> 'Thou hast maad a ful gret lesyng heere.   (479)
> Thou seyst they princes han thee yeven myght
> Bothe for to sleen and for to quyken a wight;
> Thou, that ne mayst but oonly lyf bireve,
> Thou hast noon oother power ne no leve.'

Almachius claims to be unmoved by what she says, for he is a
'philosopher': doubtless referring to the stoicism which, seeing
nothing beyond death, praises only the resolute acceptance of
fleshly vicissitudes. Yet Almachius still demands respect for

his 'gods'—the dead images of stone. He is the prey of power and superstition. His false reality is denounced by Cecilia:

> 'Ther lakketh no thyng to thyne outter eyen   (498)
> That thou n'art blynd; for thyng that we seen alle
> That it is stoon, that men may wel espyen,
> That ilke stoon a god thow wolt it calle.
> I rede thee, lat thyn hand upon it falle,
> And taste it wel, and stoon thou shalt it fynde,
> Syn that thou seest nat with thyne eyen blynde.'

There are two stages to Cecilia's martyrdom. First she is burnt in a bath of flames—only, miraculously, she suffers no pain. This signifies the predominance of the soul over the passions and frailties of the flesh. The image Chaucer employs to describe her immunity is to be given a startling new twist when it reappears in *The Canon's Yeoman's Prologue*:

> It made hire nat a drope for to sweete.   (522)

The second phase of her martyrdom comes with the wounding in the neck, and her lingering for three days in 'torments' before dying. But her living for three days after the mortal blows had been struck is a gift she had asked of God, that she might preach and do His work. Her death is thus voluntarily sought, and she is not merely the helpless victim of Almachius' whims. And, above all, in the three days we are expected to recognise the parallel to Christ's sacrifice on the cross. Every martyrdom is an analogue of the Passion. Cecilia follows the path of the Master she serves.

In this tale, as elsewhere, Chaucer has written some of the most notable religious poetry of Middle English literature. But what was his attitude to this tale 'told' by the second Nun? The creator of the Wife of Bath with her exuberant rejection of the life of chastity, of the Miller with his hugging of fleshly pleasures, and even of the Knight with his acceptance of the fortunes of this world: what did the creator of these characters and their stories really think about this tale? To what extent did he endorse the Nun's vision?

The Second Nun's Tale

The second Nun is not described, nor need she be. She is any 'sone of Eve' who, by her life of celibacy and acts of devotion, witnesses to the faith she holds. 'That am nat I', says the Wife of Bath; and this Nun could never live like the Wife either. But which is right? Chaucer's answer, implicit I think in the whole design of the *Canterbury Tales*, is that all are God's creatures, and there are many ways to Him. Indeed, the Parson is made explicitly to preach it: 'Manye been the weyes espirituels that leden folk to oure Lord Jhesu Crist, and to the regne of glorie.'

CHAPTER 19

The Canon's Yeoman's Tale

THE dangers, in reading the *Canterbury Tales*, of attending mainly to story-line, characterisation and comic-timing, and neglecting other aspects of the poetry, must again be guarded against when turning to *The Canon's Yeoman's Tale*. T. W. Craik, for example, whose approach is limited to reading with this emphasis, is forced to regret that the tale 'is like the two fragments in its comparative lack of interest as a story'.[1] But due attention, I think, to other things—the tale's intellectual argument, its allegorical nature, its place in the pilgrim's debate, and the symbolic working of much of the poetry—will reveal that here we have one of the finest and most satisfying achievements of Chaucer's art.

The theme of the *Prologue* and *Tale* is the misuse of men's intelligence in the obsessive pursuit of false and meretricious goals. In *The Nun's Priest's Tale* the unreliability and vanity of human reason were laughed at. Chauntecleer closed his eyes to danger in the proud display of his own voice. In the confession of the Canon's Yeoman we are again shown how the single-minded pursuit of a trivial object can destroy a man. The tone is comic, the treatment partly realistic and partly allegoric. The Canon himself is presented as an actual individual case-history, but the poetry also opens out an allegorical realm wherein the nature and effects of sin are dramatised. One of the most remarkable qualities of the poem is the way it manages to create the allegorical superstructure without ever destroying the credibility of the specific human beings who are portrayed.

The opening description of the arrival of Canon and Yeoman on the scene begins at once to establish the symbolic implications of the incident. The frenzy of their pursuit of

---

[1] Craik, *op. cit.* p. 92.

alchemy is already given an 'objective correlative' in the sweating horses.

> The hors eek that his yeman rood upon   (562)
> So swatte that unnethe myghte it gon.
> Aboute the peytrel stood the foom ful hyre;
> He was of foom al flekked as a pye.
> A male tweyfoold on his croper lay...

The condition of the Canon is indeed identified with the horse here described: the reference changes from one to the other so rapidly that we are not sure which is being referred to (Robinson takes it that the line 'He was of foom al flekked as a pye' refers to the Canon).[1] The explicit comment on the Canon's sweating a few lines later contrasts his condition—and surely the contrast is as much spiritual in implication as physical—with Saint Cecilia's burning in the bath of fire. At the same time the line also expresses the basic attitude of the whole poem: an amused but compassionate enjoyment of the frenzy of mankind—

> But it was joye for to see hym swete.   (579)

At first the Host accepts the reason they give for spurring to catch up with the pilgrims, that they wished to ride 'in this myrie compaignye'; but the reason sounds implausible and the reader is anxious for the real motive to emerge. The truth is rapidly uncovered as the Host begins to query the lies of the Yeoman—in the question-and-answer exchange the deceits are skinned away till the Yeoman can, with evident relief, confess the true nature of himself and his master.

Initially the Yeoman highly praises his master, emphasising his great talents which seem so belied by his appearance. At last, after ascribing many other virtues to him, the Yeoman mentions his master's alchemy.

> 'I seye, my lord kan swich subtilitee—   (620)
> But al his craft ye may nat wite at me,
> And somwhat helpe I yet to his wirkyng—
> That al this ground on which we been ridyng,

---

[1] Robinson, *op. cit.* p. 867.

Til that we come to Caunterbury toun,
He koude al clene turne it up-so-doun,
And pave it al of silver and of gold.'

The extravagance of the claim points its absurdity, the notion of the road turned upside-down preparing for the futility as well as the impossibility of their endeavours (what could one do with a road turned upside-down?). The Host wonders at the bedraggled appearance of the Canon on whose behalf these claims are being made: 'Why is thy lord so sluttish, I the preye?' The Yeoman's evasions of this question carry their own ironic commentary.

'God help me so, for he shal nevere thee!' (641)

'For whan a man hath over-greet a wit, (648)
Ful oft hym happeth to mysusen it.'

Each step in the interrogation delineates something further about the Canon, but often in a way that intrigues and puzzles. For example, why does he choose to live where he does? Only later do we fully appreciate how the Canon's habitation depicts his haunted state.

'Telle how he dooth, I pray thee hertely, (654)
Syn that he is so crafty and so-sly.
Where dwelle ye, if it to telle be?'
'In the suburbes of a toun', quod he,
'Lurkyng in hernes and in lanes blynde,
Whereas this robbours and thise theves by kynde
Holden hir pryvee fereful residence,
As they that dar nat shewen hir presence;
So faren we, if I shal seye the sothe.'

But it is with the Host's turning his attention to the discoloured appearance of the Yeoman's face that the Yeoman at last confesses to their bootless struggle in the mazes of alchemy. The lure of transforming baser metals into gold torments them with sufferings akin to those of Tantalus:

'. . .ay we han good hope (678)
It for to doon, and after it we grope.
But that science is so fer us biforn,

We mowen nat, although we hadden it sworn,
It overtake, it slit awey so faste.
It wole us maken beggers atte laste.'

True the Canon and his Yeoman are suffering from an obsession; but, though the poetry presents all the psychological
symptoms of such a state, what is most important is that it portrays the two as sinners and their torments as the consequence
of sin. The suspiciousness of the Canon at what his servant is
saying about him depicts the way guilty people feel that others
must be talking ill of them. We are shown the pathological
desire of the guilty to hide their secrets, and the shame and
sorrow which make them flee from company when their
actions are discussed. Clearly such moments frequently occur,
and this is why the Canon has ended up living in the haunts of
thieves and others who have misdemeanours to conceal. The
Canon has not yet reached the later stage of guilt, where the
evil-doer grows shameless and numb to his own self-debauch-
ery. He has not yet become like the canon of whom the second
part of the *Tale* speaks.

With the departure of the Canon the Yeoman's real feelings
about his master, long suppressed and mounting, break forth
in almost uncontrolled denunciation. In the presentation of the
Yeoman's speech Chaucer's insight into the psychology of
obsession never falters. It is all here: the compulsive repetition
as if the only way to escape the bondage of the past is by
unwinding each crooked turn again and again; the confessing
and reliving of parts of the experience, punctuating the recital
by sudden outbursts of condemnation; the mocking of one's
own folly by noting it in others; the hope that self-laceration
and humiliation will bring relief. Finally, as the process works
itself out, the steadying recognition of what one has been,
what one was becoming. We see it all in the Yeoman's account
of his pursuit of alchemy. Usually *The Canon's Yeoman's
Tale* is read by critics and scholars as an exposé of alchemy;
it is that, but more important, through every detail about
the procedures of alchemists, the poetry dramatises the

Yeoman's morbid psychological state. Nor, as I shall try to demonstrate, does the significance stop here, but the events become an allegorical representation of the workings of sin and guilt.

Before starting on the *Tale* proper, one further point in the *Prologue* is worth mentioning. That is, the play on the words 'game' and 'ernest'. The Yeoman was initiated into the 'game' of alchemy (a pursuit, a trade, an activity with its own set rules, a sport which offered pleasure and reward without much effort), and soon he found it 'ernest' for himself (a thing to which one is utterly committed, a kill-joy, a pursuit which is disproportionately valued); now with the departure of his master he sees that *game* can arise again (a merry story at the Canon's expense, but also the carefree joy which is a gift of life and which he had lost). As elsewhere, Chaucer rings changes on these words 'game' and 'ernest', with the most approved meaning pointing to that joy which accompanies truth and self-knowledge.

The Yeoman, who had neglected to look in on himself in the pursuit of a delusion ('I am nat wont in no mirour to prye'), begins his story with a glance at his own portrait before and after.

> With this Chanoun I dwelt have seven yeer,   (720)
> And of his science am I never the neer.
> Al that I hadde I have lost therby,
> And, God woot, so hath many mo than I.
> Ther I was wont to be right fressh and gay
> Of clothyng and of oother good array,
> Now may I were an hose upon myn heed;
> And wher my colour was bothe fressh and reed,
> Now is it wan and of a leden hewe—
> Whoso it useth, soore shal he rewe'—
> And of my swynk yet blered is myn ye.
> Lo! which avantage is to multiplye!

Literally, when he says many more than himself have lost by this pursuit, he is probably thinking of the many creditors never paid, but the phrase also suggests the larger context where many are undone by their own fanatical activity. The outward change in the Yeoman obviously mirrors the inward, from health and confidence to haunted death-in-life. His eyes are 'blered' from poring over stinking chemicals in dark rooms —but the phrase also suggests the spiritual blindness possessing him. 'Multiplye' is a technical term for transmuting baser metals into gold—but, with the memory of the repeated phrase 'More for delit than world to multiplye' carried over from other tales, the word perhaps acquires an ironical tinge which contrasts the barren search of alchemists with the rewarding harvest of natural procreation.

After the fall into personal despair and misery the next stage is to ease the pains of this self-fabricated hell by dragging others into a like condition. The Yeoman remembers that a clerk once preached this lesson to him that the wicked wish company in their wretchedness, but only now does he recognise its truth. Next he plunges into an account of the curious practices of alchemy giving much of its absurd jargon. At moments in the Yeoman's monologue flashes of pride flicker still as he demonstrates the hard-won products of his years of labour. In passages such as the following he is reliving his period of arduous toil as much as he is exhibiting the learning he has acquired. The poetry, however, by relentlessly piling fact upon fact, term upon term, imitates the meaningless accumulation of worthless knowledge which buries humanity beneath mounds of rubbish.

> Oure fourneys eek of calcinacioun, (804)
> And of watres albificacioun;
> Unslekked lym, chalk, and gleyre of an ey,
> Poudres diverse, asshes, donge, pisse, and cley,
> Cered pokkets, sal peter, vitriole,
> And diverse fires maad of wode and cole;
> Sal tartre, alkaly, and sal preparat,
> And combust materes and coagulat;
> Cley maad with hors or mannes heer, and oille
> Of tartre, alum glas, berme, wort, and argoille . . .

Failure and frustration no more deter the alchemists than the filthiness of some of their ingredients. Hope always drives them on.

> But that good hope crepeth in oure herte,   (870)
> Supposynge evere, though we sore smerte,
> To be releeved by hym afterward.
> Swich supposyng and hope is sharp and hard;
> I warne yow wel, it is to seken evere.
> That futur temps hath maad men to dissevere,
> In trust therof, from al that evere they hadde.

The first half of the *Tale* reaches its climax with the explosion of the alchemists' pot. The frenzied accumulation of chemical materials and the equally frenzied accumulation of the alchemists' tribulations culminate in this disastrous (and comically dramatised) experiment. The reader has been made to feel something of the suffocating confinement that characterises obsessive behaviour, and the explosion comes as a psychic relief—an outburst of comedy that blasts apart all the false pretensions of alchemy, and restores the sanity of good humour. The passage also illuminates the behaviour of the Yeoman: for so long all his ills have fermented and boiled like the chemicals in the pot, till the inevitable bursting point is reached and he spews forth in a spate of words his bubbling indignation. Thus Chaucer makes the external incidents of the story mirror the (internal) processes of the Yeoman's mental and emotional development.

> Ful ofte it happeth so,   (906)
> The pot tobreketh, and farewel, al is go!
> Thise metals been of so greet violence,
> Oure walles mowe nat make hem resistence,
> But if they weren wroght of lym and stoon;
> They percen so, and thurgh the wal they goon.
> And somme of hem synken into the ground—
> Thus han we lost by tymes many a pound—
> And somme are scatered al the floor aboute;
> Somme lepe into the roof. Withouten doute,
> Though that the feend noght in oure sighte hym shewe,

I trowe he with us be, that ilke shrewe!
In helle, where that he lord is and sire,
Nis ther moore wo, ne moore rancour ne ire.

In the last lines quoted above, the reference to the fiend
being with them though not showing himself to their sight
makes more explicit what has several times earlier in the *Tale*
been hinted at (in the Yeoman saying that he has already told
people enough about alchemy to 'reyse a feend' (l. 861) or his
speaking of folk who 'bitrayen innocence' (l. 897)). It is not
merely that the pursuit of alchemy is being likened to witch-
craft; rather it is that through the story of the alchemists we
are being given a fable of how evil—here the evil of misguided purposes—tempts and corrupts men.

The first part of *The Canon's Yeoman's Tale* ends with the
comic dialogue of the crestfallen alchemists who are trying to
explain away their failure. Explanations, even when they may
explain nothing, have a wonderful way of boosting men's
morale, and there is a resonance to the following lines which
suggests that we are to think of more than this particular group
and we are to acknowledge a basic human trait:

> We faille of that which that we wolden have,   (958)
> And in oure madnesse everemoore we rave.
> And whan we been togidres everichoon,
> Every man semeth a Salomon.

In Part 1 of *The Canon's Yeoman's Tale* there is a description of how their chemicals give the alchemists a hellish
stench.

> And everemoore, where that evere they goon,   (884)
> Men may hem knowe by smel of brymstoon.
> For al the world they stynken as a goot;
> Hir savour is so rammyssh and so hoot
> That though a man from hem a mile be,
> The savour wole infecte hym, trusteth me.

The images here evoke associations of some fiends come from
the brimstone pit, but the associations merely add to the vivid-

ness and comedy of the picture, and are not to be taken too literally. But in the second part of the *Tale*, I think, we are expected to see in the shape of the alchemist an actual fiend who tempts, betrays and destroys man. The opening lines, while still the exaggerated report of the Yeoman unloading his malice, have a greater seriousness of tone than anything in the first part.

> Ther is a chanoun of religioun   (972)
> Amonges us, wolde infecte al a toun,
> Thogh it as greet were as was Nynyvee,
> Rome, Alisaundre, Troye, and othere three.
> His sleightes and his infinite falsnesse
> Ther koude no man writen, as I guesse,
> Though that he myghte lyve a thousand yeer.
> In al this world of falshede nis his peer;
> For in his termes he wol hym so wynde,
> And speke his wordes in so sly a kynde,
> Whanne he commune shal with any wight,
> That he wole make hym doten anonright,
> But it a feend be, as hymselven is.
> Ful many a man hath he bigiled er this,
> And wole, if that he lyve may a while;
> And yet men ride and goon ful many a mile
> Hym for to seke and have his aqueyntaunce,
> Noght knowynge of his false governaunce.

The images are vaster in scope: this man infects not by the mile but by whole populations. There is fuller emphasis on the paramountcy of his evil, and the vast numbers of victims taken in by him. The exaggeration is now more sinister than comic in effect. In all this world he has no peer for falsehood; but perhaps the line also suggests that in all *this world of falsehood* he has no peer, thus stressing Man's fallen state. As the tale proceeds, further bold strokes darken the canon's portrait, emphasising his malign treachery:

> ye woot wel how   (1001)
> That among Cristes apostelles twelve
> Ther nas no traytour but Judas hymselve.

The comic tones that so marked the first part of the *Tale* are now virtually gone, and we are shown evil similar, at least in kind, to the most notorious of all betrayals. Furthermore, this evil takes place within the religious realm—a priest, not a mere yeoman, is his gull—and we are told explicitly (l. 1070) that it was 'Cristes peple' that this canon sought 'to meschief brynge'. The religious orders are bidden to cast out the Judases in their midst—perhaps at this point we are expected to think of men such as the Pardoner or the Summoner who thrive by exploiting their office. In line with this change to a greater seriousness of tone is a change in the presentation of alchemy itself: in Part I alchemy was a foolish pursuit, a symptom of vanity and venial sin; in Part II it is the device whereby the silver of truth is faked to deceive a good man, and now the alchemist acts cunningly and without conscience.

> 'What!' quod this chanoun, 'sholde I be untrewe   (1042)
> Nay, that were thyng yfallen al of newe.
> Trouthe is a thyng that I wol evere kepe
> Unto that day in which that I shal crepe
> Into my grave, and ellis God forbede.
> Bileveth this as siker as your Crede.'

At regular intervals throughout the second part of the *Tale* the Yeoman breaks forth with invective against the alchemist: once in words that recall the fox who nearly duped Chauntecleer.

> O sely preest! o sely innocent!   (1076)
> With coveitise anon thou shalt be blent!
> O gracelees, ful blynd is thy conceite,
> No thyng ne artow war of the deceite
> Which that this fox yshapen hath to thee!

(The Yeoman, of course, had not been present during the Nun's Priest's tale so this cannot be taken as an intentionally ironic reference on his part.) These lines support the interpretation that *The Canon's Yeoman's Tale* is a more specific and serious illustration of the temptations that beset man and would destroy him. *The Nun's Priest's Tale* dealt with this theme more lightheartedly.

Naturally the Yeoman's almost personal animosity towards the canon of his story leads one to wonder whether this canon was his master. But the Yeoman soon denies that.

> This chanoun was my lord, ye wolden weene? (1088)
> Sire hoost, in feith, and by the hevenes queene,
> It was another chanoun, and nat hee,
> That kan an hundred foold moore subtiltee.
> He hath bitrayed folkes many tyme;
> Of his falsnesse it dulleth me to ryme.
> Evere whan that I speke of his falshede,
> For shame of hym my chekes wexen rede.
> Algates they bigynnen for to glowe,
> For reednesse have I noon, right wel I knowe,
> In my visage; for fumes diverse
> Of metals, whiche ye han herd me reherce,
> Consumed and wasted han my reednesse.

Yet the personal nature of the Yeoman's hostility remains. The first Canon is presented as the victim of his own folly, the second as the exploiter of others' folly. I think we should detect here, and in other passages, the Yeoman's feeling (not wholly rational nor even perhaps fully conscious) that this second canon, like a fiend or like Judas, is the source of evil which spreads outwards to corrupt many only indirectly connected with it. As with the Friar's tale of a summoner, wherein Satan became the ultimate Summoner, we are made to feel there exists a hierarchy of evil. The canon himself seems to have no personality: he is simply characterised by his power to deceive.

> It dulleth me whan that I of hym speke. (1172)
> On his falshede fayn wolde I me wreke,
> If I wiste how, but he is heere and there;
> He is so variaunt, he abit nowhere.

Lines such as these intimate that the canon is something more than a vagrant trickster; that he is sinister in a supernatural way.

Yet the actual process whereby the priest is gulled of forty pounds is presented with detailed realism. The interest of this section of the *Tale* lies mainly in the exposition of a confidence trick. The formula is a classic one, and has changed little through the ages. First there is the stage of establishing the victim's confidence in the deceiver and of making him feel ashamed of ever having harboured any suspicions: this the canon does by promptly returning the money he borrowed. Next step is to introduce the trick as an act of gratitude for the victim's kindness. The victim is led to believe he is being let in on a secret, and his credulity is further strengthened by permitting him to participate in the trick: thus the priest himself performs the experiment as the canon bids. The trick is repeated to settle any doubts remaining. Finally the victim himself must ask for the secret, and then be made to feel that he is buying it cheaply because the confidence trickster is too kind or too weak-minded to refuse him. The Yeoman's story follows the classic pattern of all such deceptions, and doubtless a fool has been born this minute who will one day succumb to a variation of the trick.

The canon 'takes' the priest for forty pounds. Is the realism of this part of the narrative at odds with the allegorical content I have suggested may be found elsewhere? I do not think so. The trick played on the priest is a mundane one, but at the same time it is merely an example, a specific instance, of greater and less tangible duplicity. The canon's deceit in little figures the greater deceit of Satan—just as Macbeth's killing of Duncan is a fragment of the far greater evil filling the wide vessel of the universe and of which even the three weird sisters are only a partial representation. For the medieval mind—and in spirit *Macbeth* is Shakespeare's most medieval play—could read macrocosmic patterns in the small events of this world. Furthermore, at certain moments in the story Chaucer is at pains to give a darker tone to actions than the literal context requires. Thus, when the priest expresses his desire to know the secret of the canon's craft, he speaks in words that strongly recall a bargain being struck with the devil.

> 'Goddes blessyng, and his moodres also, (1243)
> And alle halwes, have ye, sire chanoun',
> Seyde the preest, 'and I hir malisoun,

> But, and ye vouche-sauf to techen me
> This noble craft and this subtilitee,
> I wol be youre in al that evere I may.'

The blessing with which his speech begins contrasts with his offer of himself with which it concludes, and the passage gains considerably in irony if we recognise diabolic associations in the ambiguity of the last line. A little later, after the goldsmith has confirmed that the silver is genuine, the priest's joy is described in a passage which compares his feelings to other great joys in life: yet in the course of this comparison the poetry suggests that the priest is turning his back on the ordinary pleasures of mankind for something only speciously pleasurable. Alchemy causes men to forsake the natural gifts of God for worthless rewards.

> This sotted preest, who was gladder than he? (1341)
> Was nevere brid gladder agayn the day,
> Ne nyghtingale, in the sesoun of May,
> Was nevere noon that luste bet to synge;
> Ne lady lustier in carolynge,
> Or for to speke of love and wommanhede,
> Ne knyght in armes to doon an hardy dede,
> To stonden in grace of his lady deere,
> Than hadde this preest this soory craft to lere.
> And to the chanoun thus he spak and seyde:
> 'For love of God, that for us alle deyde,
> And as I may deserve it unto yow,
> What shal this receite coste? telleth now!'

The literal answer turns out to be forty pounds—the true answer is jeopardy to his soul.

The Yeoman concludes his story by drawing certain moral lessons. This latter section of the *Tale* has been criticised on the grounds that the sermonising here makes the Yeoman speak out of character. I believe this criticism is based upon a misreading of the poem's development. The hectic speech of the Yeoman at the beginning, the obsessive outbreaks of passion, give way as the poem proceeds to a calmer tone. The agitation of a man caught in the toils of alchemy is replaced by the warning note of one who has at last freed himself and exorcised the devil possessing him and who can therefore now teach others to avoid his errors. That he has not completely shed the past is suggested, however, by his use of 'philosophers'' arguments (those of Arnoldus de Villa Nova and Hermes Trismegistus) to demonstrate the futility of pursuing alchemy.

The conclusions he draws fall into place in the thematic pattern of the *Canterbury Tales*. The vanity of human wisdom, a theme treated in *The Nun's Priest's Tale*, is freshly expressed.

> Philosophres speken so mystily (1394)
> In this craft that men kan nat come therby,
> For any wit that men han now-a-dayes.
> They mowe wel chiteren as doon thise jayes,
> And in hir termes sette hir luste and peyne,
> But to hir purpos shul they nevere atteyne.

Philosophy, in this context, refers primarily to alchemy, but the other meaning of 'seekers after knowledge' is not excluded. Another theme that reappears is that of false seeing: blindness of eye, the distortion of truth through clinging to illusions, the theme of tales as different as *The Miller's Tale* and *The Merchant's Tale*.

> Ye been as boold as is Bayard the blynde, (1413)
> That blondreth forth, and peril casteth noon.
> He is as boold to renne agayne a stoon
> As for to goon bisides in the weye.
> So faren ye that multiplie, I seys.
> If that youre eyen kan nat seen aright,
> Looke that youre mynde lakke noght his sight.

Above all, in the final lesson (ascribed to Plato) the inviolable 'privitee' of God's mysteries is emphasised: to seek to understand and exploit what God has hidden is to reject the gifts He has lavished upon man for his enjoyment, and to commit

the final blasphemy—the pride of egoism that sets up the part
as worth more than the whole.

> Thanne conclude I thus, sith that the God of hevene   (1472)
> Ne wil nat that the philosophres nevene
> How that a man shal come unto this stoon,
> I rede, as for the beste, lete it goon.
> For whoso maketh God his adversarie,
> As for to werken any thyng in contrarie
> Of his wil, certes, never shal he thryve,
> Thogh that he multiplie terme of his lyve.
> And there a poynt; for ended is my tale.
> God sende every trewe man boote of his bale!

Though these didactic conclusions grow out of the portrayal
of the character, experience and psychological development of
the Canon's Yeoman, and are not just grafted on, their explicitness gives them a certain sermonising authority. Their similarity to conclusions drawn or implied elsewhere in the
Canterbury Tales suggests that they embody much of Chaucer's
own beliefs. This raises an interesting and important question.
Living in an age today where secular values are on the whole
triumphant, where man's inventive and rational powers are
supremely prized, and where his right to probe and explore
all realms of experience is unquestioned, how shall we take
this moral teaching? I do not mean that the literary merit of
the *Tale* is wholly dependent on the didactic conclusions.
Clearly a writer may employ a set of beliefs which are not
acceptable to organise his material (for example, Coleridge
using superstitions he did not himself hold, for significant
effects in *The Ancient Mariner*), without lessening the truth
of his poetry. Clearly, too, much of *The Canon's Yeoman's Tale*
still remains valid irrespective of what we may think of its
conclusions: the characterisations of the Yeoman, the insight
into obsession, the informed reportage of the ways of alchemists, the comedy of frustration, and so on. But, since it would
seem Chaucer endorses the moral of the *Tale*, and much of
the intention of the *Tale* is bound up with the moral, our

final judgment must be coloured by our acceptance or rejection of its validity. I suspect Stephen Toulmin and June Goodfield are right when they suggest that Chaucer would tar much twentieth-century research with the same brush he tars the alchemists.[1] We know that science owes a great debt to the alchemists, particularly for their development of chemical apparatus and their creation of an intellectual environment that could foster scientific discovery. Few of us would be willing today to turn our back on the benefits brought by scientific and technological advance. Should we be patronising towards Chaucer, and regret that he belongs to that 'traditional' culture which, according to C. P. Snow, has always been anti-scientific, reactionary and has in general responded by wishing the future did not exist?[2]

Chaucer's attitude towards alchemy is in line with medieval religious thinking on the subject. Apart from any orthodox scepticism about the purpose of alchemy, doubtless many of its practitioners were alchemists for motives of greed and power, and hence were likely to alienate responsible opinion. Common sense too despised alchemy for its blatant record of failure. Furthermore, by Chaucer's time alchemy had fallen into a state of senility:[3] it had pursued a dead end for too long. Chaucer had good grounds for condemning alchemy. But what of the implications of what he has to say for modern research? Chaucer's thinking followed the current of his own times, just as it goes completely against the current today. And this may be the very reason why *The Canon's Yeoman's Tale* has more relevance and importance today than it could have had for Chaucer's own audience. Today we do accept, with far too little questioning, the validity of isolating a branch of knowledge and pursuing discoveries as far as we can go with little consideration of the consequences to the lives of our fellow-men. Traditional patterns of society are being disrupted with

[1] Stephen Toulmin and June Goodfield, *The Architecture of Matter* (Hutchinson, 1962), p. 109.

[2] Snow, *The Two Cultures and the Scientific Revolution* (C.U.P. 1959), p. 11.

[3] Toulmin and Goodfield, *op. cit.* p. 132. 'Senility' is the actual word they use in describing medieval alchemy.

effects of anxiety and insecurity as debasing as the obsessive urges wrecking the Canon and his Yeoman. Much specialisation too is as futile as the alchemists' search for the philosopher's stone: not only because of the many footling topics chosen for research, but also because the ever-increasing churning out of articles, books, reports, findings, experiments, proposals, digests, digests of digests, proofs and refutations exceeds our ability to assimilate the material and set it in perspective. A frequent anxiety expressed by research workers in many branches of science is whether all their experiments may be worthless because somewhere or other the work has been done before. Arising from this outpouring of specialisation too is the frustration brought about by being cut off from work in other fields: the danger is not a division into two cultures but a fragmentation produced by innumerable specialisations, each isolated from its neighbour. Here the disastrous effect of technical terms is seen: many practitioners take as much delight in the esoteric jargon of their field as the Yeoman did in the language of alchemy. But most important of all—and this question is at the very core of Chaucer's poem—is the question of the motive driving men on. Scientific research and technology are often justified in terms of greater goods for all—two blades of wheat where only one could be grown before—but for many this is no more than a materialism which wishes to transmute stinking chemicals into smooth nylon, labour into leisure, knowledge into power, relationship into possession, investment into profit, lead into gold. And where does this take us? What do our motives do to us? Shall we be grateful in the end for the Midas touch[1] when technology has transformed the world with its success? Can science and technology even succeed in producing more for all, or is this millennium ('jam tomorrow') another illusion pursued at a cost not yet reckoned? Precisely because *The Canon's Yeoman's Tale* can

---

[1] I was led to use this phrase by an article entitled 'The Midas Touch' by M. M. Carlin in *Makerere Journal*, 9. The article deals with the assumptions underlying the financing of university education in East Africa, and shows how utilitarian clichés direct the thinking of financial advisers assisting the new 'emerging' countries.

open up such considerations as these its didacticism remains valid, and challengingly relevant.

F. R. Leavis has remarked: 'In coming to terms with great literature we discover at bottom what we really believe. What for—what ultimately for? what do men live by—the questions work and tell at what I can only call a religious depth of thought and feeling.'[1] Chaucer's poem exemplifies the truth of Leavis's dictum.

[1] F. R. Leavis and Michael Yudkin, *Two Cultures? The Significance of C. P. Snow* (Chatto and Windus, 1962), p. 23.

CHAPTER 20

The Manciple's Tale and the Parson's Tale

AT the outset of the pilgrimage the Host had suggested that each pilgrim tell two tales on the way to Canterbury, and two on the return journey, and this must have been Chaucer's original intention. With the conclusion of *The Manciple's Tale* we are given to understand that all the pilgrims bar the Parson have told one tale, and that the company is now close to Canterbury. This suggests that Chaucer had cut the stories on the way to Canterbury down to one each. Whether he further intended to end the work with *The Parson's Tale*, and not transcribe the tales of the return journey, or whether there was to be a second series which he never commenced, we cannot know for sure. But undoubtedly *The Parson's Tale* ends one stage of journeying and story-telling, and hence is intended to 'knytte up wel a greet mateere'. A pilgrimage is a penitential journey, and fittingly the Parson preaches a sermon on Penitence. It is easy to see why *The Parson's Tale* should conclude the pilgrimage to Canterbury. What is not so obvious is why Chaucer considered it appropriate to have *The Manciple's* as the second last of the series.

The Manciple's Tale immediately precedes *The Parson's Tale* because it is intended, I think to offer a contrast. Certainly the Manciple and the Parson are themselves contrasting figures. The Manciple is a secular person, worldly-shrewd to a great degree. Though more than thirty lawyers employed him, men of great learning and wise judgment, yet 'this Manciple sette hir aller cappe'. Undoubtedly he knew how to exploit others for his own benefit, yet he also knew how to avoid being found out. He is cunning, capable and self-seeking. The Parson, on the other hand, is presented by Chaucer as an ideal pastor.

Although poor and simple in living, he is a learned man. He teaches by example first, and words afterwards. His life is centred on serving others, guiding their souls that they may find their way to God. 'He was a shepherde and noght a mercenarie.' It is the Manciple who, by profession and character, is a 'mercenarie'. The tales they tell suitably exemplify the values by which they live. The Manciple tells the story of how the crow became black: foolishly he told others the truth about themselves, and hence was punished. The moral of his story is that one should keep one's mouth shut, and not give anything away. But to tell men the truth about themselves, and call upon them to reform, is the very essence of the Parson's calling. He has already been attacked by the Host— also one of the most worldly of figures—for reprimanding him for swearing.[1] In the *General Prologue* Chaucer presents, clearly with admiration, the candour of the Parson.

> He was to synful men nat despitous,   (514)
> Ne of his speche daungerous ne digne,
> But in his techyng discreet and benygne.
> To drawen folk to hevene by fairnesse,
> By good ensample, this was his bisynesse.
> But it were any persone obstinat,
> What so he were, of heigh or lough estat,
> Hym wolde he snybben sharply for the nonys.

And in his tale the Parson does the exact opposite of what the Manciple advises: he describes at length the deadly sins that men possess, and calls on all to cast out their vices by repentance.

The Manciple's Tale expresses the compromising values of worldly people: *The Parson's Tale* teaches the rigours of self-examination, the hard road to salvation and the celestial city.

What occasions the Manciple's story with its cautioning moral is his hasty rebuke of the drunken Cook. (Traditionally Cooks and Manciples, like Reeves and Millers, were supposed

---

[1] See the *Epilogue to the Man of Law's Tale*, ll. 1172–7.

to dislike and distrust one another; this probably explains why
the Manciple criticised the Cook in the first place.) But when
the host suggests that the Cook may remember his insulting
words, and one day pay him back, the Manciple quickly
changes tack.

> 'But yet, Manciple, in feith thou art to nyce,　　　(69)
> Thus openly repreve hym of his vice.
> Another day he wole, peraventure,
> Reclayme thee and brynge thee to lure;
> I meen, he speke wole of smale thynges,
> As for to pynchen at thy rekenynges,
> That were nat honest, if it cam to preef.'
> 'No', quod the Manciple, 'that were greet mescheef!
> So myghte he lightly brynge me in the snare.'

Clearly the Manciple has reason to avoid an investigation into
his accounts. So instead of condemning the Cook any more
for his drunkenness, to conceal his own malpractices he
encourages the Cook in his drinking by offering a gourd
of wine.

Though this incident is dramatised with the realism cus-
tomary in the links between the tales, one or two touches give
an allegorical edge to the exchange. For example, the Manciple in jeering at the Cook's drunken condition employs some
expressions the Canon's Yeoman used in depicting the sinfulness of the alchemist.

> 'thy visage is ful pale,　　　(30)
> Thyne eyen daswen eek, as that me thynketh,
> And, wel I woot, thy breeth ful soure stynketh...'

> 'Hool cloos thy mouth, man, by thy fader kyn!　　　(37)
> The devel of helle sette his foot therin!
> Thy cursed breeth infecte wole us alle.'

This can be read as a deliberate joke on the Manciple's part:
but it also serves to suggest that we should recognise that the
Cook, like the Canon, is possessed by sin. Again, when the
Host laughs at the method chosen by the Manciple to reconcile

himself to the Cook, he echoes the play on the words
'ernest' and 'game' which appears in *The Canon's Yeoman's
Prologue.*

> 'I se wel it is necessarie,   (95)
> Where that we goon, good drynke with us carie;
> For that wol turne rancour and disese
> T'acord and love, and many a wrong apese.
>   O thou Bacus, yblessed be thy name,
> That so kanst turnen ernest into game!'

Although he finds a joke here, basically in what he is saying the
Host endorses the attitude of the Manciple: less trouble is
stirred up if one tolerates and even encourages the vices of
others. What he envisages by accord and love are far indeed from
those qualities as the Parson would understand them. Like the
Manciple the Host is a secular figure, and his values are worldly
ones. 'Game' for him means merely something jolly and entertaining: things 'ernest' are on the whole unpleasant. He is
always calling for 'myrthe' or a 'myrie tale'—so that when the
Parson's turn comes he offers to tell a 'myrie tale in prose',
only ironically he means a very different kind of joy from that
loved by the Host.[1] By means such as this Chaucer emphasises
the distinction between secular and divine ways of seeing
things, and suggests the ever-present importance of judging
things *sub specie aeternitatis.*

The Manciple's Tale is very short. The plot is scarcely more
than a brief incident, and there is little characterisation. The
bulk of the *Tale* consists of the Manciple's sermonising. He
airs his opinions on a number of topics which have been debated in earlier tales: the perfidy of women, the sinfulness of
man, the language of story-telling. In lines which are reminis-
cent of some of the imagery of *The Miller's Tale* the Manciple

---

[1] 'The "myrie tale" proves to be nothing less than a baldly homiletic, sober-
sided preachment, a doctrinal sermon whose merriment can be called so only
in Bernardian and ascetical terms, not in the lexicon of the Host at all. That
is, since it purposes to predispose its hearers to the "knoweleche of hym
(God)" and "to the blisful life that is perdurable" then is it signally "myrie"
with a celestial *gaudium*' (Baldwin, *op. cit.* p. 87).

argues that a natural creature cannot be constrained, and that the innate qualities will always come out.

> But God it woot, ther may no man embrace   (160)
> As to destreyne a thyng which that nature
> Hath natureelly set in a creature.

He supports this with examples of a caged bird which will always try to escape; a cat which will always prefer a mouse to sweeter dainties; and a she-wolf which will always seek 'the lewedest' wolf for mate. But the Manciple has nothing of the Miller's rejoicing in the vigour of the natural life: rather he sees the natural passions and desires as debased and debasing. Thus, in his example of the cat, he says,

> Lo, heere hath lust his dominacioun,   (181)
> And appetit fleemeth discrecioun.

And a few lines later, he doubts whether virtue can ever flourish.

> For men han evere a likerous appetit   (189)
> On lower thyng to parfourne hire delit
> Than on hire wyves, be they never so faire,
> Ne never so trewe, ne so debonaire.
> Flessh is so newefangel, with meschaunce,
> That we ne konne in nothyng han plesaunce
> That sowneth into vertu any while.

Even when he argues that in telling a story the word must be cousin to the deed, the same bias can be discerned. What he is objecting to is the way a poor woman who commits adultery is abused with vicious names, while a lady of high degree committing the same offence is free of such appelations. Similarly, he sees no difference between an outlaw and a tyrant, except the tyrant with the larger following and the more destructive character is not depised as the outlaw is. Perhaps we can detect something akin to modern class bitterness in the Manciple's diatribes here. He works for lawyers and no doubt has ample opportunity to observe their sharp practices; they are honoured while he, who cheats and outsmarts them when he can, has to be constantly on guard lest his accounts be called into question. No doubt his position also gives him opportunity to observe how the unscrupulous among his employers' clients fare, the high-born getting away unpunished, the low-born having the sentence go against them. But his sense of the injustice of such things merely makes him more cynical.

The story the Maniple chooses fits his attitude. Apollo, who is traditionally the god of civilisation, of law, of high moral and religious principles, is presented in the Maniple's story as a spoilt nobleman. When the crow tells him the truth about his wife's infidelity he first of all kills her in a fit of rage; then, when remorse sets in, he convinces himself that she was innocent and the crow lied. It appears, from the way the Maniple ends his tale, that this was a story taught him by his mother. The moral of it was drummed into him: the constant repetition of 'my sone' is ridiculous, and suggests a mother fatuously concerned with passing on to her son her own base-minded ethics.[1]

The interest of *The Maniple's Tale* lies not in the story itself (which is poor), but in the way the Maniple reveals himself. Cynical and mean-spirited, he is highly conscious of man's sinful state, but sees no better course of action than a conspiracy of silence. There is a touch of bitterness in his narration which partly arises from guilty self-justification: perhaps it hints at a core of dissatisfaction at his spiritual condition somewhere in him yet scarcely recognised. Penitence is a possibility he has probably never considered.

The Parson's Tale is straightforwardly a sermon preached to his fellow pilgrims. Because a medieval sermon is somewhat heavy going for the modern reader—several critics have attested to its dullness[2]—it may be worth-while, before commenting on the *Tale* and attempting to deal with its significance

[1] In Gower's version of the story (see *Confessio Amantis, op. cit.* Book III, ii, 768–835). 'Mi Sone' is repeated only a few times, with restraint, and the effect is quite different.

[2] E.g. Robinson, *op. cit.* p. 873; and Baldwin, *op. cit.* p. 98.

in the pattern of the *Canterbury Tales*, briefly to outline the main branches and sub-divisions of the Parson's argument.

The Main Theme of the Parson's sermon: the way to the Celestial City.

The right way is via *Penitence*.
    Definitions of Penitence.
        3 Actions of Penitence.
        3 Species of Penitence.
        3 things necessary for perfect Penitence:
            (*A*) Contrition of Heart.
            (*B*) Confession of Mouth.
            (*C*) Satisfaction.

(*A*) *Contrition* has 6 causes:
    (1) Remembrance of sin.
    (2) Disdain of sin.
    (3) Dread of doom and the pains of hell.
    (4) Sorrowful remembrance of good deeds omitted.
    (5) Remembrance of the Sacrifice on the Cross.
    (6) Hope of 3 things:
        (i) forgiveness of sin;
        (ii) gift of grace to come;
        (iii) the glory of heaven.

(*B*) *Confession:*
    (1) Showing of sins to the priest.
    (2) Understanding of sin:
        (*a*) Whence they come:
            (i) from the suggestion of the devil;
            (ii) then from the delight of the flesh;
            (iii) finally from the consenting of reason.
        (*b*) How sins increase:
            (i) *concupiscence* (which Man inherits from Adam) nourishes it;
            (ii) the devil fans it;
            (iii) the will chooses it.
        (*c*) What they are:
   Sin: There are two manners of sin:
    Venial sins.
    Deadly sins of which there are 7:

(1) *Pride*—the twigs of which are:

   (*a*) The products of pride: Disobedience, Boasting, Hypocrisy, Scorn, Arrogance, Shamelessness, Swelling of Heart, Contempt, 'Elation', Impatience, Rebelliousness, Strife, Presumption, Irreverence, Obstinacy, Vainglory, Chattering.

   (*b*) The kinds of pride:

      (i) inner,

      (ii) outer.

   (*c*) The sources of pride:

      (i) from the good things of nature:

         gifts of the *body*: health, strength, dexterity, beauty, noble birth, freedom;

         gifts of the *soul*: wit, intelligence, understanding, skill, 'vertu natureel', good memory;

      (ii) from the good things of *fortune*: wealth, advancement, reputation;

      (iii) from the good things of *grace*: knowledge, endurance, kindliness, virtuous contemplation, withstanding of temptation.

   (*d*) The *remedy* against pride—humility:

     in the heart (4 kinds);

     in speech (4 kinds);

     in works (4 kinds).

(2) *Envy:*

   Defined—attacker of good and truth.

   (*a*) Kinds:

      (i) sorrow at others' goodness or prosperity;

      (ii) joy at others' harm.

     These lead to backbiting; *backbiting* (given 5 subdivisions and illustrated) leads to grumbling; grumbling leads to bitterness of heart; bitterness of heart leads to discord; discord leads to scorning one's neighbours; scorning one's neighbours leads to accusations; accusations lead to malignity.

   (*b*) *Remedy:* to love God, and to love thy neighbour like thyself. Explanations with accounts of how the love may be expressed, particular emphasis being given to love of enemies.

(3) *Anger:*

Defined. Two kinds:

(*a*) Good anger directed against wickedness.

(*b*) Bad anger:

    (i) hasty and unpremeditated,

    (ii) cold and calculated.

Often caused by pride, nourished by rancour, and further assisted by pride, envy and strife. Consequences of anger: hate, discord, war, manslaughter (spiritual or bodily); as well as accusations against God, venomous rage, excuses, blasphemy (or swearing), lies, flatteries, curses, scolding and reproach, scorn, wicked counsel, spreading of discourse, speaking with double tongue, betrayal, threats, idle words, idle talk, jesting.

Remedy: meekness, also patience: what they are and how they work.

(4) *Sloth:*

How related to previous deadly sins. Defined.

It undermines man in his three conditions:

    the state of innocence,

    the state of fallen man,

    the state of grace.

It is resisted by good works.

Its branches: dread of working, despair, somnolence, carelessness (negligence), idleness, tardiness, laziness, poverty and destruction (spiritual and temporal), coldness of heart, lack of devotion, worldly sorrow (*tristicia*).

Remedy: fortitude: great courage, faith and hope, assurance (confidence), magnanimity, constancy.

(5) *Covetousness and Avarice:*

Definition: Covetousness the desire to possess what one has not. Avarice the desire to hold what one has.

Explanation and justification of 'degree' in society.

Trade:

    (i) Temporal:

        good is sharing of wealth,

        evil is trading by fraud, treachery and deceit.

    (ii) Spiritual: simony breeds gambling, reproaches, thefts, blasphemy, hate, waste, sometimes manslaughter, and sacrilege.

Avarice also breeds lies, thefts, false witness (and false oaths).

Remedy: mercy and pity (with definitions and species). Also reasonable liberality (but not foolish prodigality).

(6) *Gluttony:*

Defined.

   Species:
    (i) drunkenness,
    (ii) loss of discretion,
    (iii) bad table manners,
    (iv) illness through excess,
    (v) forgetfulness through drunkenness.

St Gregory's analysis of 5 species of gluttony.

Remedy: Abstinence, with its companions: temperance, shame, sufficiency, moderation, sobriety.

(7) *Lechery:*

   Species:
    Adultery: both deed and desire condemned; effects on soul and body.
    Fornication.
    Seduction of a maiden.
    Harlotry: breaking of faith, theft, filth, illegitimate children, incest, prostitution and pimping.
    Concupiscence (delight in sexual act between husband and wife).
    Sexual perversions.
    Self-pollution.

Remedy: Chastity and continence:
   (i) in marriage: the nature of marriage, and in particular how wives should be subordinate to their husbands;
   (ii) in widowhood: to avoid the embraces of man and desire the embraces of Christ;
   (iii) in virginity: holy of heart, clean of body, the glory of the world.

Avoid opportunities for temptation (e.g. sleeping long in great quiet).

Confession (continued):

Consider your sins, and all the 7 circumstances pertaining to them. Then for true confession there are 4 conditions:
(1) sorrowful bitterness of heart, of which there are 5 signs:
   (i) the feeling of shame,
   (ii) humility in confession,

    (iii) tears,
    (iv) not to be held back by shame,
    (v) obedience to the penance given;
  (2) that it be done quickly;
  (3) that it be done by free choice;
  (4) that it be performed lawfully.

(C) *Satisfaction:*
    Consists generally in alms and bodily pain.
    Alms:
    (1) contrition of heart,
    (2) pity on the defects of neighbours,
    (3) giving of good counsel and comfort (spiritual and material).
    They should be given from thy own store promptly and secretly.
    Bodily Pain:
    (1) prayers (and the conditions of saying them);
    (2) vigils;
    (3) fasting: forbearance of
      (i) meat and drink,
      (ii) worldly amusement,
      (iii) deadly sin;
    (4) virtuous teaching of prayer.
    There are other things in which bodily pain may manifest itself (e.g. using hairshirts, scourging oneself, etc.).
Four things interfere with penance:
  (1) dread,
  (2) shame,
  (3) hope,
  (4) despair,

The Parson's sermon concludes with a brief promise of the joys of the Kingdom.

    The sermon is exceedingly, if not excessively, long: any summary must be inadequate, and mine gives but the barest bones. Yet it will suffice, I hope, to emphasise the thoroughness, complexity and scope of the Parson's preaching. In reading it we are reminded that the Parson was a learned man. There are two questions about *The Parson's Tale* which particularly

I wish to consider. How does the *Tale* fit into the plan of the *Canterbury Tales*? What is Chaucer's attitude to the Parson's teaching? The last question leads on to a consideration of the poet's *Retraction*.

It has been suggested that the Parson's presentation of the Seven Deadly Sins provides the unifying theme of the *Canterbury Tales*, and that each pilgrim represents in his person a sin which the Parson condemns.[1] One of the difficulties about this suggestion is that *The Parson's Tale* is too wide and general in reference: no doubt comments could be found in it which would fit one pilgrim or another, but so inclusive are the sins (counting the minor as well as the major ones) mentioned by the Parson there is no book written whose characters could not be said to exemplify something described by the Parson. (Even Hamlet describes himself as proud, revengeful and ambitious.) We need not pursue this proposal further.[2]

Much finer, I think, is the interpretation put forward by Ralph Baldwin in his book *The Unity of the Canterbury Tales*. He suggests that the pilgrimage which brings together the motley crowd of people is not to be taken as merely a device to link a collection of disparate stories, but is the very subject of the poem. Through the pilgrimage to Canterbury we are being shown mankind (or a portion of mankind) on its pilgrimage through life, and the whole action of the poem is enfolded in religious understanding.

This very pilgrimage to Canterbury is to be the spiritual, that is, anagogical, figure for the pilgrimage to the heavenly Jerusalem... the Canterbury Pilgrimage becomes by metaphorical 'pressure' the pilgrimage to the Celestial City. Canterbury, the destination of the pilgrims, becomes the City of God; the *wey* to Canterbury becomes the way to the City of God; the pilgrims, wayfarers in time, become *potius mystice quam chronice*, wayfarers to eternity. Chaucer's Canterbury Pilgrimage becomes, and this is the *sovransenso*, the pilgrimage of the life of man. This makes the diversity of the tales part of its

[1] See Frederick Tupper, 'Chaucer and the Seven Deadly Sins', *PMLA*, XXIX (1914), 93–128.

[2] For a refutation of Tupper's suggestion see John Livingstone Lowes, 'Chaucer and the Seven Deadly Sins', *PMLA*, XXX (1915), 273–371.

structure. The waywardness and frailty of the characters, the too human gropings and anguish, the tears and tumult, diversions and banter, the self-indulgences and the heroism, tensions and tenderness, the hypocrisies and rue: these are the actions of that feckless creature man in his human comedy. And if the postlude to this comedy is beatitude, the last scene is playable for the medieval Christian only with that dramatic propriety sanctioned by the Parson...[1]

...If the pilgrims could forget themselves, under the hearty encouragings of the Host, so far as to 'pleye by the weye', then it behooved the Parson, the professional admonisher and mediator, to recall them to the realization that the *weye* was a *via*, that play had to be remedied by a Christian work, that *fable* had to give place to *morality*, that the readiness is all; that death is precarious for Christians not so much in its inevitability as in its unexpectedness, because the state of grace must be maintained up to and at the moment of death. The Parson becomes, supremely, the Pastor in the actual as well as the parabolic sense.[2]

On the whole this interpretation of Baldwin's fits in with what I have felt in my reading of the *Canterbury Tales*. A religious regard is nearly always present, whatever the subject or the character of the pilgrim narrating the story. In my analysis I have frequently drawn attention to the symbolic overtones of the poetry, even in passages bustling with 'realism'. Another example of this comes aptly here: the Host's words to the Parson before he commences his tale. All the pilgrims agree that the series of tales should rightly end 'in som vertuous sentence';

> Oure Host hadde the wordes for us alle: (67)
> 'Sire preest', quod he, 'now faire yow bifalle!
> Telleth', quod he, 'youre meditacioun.
> But hasteth yow, the sonne wole adoun;
> Beth fructuous, and that in litel space,
> And to do wel God sende yow his grace!'

Do we not feel here that the Host perhaps speaks better than he knows: that in his reference to the sun setting soon there is a suggestion of the coming of dark and death and mystery?

---

[1] Baldwin, *op. cit.* p. 92   [2] *Ibid.* pp. 93–4.

The pilgrimage of life, as well as the Canterbury Pilgrimage, has an ending: and fitting meditation should be found for it.

In one way I would emphasise the religious meaning of the Pilgrims' tales even more than Baldwin. He suggests, by omission more than by direct statement, that some of the tales are to be taken at their face value: mere stories that signify no more than playing 'by the weye'. I would rather insist that we are always invited to see them against a divine background, and, through the story that each pilgrim tells, enabled to understand something of his spiritual condition. Chaucer, through his descriptions and the stories he has them tell, not only shows the characters of the pilgrims but also makes explicit the spiritual values by which they live. Further, he does this with such compassion and wisdom that we seem to view their very souls. Or to put it another way: when we imagine how God would see his fallible creatures, with what infinite sympathy, undeceived patience, rigour of judgment, and what benign forgiveness, the nearest guess we can make is to apprehend the way Chaucer regards his characters. And it is the all-pervading presence of this quality in Chaucer's poem, rather than the mention of any specific ideas or doctrines, which makes it so religious.

It is here that I find myself parting company with Baldwin. Clearly it is right that on a pilgrimage, in which all the Pilgrims confess their spiritual state, the last words should be spoken by the Parson, that ideal shepherd; that his words should express bluntly and simply the teaching of the faith on penance and the soul's salvation. It is an artistic rightness. But this is not to say that *The Parson's Tale* is more valid than any other, and that its doctrines are truer than the thoughts explored in other *Tales*. Yet this seems to be Baldwin's implication; he writes, 'But, word for word, principle for principle, it is not too much to say that Chaucer himself might have claimed it the most meaningful, and in a dialectical, perhaps even a dramatic sense, the most artistic of the Tales'.[1] Chaucer was undoubtedly a Christian, and in the main held by the tenets

[1] *Ibid.* p. 98.

of the Christian faith; but he was also an artist, and his genius led him to perceive truths not always sufficiently acknowledged by Christianity. Because Chaucer was an artist he could create the Parson, and was under obligation to treat him without falsification. How would the Parson's character emerge in any sermon he preached? Surely scarcely at all, for the Parson's character at such a moment would be to be without character: he would surrender his own personality pursuing selflessly the performance of his calling. The teaching would be everything. Therefore the sermon he preached must be a genuine sermon: one that can be attended to without thought of the man delivering it. Thus Chaucer composed a genuine sermon, faithfully recording the doctrines of the Church as honest pastors taught them. This is one side of the *Tale's* truth. Another side is the truth of the doctrines themselves, and they are as true as the Church's authority. As a Christian Chaucer was obliged to accept these doctrines, though doubtless like most thinking Christians at any time on certain matters he had misgivings, qualifications or doubts (for example, I wonder if Chaucer really shared the Parson's orthodox anti-feminist bias). Even authority, sincere and orthodox, is fallible, like all human wisdom. In a number of the *Canterbury Tales* we have seen God's 'privatee' touched upon: one thing we can believe is that Chaucer had a very strong sense of God's *mystery*, and possessed a profound humility about the claims of human knowledge. Have we not here perhaps a clue as to why he is as cunning as a serpent? His whole method, throughout the *Canterbury Tales*, is to show an aspect of truth, criticise it, suggest its partiality, set up a counter-truth, explore that, call for a revaluation, move on to further considerations, never quite settle, never give a conclusive answer. His techniques have been the debate of the Pilgrims (each one with his own vision), the juxtaposing of argument, of style, of genre, of tones. Even his aphorisms, such as 'pitee runneth soon in gentil herte', even his key words, such as 'ernest', or 'game', or 'gentilesse', shift in meaning from context to context, growing more complex with every reappearance. Despite

all this, when he came to write *The Parson's Tale* shall we say
that Chaucer at last settled for a didactic literalism, or shall we
suspect even here we shall find Chaucer's own multidimensional
ambiguity? Baldwin advocates the first answer. I wish to propose that the second answer is the true one.

Chaucer, as he emerges from his writing, appears to be
almost at the opposite pole in character to his own Parson.
The more bland, the more naive Chaucer makes himself sound,
the more the ironies and complexities grow. His is the very
essence of the quick, poetic mind. The Parson, on the other
hand, is presented as possessing a firm and literal mind. This
appears in the way the Parson rejects *fable*.

> 'Thou getest fable noon ytoold for me;   (31)
> For Paul, that writeth unto Thymothee,
> Repreveth hem that weyven soothfastnesse,
> And tellen fables and swich wrecchednesse.
> Why sholde I sowen draf out of my fest,
> Whan I may sowen whete, if that me leste?'

For the Parson 'moralitee and vertuous mateere' suffice, but
can they ever suffice for an artist? For the poet can didactic
instruction ever be the only way to moral truth? Chaucer
could never have believed so or the *Canterbury Tales* could
never have been written in the first place. Something of the
flexibility of Chaucer's mind is demonstrated by setting beside
these words he granted the Parson some he set in the mouth
of the Wife of Bath.

> 'I nyl envye no viginitee.   (142)
> Lat hem be breed of pured whete-seed,
> And lat us wyves hoten barly-breed;
> And yet with barly-breed, Mark telle kan,
> Oure Lord Jhesu refresshed many a man.'

For all her laughable impudence, the Wife of Bath has here a
pious truth of her own, and Chaucer can recognise it. And
Chaucer could love, as he believed God could love, the truth
of the Wife as well as the truth of the Parson. This is the

wisdom of the fox, to know many things, to perceive many paths: and Chaucer is a fox. Through fables he guides us to many spiritual discoveries: the Parson leads us along one path only. This is explicitly made clear in the very opening paragraph of *The Parson's Tale*.

Oure sweete Lord God of hevene, that no man wole perisse, but wole that we comen alle to the knoweleche of hym, and to the blisful lif that is perdurable, / amonesteth us by the prophete Jeremie, that seith in thys wyse: / Stondeth upon the weyes, and seeth and axeth of olde pathes (that is to seyn, of olde sentences) which is the goode wey, / and walketh in that wey, and ye shal fynde refresshynge for youre soules, etc. / *Manye been the weyes espirituels that leden folk to oure Lord Jhesu Crist, and to the regne of glorie.* / Of whiche weyes, ther is a ful noble wey and a ful covenable, which may nat fayle to man ne to womman that thurgh synne hath mysgoon fro the righte wey of Jerusalem celestial; and this wey is cleped Penitence . . . (My italics.)

Chaucer does not despise or underrate the one path preached by the Parson. He even accentuates its importance by contrasting the Parson's message with the devious discretions advocated in *The Manciple's Tale*. Doubtless the parson's doctrinaire directness is just what such erring men as the Manciple need to set them right. But as an artist Chaucer knows he must explore some of the many other paths (and there may even be dead ends), and this is the task he performs throughout the *Canterbury Tales*. To say this is again to insist that for Chaucer the poet's function is a religious one. *The Parson's Tale* is then only one of the many paths explored within the *Canterbury Tales*. Nor is it pre-eminent among the *Tales*. Can we say that its literalness is truer than the fable of *The Nun's Priest's Tale*, that the Parson's 'ernest' is wiser than the Nun's Priest's 'game'? I doubt it. Chaucer's spiritual didacticism is to be found in every corner of the great work, not merely set out in the final sermon.

Yet there is one sense in which the doctrine of *The Parson's Tale* does have special importance. It is the received guidance of the Church on the matter of personal salvation: it is instruction in what to *do* to be saved. The Parson's sermon has its place within the art of the *Canterbury Tales*, but it also steps outside that art as a literal exhortation. There comes a stage when art seems not enough, when the wisdom and even the spiritual transformations it can render seem inadequate before the urgent demands of life itself. The time when what is wanted is not sensitivity, understanding, even tragic joy, but simple guidance in what to do and what not to do.[1] For a Christian, who believes his soul is at stake, wants precepts based on revelation; and where the precepts taught by the authority of the Church conflict with the perceptions of art, he has little choice but to obey Christian teaching. Perhaps for all men there is this dilemma, but for the Christian, and the Christian artist, who finds his art incompatible with orthodoxy, the problem is especially harsh. This too was Chaucer's predicament. I am, of course, coming on to the *Retraction*. Whether the *Retraction* was written immediately after *The Parson's Tale*, or whether it was added much later, the recantation follows naturally on the sermon preceding it, and there is no reason for not accepting Chaucer's authorship. Indeed, the very humility that, I suggested earlier, gave Chaucer the cunning of the fox, the slyness of the serpent in his art, and enabled him to see the multidimensional aspects of truth, this same profound humility must also have led him to question the very validity of his own art, and certainly those aspects of it condemned by the morality of the Church. Could he not have wondered whether the composition of his bawdier tales brought his soul into jeopardy? Yet as artist must he not have

[1]
   Art opens the fishiest eye
   To the Flesh and the Devil who heat
   The Chamber of Temptation
   Where heroes roar and die.
   We are wet with sympathy now;
   Thanks for the evening; but how
   Shall we satisfy when we meet,
   Between Shall-I and I-Will,
   The lion's mouth whose hunger
   No metaphors can fill?
  W. H. Auden, from *The Sea and the Mirror* (Faber, 1945), p. 8.

felt that to speak the truth about the world as it was, with its inherent bawdy, was justifiable? The conflict was real to him, and it can be detected in the *Retraction*. For, though he does recant and ask forgiveness for those *Canterbury Tales* that 'sownen into synne' the *Recantation* contains what seem to be two quite different standpoints. On the one hand Chaucer expresses in it an attitude similar to the Parson's: asking pardon for his 'translacions and enditynges of worldly vanitees' and for many 'a song and many a leccherous lay,' and thanking Christ and the Virgin for his books of meditation, homilies, moralities, devotions and legends of saints only. On the other hand he offers pleasure as a test of his works, and apologises only for his lack of skill.

Now Preye I to hem alle that herkne this litel tretys or rede, that *if ther be any thyng in it that liketh hem, that therof they thanken oure Lord Jhesu Crist, of whom procedeth al wit and al goodnesse.* And if ther be any thyng that displese hem, I preye hem also that they arrete it to *the defaute of myn unkonnynge*, and nat to my wyl, that wolde ful fayn have seyd bettre if I hadde had konnynge. Four oure book seith, '*Al that is writen is writen for oure doctrine*', and that is myn *entente.* Wherfore... (My italics.)

This is more like a poet's creed: Chaucer could well say of all his works and not only of *The Pardoner's Tale*, that they were written to give pleasure and instruction ('game' and 'ernest' again) and where they have succeeded it was with inspiration from Christ and hence with His approval. The part of the *Retraction* that follows this puts forward a narrower interpretation of virtuous writing, and one not wholly compatible with this. Perhaps this conflict points to a division in Chaucer's mind, a division brought about by the gap between the demands of orthodoxy and the claims of his poetic gift, which at the last resort he was not quite able to bridge. Or perhaps the bland setting down of contrary criteria shows Chaucer the fox at work again, leaving the reader to draw his own conclusions. What is worth noting is that the first apology is for the work only, asking pardon for botched jobs; the second recantation refers to himself, asking pardon for himself. As man and Christian Chaucer felt concern for what Yeats called 'perfection of the life'; as poet, and a religious poet at that, Chaucer felt concern for 'perfection of the work'.[1] It is the latter concern, the struggle to reveal joyfully the truth of things, working at a religious depth of thought and feeling, which permeates the whole of the *Canterbury Tales*. By the perfection of his work succeeding ages have come to know him best, and indeed will pardon him his rare moments of 'unkonnynge'.

[1] See W. B. Yeats, 'The Choice', *op. cit.* pp. 278–9.

Bibliography

The edition of Chaucer used is the *Complete Works of Geoffrey Chaucer*, ed. F. N. Robinson, 2nd edition, Oxford University Press, 1957.

Aristotle. *Poetics*, trs. Ingram Bywater in *Introduction to Aristotle*. Modern Library, 1947.

Atkins, J. W. H. *English Literary Criticism, the Medieval Phase*. Methuen, 1943.

Bailey, Sherwin. *The Man–Woman Relation in Christian Thought*. Longmans, 1959.

Baldwin, C. S. *Medieval Rhetoric and the Poetic to 1400*. Peter Smith, 1959.

Baldwin, Ralph. *The Unity of the Canterbury Tales*. Rosenhilde and Bagger, Copenhagen, 1955.

Baum, Paull F. *Chaucer: A Critical Appreciation*. Duke University Press, 1958.

Bayley, John. *The Characters of Love*. Constable, 1960.

Beichner, Paul E. 'C.S.C., Chaucer's Man of Law and *Disparitus Cultus*', *Speculum*, XXIII (1948).

Bennett, H. S. *Chaucer and the Fifteenth Century*. Oxford History of English Literature, II, 1, 1947.

Birney, Earle. '*After His Ymage*—The Central Ironies of *The Friar's Tale*', *Medieval Studies*, XXI (1959).

Blanchard, H. H. (ed.). *Prose and Poetry of the Continental Renaissance in Translation*. Longmans, 1949.

Bowden, Muriel. *A Commentary on the General Prologue to the Canterbury Tales*. Collier-Macmillan, 1948.

Bradley, Sister Ritamary, C.H.M. '*The Wife of Bath's Tale* and the Mirror Tradition', *Journal of English and Germanic Philology*, LV (1956).

Brewer, D. S. *Chaucer*. Longmans, 1953.

Brewer, D. S. *Chaucer in his Time*. Nelson, 1963.

Broadbent, G. B. *Poetic Love*. Chatto and Windus, 1964.

Bronson, Bertrand H. 'Chaucer's Art in Relation to his Audience', in *Five Studies in Literature* by B. H. Bronson *et al.* University of California Press, 1940.

Bryan, W. F., and Germaine Dempster (eds.). *Sources and Analogues of Chaucer's Canterbury Tales*. Routledge and Kegan Paul, 1941.

Capellanus, Andreas. *The Art of Courtly Love*, trs. John Jay Parry. Columbia University Press, 1941.

Chambers, E. K. *English Literature at the Close of the Middle Ages*. Oxford History of English Literature, 1945.

Chesterton, G. K. *Chaucer*. Faber, 1932.

Chute, Marchette. *Geoffrey Chaucer of England*. Dutton, 1945.

Clemen, Wolfgang. *Chaucer's Early Poetry*, trs. C. A. M. Sym. Methuen, 1963.

Cleugh, James. *Love Locked Out*. Crown Publishers, N.Y., 1963.

Coffman, George T. 'Chaucer and Courtly Love Once More— The Wife of Bath's Tale', *Speculum*, XX (1945).

Coghill, N. *The Poet Chaucer*. O.U.P., 1949.

Coulton, G. G. *Chaucer and his England*. Methuen, 1908.

Coulton, G. G. *Medieval Panorama*. C.U.P., 1938.

Craik, T. W. *The Comic Tales of Chaucer*. Methuen, 1964.

Curry, W. C. *Chaucer and the Medieval Sciences*. Allen and Unwin, 1960 (revised edition).

Danby, John F. 'Eighteen Lines of Chaucer's Prologue', *Critical Quarterly*, II (1960).

Dante. *The Divine Comedy*, trs. Carlyle-Wicksteed. Modern Library, 1932.

D'Arcy, M. C. *The Mind and Heart of Love*. Meridian, 1947.

Davies, Hugh Sykes. *The Poets and their Critics*. Hutchinson, 1960 (revised edition).

Dawson, Christopher. *Medieval Religion and Other Essays*. Sheed and Ward, 1935.

de Rougemont, Denis. *Passion and Society*. Faber, 1940.

Dodd, William George. *Courtly Love in Chaucer and Gower*. Peter Smith, 1913.

Everett, Dorothy. *Essays on Middle English Literature*. O.U.P., 1955.

Ford, Boris (ed.). *A Guide to English Literature*, vol. 1: *The Age of Chaucer*. Cassell, 1954.

French, Robert Dudley. *A Chaucer Handbook*. Appleton, 1936.

Gardner, Helen. *The Business of Criticism*. O.U.P., 1959.

Gerould, Gordon Hall. *Chaucerian Essays*. Princeton University Press, 1952.

Giffin, Mary. *Studies on Chaucer and his Audience*. Editions 'L'Éclair', 1956.

Gist, Margaret Adlum. *Love and War in the Middle English Romances*. University of Philadelphia Press, 1947.

Gower, John. *Complete Works*, ed. G. C. Macaulay. O.U.P., 1899–1902.

Grierson, Herbert and J. C. Smith. *A Critical History of English Poetry*. Chatto and Windus, 1944.

Guillaume de Lorris and Jean de Meun. *The Romance of the Rose*, trs. Harry W. Robbins, ed. Charles W. Dunn. Dutton, 1962.

Hadow, Grace E. *Chaucer and his Times*. Penguin, 1941.

Hauser, Arnold. *The Social History of Art*, vol. I. Routledge, 1951.

Heer, Friedrich. *The Medieval World*, trs. Janet Sondheimer. Weidenfeld and Nicolson, 1962.

Huizinga, J. *The Waning of the Middle Ages*. Edward Arnold, 1924.

Hulbert, J. R. '*The Canterbury Tales* and Their Narrators', *Studies in Philology*, XLV (1948).

Hunt, Morton M. *The Natural History of Love*. Knopf, 1959.

Huppé, Bernard F. and D. W. Robertson, Jr. *Fruyt and Chaf: Studies in Chaucer's Allegories*. Princeton University Press, 1963.

Jarrett, Bede. *Social Theories of the Middle Ages*. Ungar, 1926.

Jusserand, J. J. *English Wayfaring Life in the Middle Ages*, trs. Lucy Toulmin Smith. Benn, 1950.

Kelly, Amy. *Eleanor of Aquitaine and the Four Kings*. Harvard University Press, 1950.

Ker, W. P. 'Chaucer' in *English Prose*. vol. I: *Fourteenth to Sixteenth Centuries*. Macmillan, 1893.

Ker, W. P. *Epic and Romance*. Constable, 1896.

Ker, W. P. *Medieval English Literature*. O.U.P., 1912.

Ker, W. P. *Form and Style in Poetry*. Macmillan, 1928.

Kirby, Thomas A. *Chaucer's Troilus: A Study in Courtly Love*. Louisiana State University Press, 1940.

Leach, MacEdward (ed.). *Studies in Medieval Literature in Honor of Albert Croll Baugh*. University of Philadelphia Press, 1961.

Leclercq, Jacques. *Marriage and the Family*, trs. Rev. Thomas B. Hanley. Frederick Pustet, 1941.

Lewinsohn Richard. *A History of Sexual Customs*, trs. Alexander Mace. Longmans, 1958.

Lewis, C. S. *The Allegory of Love*. O.U.P., 1946.

Lord, Albert B. *The Singer of Tales*. Harvard University Press, 1960.

Lowes, J. L. *Geoffrey Chaucer*. O.U.P., 1934.

Lumiansky, R. M. 'Chaucer and the Idea of Unfaithful Men', *Modern Language Notes*, LXII (1947).

Lumiansky, R. M. *Of Sondry Folk: The Dramatic Principle in the Canterbury Tales*. University of Texas Press, 1955.

Malone, Kemp. *Chapters on Chaucer*. Johns Hopkins Press, 1951.

Murry, J. Middleton. *The Problem of Style*. O.U.P., 1960.

Murry, J. Middleton. *Selected Criticism 1916–1957* O.U.P., 1960.

Murry, M. A. *The Witch-Cult in Western Europe*. O.U.P., 1921.

Muscatine, Charles. *Chaucer and the French Tradition*. University of California Press, 1960.

Myers, A. R. *England in the Late Middle Ages*. Pelican, 1952.

Owen, C. A., Jr. 'Chaucer's *Canterbury Tales*: Aesthetic Design in the Stories of the First Day', *English Studies*, XXXV (1954).

Owen, Charles A. 'The Earliest Plan of the *Canterbury Tales*', *Medieval Studies*, XXI (1959).

Owst, G. R. *Literature and Pulpit in Medieval England*. O.U.P., 1961.

Painter, Sidney. *French Chivalry*. Johns Hopkins Press, 1940.

Patch, H. H. *On Rereading Chaucer*. Harvard University Press, 1939.

Payne, Robert O. *The Key of Remembrance: A Study of Chaucer's Poetics*. Yale University Press, 1963.

Power, Eileen. *Medieval People*. Methuen, 1924.

Pratt, R. A. 'The Order of the Canterbury Tales', *PMLA*, LXVI (1951).

Preston, Raymond. *Chaucer*. Sheed and Ward, 1952.

Pursell, Willene van Loenen. *Love and Marriage in Three English Authors*. Stanford Honors Essays in Humanities, 1963.

Raynelda, Sister Mary Makarewicz. *The Patristic Influence on Chaucer*. Catholic Universities of America Press, 1953.

Rickert, Edith (compiled). *Chaucer's World*. Columbia University Press, 1948.

Robertson, D. W., Jr. *A Preface to Chaucer*. Princeton University Press, 1963.

Salter, Elizabeth. *Chaucer: The Knight's Tale and the Clerk's Tale*. Edward Arnold, 1962.

Sayers, Dorothy L. *Introductory Papers on Dante*. Methuen, 1954.

Sayers, Dorothy L. *Further Papers on Dante*. Methuen, 1957.

Schoek, Richard and Jerome Taylor (eds.). *Chaucer Criticism*, vols. I and II. University of Notre Dame Press, 1960 and 1961.

Shelly, Percy Van Dyke. *The Living Chaucer*. University of Pennsylvania Press, 1940.

Silverman, Albert H. 'Sex and Money in Chaucer's *Shipman's Tale*', *Philological Quarterly*, XXXII (1953).

Southworth, James G. *Verses of Cadence: Chaucer's Prosody*. Blackwell, 1954.

Southworth, James G. *The Prosody of Chaucer and His Followers*. Blackwell, 1962.

Spearing, A. C. *Criticism and Medieval Poetry*. Edward Arnold, 1964.

Speirs, John. *Chaucer the Maker*. Faber, 1951.

Speirs, John. *Medieval English Poetry*. Faber, 1957.

Spurgeon, Caroline. *Five Hundred Years of Chaucer Criticism and Allusion, 1357–1900*. C.U.P., 1925.

Stenton, Doris Mary. *English Society in the Early Middle Ages: 1066–1307*. Pelican, 1951.

Stillwell, Gardiner. 'Chaucer in Tartary', *Review of English Studies*, XXIV (1948).

Tatlock, J. S. P. *The Mind and Art of Chaucer*. Syracuse University Press, 1950.

Taylor, G. Rattray. *Sex in History*. Thames and Hudson, 1953.

Ten Brink, Bernhard. *History of English Literature*, trs. Wm. Clarke Robinson. George Bell, 1895.

Tillyard, E. M. W. *Poetry Direct and Oblique*. Chatto and Windus, 1948.

Tolkien, J. R. R. and E. V. Gordon (eds.). *Sir Gawain and the Green Knight*. O.U.P., 1925.

Trevelyan, G. M. *English Social History*. Longmans, 1962 (second edition).

Trilling, Lionel. *Freud and the Crisis of our Culture*. Beacon Press, Boston, 1955.

Tupper, F. 'Chaucer and the Seven Deadly Sins', *PMLA*, XXIX (1914).

Utley, Francis Lee. *The Crooked Rib*. Ohio State University, Columbus, 1944.

Valency, Maurice. *In Praise of Love*. Collier-Macmillan, 1961.

van Heyningen, Christina. *Clarissa, Poetry and Morals*. University of Natal Press, 1963.

Wagenknecht, Edward (ed.). *Chaucer: Modern Essays in Criticism*. Galaxy Books, 1959.

Webb, Henry J. 'A Reinterpretation of Chaucer's Theseus', *The Review of English Studies*, XXIII (1947).

Woolf, Rosemary. 'Chaucer as a Satirist in the General Prologue to the *Canterbury Tales*', *Critical Quarterly*, XLI, 2 (1959).

Index

307

Index

139

8